SELECTIONS FROM *YSTORY*

THE LIBRARY OF MEDIEVAL WELSH LITERATURE

General Editors

Nerys Ann Jones
Erich Poppe

previous volume
Welsh Court Poems
edited by Rhian M. Andrews (2007)

SELECTIONS FROM
YSTORYA BOWN O HAMTWN

Edited by

Erich Poppe and Regine Reck

UNIVERSITY OF WALES PRESS
CARDIFF
2009

www.uwp.co.uk

British Library Cataloguing-in-Publication Data
A catalogue record for this book is available from the British Library.

ISBN 978-0-7083-2171-3
e-ISBN 978-0-7083-2245-1

Printed in Wales by Dinefwr Press, Llandybïe

Contents

Preface

Translations of foreign texts into Middle Welsh are a somewhat neglected and underrated genre, in comparison with native productions such as the *Four Branches of the Mabinogi* or the poetry of the Welsh courts. However, translations and adaptations of foreign narratives, as well as of a wide range of historical and religious writings, constitute a substantial portion of the corpus of Middle Welsh prose. For the literary historian, medieval translations have a special attraction. Since the translators as a rule followed an approach that intended to facilitate the reception of their sources by the new audiences, they transformed and rewrote them, sometimes quite dramatically. The differences between foreign source and Welsh adaptation vividly reflect the formative stylistic and literary conventions which medieval Welsh authors followed, as well as the expectations of their audiences.

In this volume of the Library of Medieval Welsh Literature we present selections from *Ystorya Bown o Hamtwn*, the Welsh adaptation of the Anglo-Norman *Geste de Boeve de Haumtone*. *Boeve de Haumtone*, dating to about the last decade of the twelfth century, was a hugely successful work, not only in the Insular context, where it was translated into Welsh, Norse, Middle English and, on the basis of a Middle English text, into Irish, but also on the Continent. *Ystorya Bown* therefore gives modern readers a good idea about what a medieval Welsh audience found fascinating and entertaining in a narrative and introduces them to the genre of adaptations of foreign works in which the storyline of the source is preserved, but rewritten using predominantly Welsh narrative techniques. Comparison between source and adaptation is now greatly facilitated by Judith Weiss's English translation of *Boeve de Haumtone*.

Ystorya Bown is a very long text, and we have therefore decided to give a selection of passages. These follow the development of the story and of Bown's biography, and we have also included what we consider to be some narrative highlights.

We wish to thank the Deutsche Forschungsgemeinschaft for financial support in the initial stages of the preparation of this work; Vera Eilers, Nerys Ann Jones, Ceridwen Lloyd-Morgan and Ingo Mittendorf for all their help and advice; and the National Library of Wales for permission to use for the cover the first page of *Ystorya Bown* in NLW Ms. 19900 B, formerly MS Gwenogvryn Evans 1A, which was written *c*.1608 by John Jones of Gellilyfdy.

Erich Poppe and Regine Reck

Abbreviations

MIG   Mary Williams, 'Llyma Vabinogi Iessu Grist', *Revue Celtique* 33 (1912), 184–248.

Ow.   *Owein or Chwedyl Iarlles y Ffynnawn*, ed. Robert L. Thomson (Dublin, 1975).

PKM   *Pedeir Keinc y Mabinogi*, ed. Ifor Williams (Caerdydd, 1930).

Pwyll *Pwyll Pendeuic Dyuet*, ed. Robert L. Thomson (Dublin, 1957).

R   the text of *Ystorya Bown de Hamtwn* in Llyfr Coch Hergest/ Red Book of Hergest.

SC   *Studia Celtica.*

SDR   *Chwedleu Seith Doethon Rufein*, ed. Henry Lewis (Caerdydd, 1925).

VGFC   *Vita Griffini Filii Conani. The Medieval Latin Life of Gruffudd ap Cynan*, ed. Paul Russell (Cardiff, 2005).

W   the text of *Ystorya Bown de Hamtwn* in Llyfr Gwyn Rhydderch/White Book of Rhydderch.

YBH   *Ystorya Bown de Hamtwn*, ed. Morgan Watkin (Caerdydd, 1958).

YCM   *Ystorya de Carolo Magno*, ed. Stephen J. Williams (Caerdydd, 1968).

YSG   *Ystorya Seint Greal. Rhan I: Y Keis*, ed. Thomas Jones (Caerdydd, 1992).

Introduction

The purpose of these selections from *Ystorya Bown o Hamtwn* is to introduce students with some knowledge of Middle Welsh to an important and interesting but still somewhat underrated genre of medieval Welsh literature, namely adaptations of foreign secular narratives. We do not intend to supersede Morgan Watkin's scholarly diplomatic edition of the full text of *Ystorya Bown* in the White Book of Rhydderch,[1] to which we are heavily indebted in many respects, but rather to provide a more accessible text for selected passages.

Ystorya Bown is the Middle Welsh adaptation of the Anglo-Norman *Geste de Boeve de Haumtone*. The story of Boeve de Haumtone was very popular in the Middle Ages and the early modern period, particularly so in the insular literatures of England, Wales, Ireland and Iceland, but there are also Continental French, Italian, Dutch, Yiddish, Rumanian and Russian versions. Its origins, however, appear to be Anglo-Norman French.[2] *Ystorya Bown* is based on an Anglo-Norman source which was close to, but probably not identical with, any of the three known incomplete Anglo-Norman texts of the *Geste de Boeve de Haumtone*. The two major Anglo-Norman fragments overlap and together provide the complete story but the approximately 350 verses common to both show how different they are in detail.[3] The remains of a single sheet make up the tiny third fragment.[4] The Anglo-Norman version 'as a whole in its existing shape (though not in its existing, thirteenth-century, language)' has been dated to the last decade of the twelfth century.[5]

The Welsh *Ystorya Bown* is now known from five manuscripts, two medieval and three post-medieval.[6] The two medieval manuscripts are Aberystwyth NLW Peniarth 4–5, the White Book of Rhydderch, compiled about 1350, and Oxford Jesus College 111,

the Red Book of Hergest, produced probably quite soon after 1382.
In the White Book, *Ystorya Bown* is in the hand of scribe C, one
of the manuscript's five scribes, and is his only contribution to it;
the text in the Red Book is in the hand of Hywel Vychan, the manu-
script's main scribe.

The final sentence of the text in the White Book of Rhydderch
calls the tale *Ystorya Bown*; the Red Book of Hergest adds *o
Hamtwn*. Middle Welsh tales are not normally given titles in the
manuscripts but are named in their final sentences, and we have
opted to use the Red Book's fuller version as our title. Morgan
Watkin preferred *Ystorya Bown de Hamtwn* but since there is a
slight preference in the White Book for *Bown o Hamtwn* over *de
Hamtwn*, we feel justified in using the Welsh form. Furthermore,
there are a few other instances in the text in which an Anglo-
Norman name with *de* is rendered by the Welsh redactor with
o, for example Welsh *Brice o Vristeu*, but Anglo-Norman *Brise de
Bretoue*.

The White Book and the Red Book share a number of prose
texts, *Ystorya Bown* among them, and the relationship between
these is a difficult issue. The general drift of modern scholarship
in this matter inclines to the view that it is more likely that they
derive from a common source, rather than that the texts in the Red
Book are derived directly from the White Book. The orthographic
and stylistic differences between the texts of *Ystorya Bown* in the
two manuscripts are slight and it would be difficult to argue on
this basis that one manuscript preserves a significantly superior
text. The White Book, however, has two different beginnings for the
narrative: the first beginning, forty-nine lines in the manuscript,
ends in the middle of the second column of folio 118, the rest of
which is then left blank. The tale starts again on folio 119. The
first twenty-one lines of the two beginnings agree very closely but
the remaining lines of the first version deviate significantly from the
second. The narrative in this second part of the first beginning is
much more condensed and, in contrast to the Anglo-Norman text
and the second beginning, does not employ direct speech, an import-
ant feature also of native Welsh tales. Some details in the second
part of the second beginning cannot be deduced from the first and
also occur in the Anglo-Norman text, particularly the references to
the first day of May and to the presents which the messenger
receives from the German emperor. The second beginning therefore

represents a different translation, rather than a creative and expanded retelling of the first. The structural and stylistic differences between the two versions appear to be impressive testimony to the freedom with which medieval translators and redactors treated their sources. Unfortunately, it remains unclear why scribe C of the White Book discarded the first beginning and switched to a different version.

Morgan Watkin is the only scholar so far to venture a view on the date of the original adaptation of the Anglo-Norman *Geste de Boeve de Haumtone* into Welsh. On the basis of some orthographic features and of the treatment of Anglo-Norman loan-words, he suggested as most likely a date not long after the middle of the thirteenth century,[7] and this dating has not been challenged since. Such a date would be supported by the occurrence in *Ystorya Bown* of two examples of 'pseudo-argument' *dim* with negated intransitive verbs, an innovation which has been dated by David Willis to the late thirteenth century.[8] *Ystorya Bown* would thus belong, together with the Welsh versions of three texts about Charlemagne, *Cronicl Turpin*, *Cân Rolant* and *Pererindod Siarlymaen*, to the early group of adaptations of foreign narratives into Welsh. In the most recent systematic discussion of regional features in the language of Middle Welsh prose texts, Peter Wynn Thomas tentatively assigned *Ystorya Bown* to 'an historical transition zone between the south-western and northern areas' but did not want to rule out the possibility of some scribal interference.[9] Watkin identified a number of Christian additions in *Ystorya Bown* and he therefore suggested that the translator was most likely a monk.[10]

The passages from *Ystorya Bown* given here represent approximately 40 per cent of the complete tale. A selection was deemed necessary because *Ystorya Bown* is a long text, probably much too long to be read in its entirety in one course. We have attempted to follow the progress of Bown's biography, from his infancy and exile, his career as a victorious warrior and his return to his patrimony to his renewed exile and wanderings and his final renown as knight and ruler.[11] In order to provide the necessary narrative context for the individual episodes we have supplied summaries of the passages omitted. Each passage included in our selections is identified by the line-numbers of Watkin's edition of *YBH* and of the corresponding passage of Kölbing's edition of *BdH* – the latter can be used to find it in Judith Weiss's translation of *BdH*.

The exile-and-return pattern gives ample opportunity for the narrator to dwell on the hero's martial exploits and, since the martial ethos is central to both the *Geste de Boeve de Haumtone* and *Ystorya Bown*, we have included some of the more thrilling and exciting combats and adventures. Another important concern in the *Geste de Boeve de Haumtone*, and perhaps even more so in *Ystorya Bown*, is the Christian foundation of the hero's life and battles: he very soon finds an opportunity to prove his steadfastness in the Christian faith at the heathen court of the king of Egypt and the religious confrontation between Christians and pagans, mainly expressed in martial terms of conflict and the destruction of heathen idols, remains one of the two leitmotifs of the plot, the other – and partly related one – being the love between him and the daughter of the king of Egypt. We have therefore included some passages in which Bown's Christian faith and piety are made explicit, for example in invocations of God or the integration of the Creed into the greeting of the English emperor. Bown is a type of the *miles christianus* and his final battle against and victory over the Saracens results in the Christianization of an entire pagan population and affirms his religious and military sovereignty. Another characteristic of the *Geste de Boeve de Haumtone* and similar romances is the presence of a love story and consequently an interest in the portrayal of women. The women in the *Geste de Boeve de Haumtone* and *Ystorya Bown* are pre-courtly figures; they are energetic, active, and resourceful as the scheming of the hero's mother to have her first husband eliminated so that she can realize her desire for the younger and more attractive German emperor bears witness. A vital and active central role in the story is assigned to Josian/Iosian, the daughter of the king of Egypt.[12] It is she who takes the initiative in courting the hero and the comic potential offered by this reversal of roles is exploited delightfully in the scene in which the hero pretends to be asleep, and even snores, in order to avoid talking to the heroine.[13] But the heroine succeeds in winning the hero's affection and the testing of their mutual love and fidelity is another sustained leitmotif, their first innocent kiss triggering an enforced separation and a further series of events and complications until they are briefly reunited, only to be separated again on two occasions. Throughout the story, the heroine's loyalty to the hero and his Christian faith as well as her resourcefulness are emphasized. A case in point is her use of a magic girdle to guard her virginity – a vital prerequisite for her eventual marriage to the hero – against two unwanted suitors. But the hero is tested too; a lady whose realm he successfully defends desires his love and this situation serves 'to enhance the hero. He is the desired, not the desiring . . ., and sufficiently self-controlled not to exploit the situation.'[14] A brief word is necessary here about the hero's horse Arwndel, which plays an important role throughout the story and forms a special link between heroine and hero: it is given by her to the hero at his knighting, on condition that he will always treat it well; it accepts him when he approaches her in disguise;[15] it is equated in two dreams with the heroine; and when she is about to die, the hero finds it dead in its stable, thus confirming his own fears about his wife.

The plot of the Anglo-Norman *Geste de Boeve de Haumtone* and its details are faithfully preserved in the Welsh *Ystorya Bown*. The interest of the Anglo-Norman author and its Welsh redactor in the text would appear to have been very similar, with regard to both the ingredients of a good story and their outlook on the world. Both want to present a series of exciting events within a framework of basic martial-Christian values. This combination is nicely encapsulated in the characterizations of Bown as 'the best knight in Christendom', and this is clearly the point of view shared and transmitted by the Anglo-Norman and Welsh narrators. The transposition of this set of literary and social ideals from the Anglo-Norman to the Welsh cultural and literary environment did not create any major problems. If there are any innovations in *Ystorya Bown* on the level of content, these are subtle and minor and do not impinge upon its basic concerns but rather, in that there may be a slightly stronger insistence on overt expressions of piety and of dedication to the Christian faith, focus the text even more within a martial-Christian social context.

On the level of form, however, the Welsh redactor changed Anglo-Norman verse into Welsh prose and he also followed the narrative and stylistic conventions of medieval Welsh prose literature in many other respects. This can already be observed on the level of narrative syntax. The passages told by the narrator consist as a rule of sequences of clauses mostly coordinated by *a(c)* 'and' or other sentence connectives. A more marked way of creating textual cohesion is the use of preposed temporal clauses which resume the verbal event of the preceding sentence. All of this is also typical of native Welsh prose. The Welsh redactor furthermore employs conventional and idiomatic narrative devices which have no obvious parallels in Anglo-Norman French, such as presentational *llyma*, the narrative verbal noun, the periphrasis with a verbal noun as the object of a preterite form of *gwneuthur*, and the various constructions with *sef*. In a characteristically Welsh way, he uses the narrative present very rarely in main clauses, where the narrative verbal noun appears to be its functional equivalent, but significantly more often in subordinate clauses. A number of idiomatic Middle Welsh expressions for oaths and similar exclamations occur in the native narrative corpus. The majority of these are also used in *Ystorya Bown*, for example *yr Duw* 'by God', *ym kyffes* 'by my confession' and *myn vyg cret* 'by my faith'. A particularly interesting case is the highly idiomatic phrase *y rof a Duw* 'between me and God', which is frequent in the native corpus. It is attested (only) six times in *Ystorya Bown* and in three instances it corresponds to functionally similar exclamations in the Anglo-Norman *Geste de Boeve de Haumtone*. This use of a native Welsh formula contrasts with an interference from the Anglo-Norman system of oaths in the phrase *myn vymphen* 'by my head'. This phrase is not part of the system found in the native corpus. It is fairly frequent in *Ystorya Bown*, with eight attestations, and more significantly it always renders Anglo-Norman *par mun chef* 'by my head'. The system of exclamations in *Ystorya Bown* thus provides in a nutshell an example of the conflicting tendencies present in the process of textual transfer from Anglo-Norman into Welsh: adaptions to native conventions, as in *y rof a Duw* 'between me and God', side by side with imitations of the foreign source, as in *myn vymphen* 'by my head'.

The accounts of single combat in *Ystorya Bown* have been thoroughly adapted, as a rule, to a pattern which characterizes the descriptions of combat in native Welsh literature. The basic pattern here consists of several more or less formulaic phrases, which are combined to describe the attack of the two opponents, the parts of the body or armour affected, the result of the blows and the falling of the defeated combatant to the ground. The realization of this pattern varies, from a skeleton description of the attack and the falling to the ground to very elaborate and detailed compositions. Syntactically, the attack and the blow delivered are typically given in main clauses, while the results of the blow are described in one or more postposed subordinate clauses introduced by the conjunction *yny* 'so that, until'. There are some fifteen accounts of single combat in *Ystorya Bown*, as well as several violent encounters, which as a rule all follow this syntactic organization. It is certainly significant that the Welsh redactor prefers a fairly fixed wording, 'so that he fell/ falls (dead) to the ground', in the result clauses which describe the defeated combatant's fall to the ground, whereas the wording varies considerably in the Anglo-Norman *Geste de Boeve de Haumtone*. It should be mentioned too that although in some instances the use of a present tense in the postposed clauses in these scenes of combat may have been conditioned by the Anglo-Norman source, on the whole it agrees quite well with what has been described as the system typical of the native corpus of texts.[16]

The narrator in the Welsh narrative tradition tends to remain invisible and it is therefore no great surprise that the Welsh narrator of *Ystorya Bown* is much less intrusive than his Anglo-Norman counterpart. What is perhaps more interesting, however, are some instances where he does make his presence felt; these would appear to be his 'lapses', in that he allowed himself to be influenced by his source and translated quite faithfully a few narrator's intrusions, comments and exclamations, a rhetorical question, and even what appears to be a reference to a written source, all of which is wholly uncharacteristic of his own native narrative tradition. Relevant examples include: 'and a pity that he did not kill him', 'and may they have a bad end' and 'that was a great loss for Bown afterwards, as will be related later'. There is even a small number of similar narrator's intrusions in *Ystorya Bown* which have no obvious parallels in the extant Anglo-Norman texts. Examples include: 'and he did wrong', 'he ate greedily like a madman – and this was no strange thing, long had he been without food', and 'and let Jesus destroy them'. It must remain an open question, however, whether these phrases were contained in the Welsh redactor's source, but not in the extant texts of the *Geste de Boeve de Haumtone*, or whether they are his own creative innovations, modelled on other instances of narrator's intrusions in the Anglo-Norman *Geste*.

A central device used by the narrator to structure and organize his text is paragraphing, the marking of narrative units. In the *Geste de Boeve de Haumtone*, expressions used frequently to mark a change of scene contain phrases in which the narrator intervenes, such as 'let us now talk of X' or 'let us now leave Y', or a combination of both. Such formulae, by means of which the narrator comments on the structure of his narrative, are not part of the Middle Welsh narrative repertoire. It is therefore not surprising that they are often not translated in *Ystorya Bown* and that the narrative transition is less explicitly marked or even left unmarked. However, in the last third of *Ystorya Bown* most of the Anglo-Norman phrases indicating transitions are quite faithfully rendered in Welsh. The Welsh redactor may even have decided on a favourite expression, namely *bellach/weithon y dywedwn am* X 'now/further we will say about X [that . . .]', which is used to render a variety of phrases of the extant Anglo-Norman source.

Medieval Welsh narrators sometimes switch quite effortlessly from indirect speech to direct speech in the same speech unit, often to emphasize the significant words which bear most emotional stress. This phenomenon is sometimes called 'slipping' and there are some examples of it in *Ystorya Bown*. Most of these follow the typical pattern identified in the native corpus. More importantly, they have no counterpart in the extant text of the *Geste de Boeve de Haumtone* and the majority appears to have been brought in artfully by the redactor to enhance the vividness of his narrative.

There is one further point to be made about the redactor's 'lapses' mentioned earlier; they tend to cluster in the last third of the text of *Ystorya Bown*, which is generally closer to the corresponding text of the *Geste de Boeve de Haumtone* than the first two thirds and which also shows some other linguistic and stylistic peculiarities. We are not yet clear about the implications of this observation.

The lexicon of *Ystorya Bown* is influenced by both the literary and learned tradition of Middle Welsh and by the Anglo-Norman source. A good example of the Welsh background is the use by the bishop of Cologne of the term *morwynwreic* for Iosian, whereas she is called *pucele* 'girl' in the Anglo-Norman text. The Welsh term has the specific legal meaning of 'a girl who has been betrothed but whose marriage has not yet been consummated' and this fits Iosian's situation, and the bishop's perception of her, very well. The term *kytknawt* 'sexual intercourse' (a compound of *cyd-* 'together' and *cnawd* 'flesh') which Iosian uses earlier when she insists that she is still a virgin and has had no intercourse with Ifor, may similarly have a specific cultural background; the other two early attestations of the word are in religious texts. There is a significant number of Anglo-Norman loan-words in *Ystorya Bown*, and nearly forty of them are thought to be first attested in this text. About thirty of these also occur at the same point in the extant Anglo-Norman texts, and it is very likely that the Welsh translator borrowed these words directly from his source.[17] This is another important indication that the source of the Welsh redactor was quite close to the extant texts of the Anglo-Norman *Geste*.

A couple of emphatic negations in *Ystorya Bown* most likely arose as imitations of Anglo-Norman idioms. A good example is the phrase *gwerth vn uanec* meaning literally 'value of a glove', a direct translation of *Boeve*'s *le vailant de un gant*, which in its new Welsh context can only have the transferred, idiomatic meaning 'no value at all'. Such emphatic negations have no counterpart in the native Welsh tales and are best treated as direct or indirect loan phrases. Similar cases are the quasi-formulaic phrases *ny chelaf ragot* and *nyt ymgelaf ragot* 'I will not hide [it] from you', which in direct speech signal polite agreement to provide desired information. These phrases correspond to three different but semantically matching Anglo-Norman expressions. Since to the best of our knowledge they do not occur in the native texts in the same formulaic way, it appears best to interpret them as loan phrases. There is, however, one significant difference between the Anglo-Norman model and its Middle Welsh realization, and this is the form of address: whereas in the *Geste de Boeve de Haumtone* the form of address in these phrases is consistently the second person plural, it is the second person singular in *Ystorya Bown*. There appears to be only one certain example in *Ystorya Bown* of a second person plural in an address, and it is probably significant that in this case the first part of the Welsh sentence has a fairly close parallel in the extant text of the Anglo-Norman *Geste*; the second part of the sentence, which does not parallel the *Geste*, reverts to the second person singular. This form of address therefore seems to be modelled on the Anglo-Norman source. For *ny chelaf ragot* and its variant this implies that, although the Welsh redactor borrowed the basic phrase from Anglo-Norman, he changed the address to the form which was more natural for him, namely the second singular. This is another illuminating example of the tensions between imitation and adaptation that we often encounter in the Welsh *Ystorya Bown*.

The foregoing brief sketch of some characteristics of the Middle Welsh adaptation of the *Geste de Boeve de Haumtone* shows how content, narrative structure and style were differently affected in the process of cultural and literary transformation. The content remains unchanged, with perhaps only a few minute modifications, in particular a stronger Christian concern. The narrative structure and the style of the source are drastically changed, with a view towards accommodation of the foreign plot to Welsh literary conventions and the expectations of the new audience. This is obvious on all levels of the text, from the macro-form and its syntactic organization down to the micro-level of specific uses of tenses and idiomatic phrases. However, the Anglo-Norman source also influenced the structure and, to a lesser extent, the style of the Welsh text. Thus the redactor probably imitated a structural device foreign to his own narrative conventions – the explicit authorial marking of transition from one scene or protagonist to another – because he found it useful in organizing the complex development of the tale. In other instances, notably occasional authorial comments and exclamations, and also loan-words and phrases, he simply followed the source; it is impossible to decide whether he did so, perhaps unconsciously, because of his bilingual competence, or whether he felt that these features would fit smoothly into their new Welsh contexts or that such slight deviations from the norm would give his text a special flavour. His adaptation is, in a sense, close both to the source and to his own literary tradition and is the result of a creative tension between them. With regard to the relative distance between the *Geste de Boeve de Haumtone* and *Ystorya Bown*, it can be said that he followed the general principle *sensus de sensu* as it was formulated by his near-contemporary Gruffudd Bola with reference to the translation of a religious core text, the Creed: *synnvyr yn lle y synnvyr heruyd mod a phriodolder yn ieith ni* 'the sense for the sense, according to the nature and diction of our language'.[18] The Welsh *Ystorya Bown* is resolutely based on the sense of the foreign source on the levels of plot and narrative intention, but on the levels of narrative techniques and strategies it is intimately informed and moulded by the nature and the diction of its redactor's language and his own literary traditions.

Our text of selected passages from *Ystorya Bown* is based on the version in the White Book of Rhydderch. Editorial interference has been kept to a minimum.[19] Word-division, capitalization, punctuation and paragraphing have been supplied; in the case of punctuation this sometimes implies considerable editorial interpretation. Watkin's diplomatic text can always be consulted for the scribe's own version. In a few instances we felt justified in deviating from the text in the White Book. These are recorded in the list of manuscript readings and variants, which follow the text and are, where necessary, more fully discussed in the notes. Since it is not the aim of this edition to document linguistic variation in Middle Welsh, we refrained from giving a full list of variants from the other manuscript texts; full variants from the Red Book are supplied by Watkin. We provide, however, a selection of variants from the Red Book where this manuscript appears to have better or more explicit readings, the latter mainly with regard to the marking of mutations, or where the Red Book substantially deviates from the White Book.

The separation of nasalizing *yn* 'in' and *vy* 'my' from the following noun presents some problems, since scribe C of the White Book uses various systems side by side.[20] The orthographic marking of nasalization is inconsistent in Middle Welsh and also in *Ystorya Bown*, and editorial consistency is therefore difficult to achieve. In the text, nasalization of <p> is spelt <-m ph-> and <-m p-> and in these cases we have separated the preposition from the following noun, but it is also spelt <-mh-> and here we have not separated the two words, thus *ym phren* (l. 377) and *ym pren* (l. 392), but *ymhren* (l. 287). In the instances of nasalization of <t> and <c, k> after *vy* (and its variant *'y*) we have separated the two words, thus *vy nhat* (l. 105), *vy ghyghor* (l. 119), *'y gyghor* (l. 359), and *'yg cledeu* (l. 325). In the case of nasalization of <t> and <c, k> after *yn* we have not separated the two words when the nasalization is spelt <-nh-> and <-gh->, as in *ynhy* (l. 716) and *yghynted* (l. 100), but we have separated them when it is spelt <-g ch->, <-g g->, or <-g c->, as in *yg charchar* (l. 494–5), *yg groc* (l. 358) and *yg cledyr* (l. 589).[21] Words with initial <b>, <d>,[22] and <g> which have undergone nasalization are separated from the preceding word.[23] In cases such as *vy galw* (l. 116, R *vyg galw*) the absence of nasalization is only apparent, since <g-> represents /ŋ/, here, as it also does word-internally in examples such as *llog* (l. 139).[24] The preposition *yn* and a following noun with initial <m> have not been separated when the scribe has written only one <m>, thus *yMwmbrawnt* (l. 905) but *ym Mwmbrawnt* (l. 867).

The following list provides a survey of some of the orthographic variations in the text of the White Book which may present problems for students:[25]

/k/: <c->, <k->; <-c->, <-k->, <-cc->, <-ck->:   *cauas, kauas; raco, racco, maccwyeit, mackwy*.

/d/: <-t->, <-d->; <-t>, <-d>:   *llityaw, llidyaw; priawt, oed*
('appointed time').

/ð/: < d->, < dd->; <-d->, <-dd->:   *yn didlawt, yn dda;*
dygwydawd, dygwyddawd.

/v/: <v->, <u->, <f->; <-u->, <-w->, <-f->, <-ff->:   *a vynnaf,*
a uynnei, a fynnei; cyuarchawd, cywarch, cyfarch, cyffarch.

/f/: <ff->, <ph->; -ff->, <-f->, <-u->; <-ff>, <-f>:   *a ffan, a phan;*
caffas, cafas, kauas; praff, praf.

/g/: <-c->, <-k->, <-g>:   *croc, crok, crog.*

/gʷ/:   <gw->, <gu->: *gwedy, guedy.*

/ŋ/:   <-ng(-)>, <-g(-)>: *llong, llog.*

/sg/: <-sg->, <-sc->, <-sk->:   *gwiscaw, gwisky, gwisgaw.*

<m>, <n>, <r>, and <s> are sometimes doubled, for example
pan/pann and *tyr/tyrr.*

Notes

[1] *Ystorya Bown de Hamtwn*, ed. Morgan Watkin (Caerdydd, 1958). The
texts of the White Book and the Red Book of Hergest are now also
available in Cardiff University's searchable corpus of Medieval Welsh
prose 1350–1425 (*http://www.rhyddiaithganoloesol.caerdydd.ac.uk*).
For a fuller discussion of our analysis of *Ystorya Bown* and details
summarized here, see Erich Poppe and Regine Reck, 'A French Romance
in Wales: *Ystorya Bown o Hamtwn*. Processes of Medieval Translations',
Zeitschrift für celtische Philologie 55 (2006), 122–80, 56 (2008), 129–64,
and id., 'Rewriting Bevis in Wales and Ireland', in Jennifer Fellows and
Ivana Djordjević (eds) *Sir Bevis of Hampton in Literary Tradition*
(Studies in Medieval Romance)(Cambridge, 2008), 37–50. Fellows and
Djordjević, *Sir Bevis of Hampton*, contains a collection of articles that
consider the Anglo-Norman *Boeve de Haumtone* and its Insular (Middle-
English, Norse, Welsh and Irish) translations and adaptations, and also
provides a comprehensive bibliography of relevant editions and research
(pp. 193–201).

[2] *Der anglonormannische Boeve de Haumtone*, ed. Albert Stimming
(Halle, 1899). For a translation of the Anglo-Norman text, see Judith
Weiss, *Boeve de Haumtone and Gui de Warewic: Two Anglo-Norman
Romances*. The French of England Translation Series 3 (Tempe, 2008).

Our translations of the Anglo-Norman text are based on hers; however, in some instances we decided to give a more literal translation in order to facilitate grammatical or stylistic comparisons.

[3] Manuscript B (= Paris, fonds français, nouv. acqu. 4532) contains lines 1–1268, D (before its destruction in 1944 in the possession of the University Library of Louvain) begins at around line 915 of B and continues until the end of the story. M. Dominica Legge (*Anglo-Norman Literature and its Background* (Oxford, 1963), p. 157) calls the two 'sufficiently different to make collation impossible' and suggests that there 'was a considerable lapse of time between the composing of the text and the making of the two copies'.

[4] For details, see Judith Weiss, 'The Anglo-Norman Boeve de Haumtone: A Fragment of a New Manuscript', *The Modern Language Review* 95.2 (2000), 305–10; the fragment contains sixty-two lines, and its text is 'marginally closer to B (the fourteenth-century manuscript) than to D (thirteenth century), especially in its preservation of lines 1008–10, missing in D, but there are at least twenty-six places in the passage where its readings are unique, notably in its addition of line 1046a' (Weiss, 'The Anglo-Norman Boeve', p. 306). Weiss thinks that the manuscript is best placed in the earlier rather than in the later part of the thirteenth century.

[5] Judith Weiss, 'The Date of the Anglo-Norman *Boeve de Haumtone*', *Medium Aevum* 55 (1986), 237–41 (p. 140); she also believes that the extant Anglo-Norman version is a compilation.

[6] The only published text contained in a post-medieval manuscript is the one from Aberystwyth NLW MS Gwenogvryn Evans 1A, written *c.*1608 by John Jones of Gellilyfdy (Nesta Jones, 'Copi ychwanegol o ddechrau *Ystorya Bown de Hamtwn*', BBCS 23 (1968–70), 17–26); the text of *Ystorya Bown* is incomplete (up to line 501 of Watkin's edition) and belongs, according to Jones, to the same textual tradition as the White Book text (Jones, 'Copi ychwanegol').

[7] Compare Morgan Watkin, 'Rhagymadrodd', 'Nodiadau', 'Geirfa', in *Ystorya Bown de Hamtwn*, ed. Morgan Watkin (Caerdydd, 1958), xxi–clxxiii, 69–182, 185–247, pp. lv–lix.

[8] David Willis, 'Negation in Middle Welsh', SC 40 (2006), 63–88; for the two examples of 'pseudo-argument' *dim* in *Ystorya Bown*, see W 1201, 2759.

[9] Peter Wynn Thomas, 'Middle Welsh Dialects: Problems and Perspectives', BBCS 40 (1993), 17–50 (p. 41). Iwan Wmffre (*Language and Place-Names in Wales. The Evidence of Toponymy in Cardiganshire* (Cardiff, 2003), p. 366) mentions subordinating *taw* and adverbial *maes* 'out' as linguistic features characteristic both of *Ystorya Bown* and of modern southern Welsh dialects.

[10] Compare Watkin, 'Rhagymadrodd', pp. xlix–lii, and Regine Reck, 'Heiligere Streiter und keuschere Jungfrauen. Religiöse Elemente in der

kymrischen Adaption des anglo-normannischen *Boeve de Haumtone*',
in Erich Poppe and L. C. H. Tristram (eds) *Übersetzung, Adaptation
und Akkulturation im insularen Mittelalter* (Münster, 1999), 289–304.

[11] The second 'proper' beginning and the divergent second part of the
beginning are included in our selections because of their methodo-
logical interest for the translators'/redactors' approaches.

[12] For discussions of her role in *Boeve*, which is closely reproduced in
Ystorya Bown, see Judith Weiss, 'The Wooing Woman in Anglo-Norman
Romance', in Maldwyn Mills et al. (eds) *Romance in Medieval England*
(Cambridge, 1991), 149–61, and ead., 'The Power and the Weakness of
Women in Anglo-Norman Romance', in Carol Meale (ed.) *Women and
Literature in Britain, 1150–1500* (Cambridge, 1993), 7–24.

[13] Judith Weiss (*Boeve de Haumtone*, p. 5) points out that the model for
the comic wooing of Boeve in bed by Josiane is probably provided by
Hue de Rotelande's *Ipomedon*. The central scene, in which Boeve is
pretending to snore when Josiane comes to his bed, 'anticipates by two
centuries the scene in Sir Gawain and the Green Knight when the Lady
of Haut Desert comes to Gawain's bedchamber and he feigns sleep'
(Weiss, 'The Wooing Woman', p. 149). Another scene in which the
burlesque potential is exploited to the full is Copart's baptism, but it
perhaps also prepares the way for his final disloyalty to the hero.

[14] Weiss, 'The Wooing Woman', p. 154.

[15] Compare Weiss, 'The Power and the Weakness', p. 12: '[T]he animal which
has attacked Josiane's husband when he wanted to mount it, joyfully
allows the hero on its back.'

[16] See also Regine Reck, *The Aesthetics of Combat in Medieval Welsh
Literature* (Wiesbaden, 2008) and ead., '*Dielwi o lyuyr y vuched* ('aus
dem Buch des Lebens löschen'). Die religiöse Inszenierung von Gewalt
in mittelalterlicher walisischer Prosaliteratur', in Ansgar Köb and Peter
Riedel (eds) *Emotion, Gewalt und Widerstand. Spannungsfelder zwischen
Geistlichem und Weltlichen Leben in Mittelalter und Früher Neuzeit*
(München, 2007), 17–30.

[17] The only exception appears to be the arming scene (W 536–47; *BdH*
532–7), in which ten items of clothing are mentioned – almost all of them
loan-words – in contrast to *BdH*'s three. The description may have been
designed to cater for an audience which was familiar with contemporary
fashions and could appreciate it, or, as Watkin notes, could have been
intended to suggest to the Welsh aristocracy the appropriate outfit of
a knight (compare *Ystorya Bown*, ed. Watkin, p. lxxvii).

[18] For some further discussion of the concept of relative distance see Erich
Poppe, '*Owein, Ystorya Bown*, and the Problem of 'Relative Distance':

Some Methodological Considerations and Speculations', in Ceridwen Lloyd-Morgan (ed.) *Arthurian Literature XXI: Celtic Arthurian Material* (Woodbridge and Rochester, 2004), 73–94.

[19] We have normalized the scribe's *Iosian* and *Josian* to *Iosian*.

[20] For the spellings of nasalization in MW, see *GMW* § 25, T. Arwyn Watkins, 'Dulliau orgraffyddol Cymraeg Canol o ddynodi'r treiglad trwynol', in *BBCS* 23 (1968–70), 7–13, and Watkin, 'Rhagymadrodd', pp. cxv–cxvi.

[21] Note *ygnhewillin* (l. 307), R *ygknewillin*.

[22] Note *yn niwycyat* (l. 444) and *vy nuw* (l. 584), but also *vyn dyw* (l. 146).

[23] Thus *y gwaet* (l. 69=R–), note *ym Bethlem* (l. 377).

[24] Compare John Morris-Jones, *A Welsh Grammar. Historical and Comparative* (Oxford, 1913), pp. 173, 23.

[25] Compare Watkin, 'Rhagymadrodd', pp. ci–cxiv, clxxxiii, for further details.

Selections from Ystorya Bown o Hamtwn

YBH 50–137 (= BdH 1–141)

Yn Hamtwn yd oed iarll a elwit Giwn. Ac aruer a wnaeth na
uynnei wreic yn y ieueigtit, a guedy hynny pan ymdreiglawd
parth a heneint y gwreickaawd. Sef gwreic¹ a uynnawd, gwreic
ieuanc tu draw y vor. A honno a oed yn karu gwr ieuanc
arderchawc a oed amherawdyr yn yr Almayn. Ac eissoes yn y   5
kyfamser hwnnw y kauas hi ueichogi o'r² racdywededic Giwn,
y gwr priawt. A ffan dyfu³ amser, mab a anet a elwit Bown. A'r
mab hwnnw a rodet ar uaeth ar⁴ varchawc kyuoethawc a elwit
Sabaoth.

A gwelet o'r iarlles y iarll yn llithraw parth ac amdrymder   10
heneint, y dremygu⁵ a'e yskaelussaw o garyat y racdywededic
amherawdyr ieuanc. Ac anuon kennat a wnaeth at amherawdyr⁶
yr Almaen ac adolwyn ydaw yr y charyat hi y uot ef a niuer o
varchogyon aruawc y gyt ac ef Duw Kalanmei yn fforest y iarll
yn ymgudyaw yndi, a hitheu a barei y'r iarll ac achydic⁷ o niuer 15
yscyuala⁸ mynet y'r fforest, ac yna⁹ y gallei ynteu llad penn y
iarll a'e anuon idi hitheu yn anrec, ac o hynny allan y gellynt
hwynteu bot y gyt yn dideruysc.

Y gennat a gerdawd y'r Almaen ac a ouynnawd yr amherawdyr.
'Y mae yn llys idaw a elwir¹⁰ Calys.' Tu ac yno y kerdawd y   20
genat, ac y'r Calys y doeth a dygwydaw ar benn y lin rac bron
yr amherawdyr a chyffarch guell idaw, ac yn dirgeledic menegi
y gennadwri idaw. A llawen fu yr amherawdyr wrth y gennat a
rodi ammws idaw a chymeint ac a uynnei o eur ac aryant yn
yghwanec, ac erchi idaw mynet drachefyn at y wreic vwyaf a   25
garei a dywedut idi y gwnaei ef pob peth o'r a archassei¹¹ hi
idaw ef yn oet y dyd. A'r gennat a doeth dracheuyn hyt yn

Hamtwn at y iarlles a menegi y gwnaei yr amherawdyr y
hewyllus hi ym phob peth o'r a archyssit idaw.

30   A llawen uu hitheu orawenus, a rywyr genthi y doei oed[12] y
dyd.

A Nos Clanmei y kymerth y iarlles cleuyt arnei ac y dywawt
wrth y iarll y bot yn claf.[13] Ac yna y doluryawd[14] yn uawr am
cleuyt y iarlles ac y dywawt wrthi, 'A oes dim a allo gwaret it[15]?
35   Ac o byd, na chel yr a gosto.' 'Oes, arglwyd,' heb hi, 'pei kawn
beth o gic baed coet yn ir, mi a gawn iechyt.' 'A wdost ti pa le
y keit kyuot ar vaed coet?' 'Gwn, arglwyd,' heb hi, 'yn yn[16]
fforest ni vch penn y mor y mae baed coet, medei y fforestwyr[17]
ymi.' 'A minneu a af auory yno yn vore.' Sef a wnaeth hitheu
40   yna, kyuodi yn y seuyll a dodi y dwylaw am y vynwgyl a rodi
kussan ydaw. A thrannoeth y gwiscawd y iarll ymdanaw ac y
kymerth y daryan a'y wayw a'e gledyf heb arueu yn angchwanec,
ac ar y petwyryd[18] marchawc yd aethant tu a'r fforest.

YBH 21–49 (= *BdH* 45–130) [second part of the first beginning]

Ac ystrywyaw a wnaeth pa vod y gallei gwplau y serchawl
45   damunedic ywyllus ymdanaw. Sef y mod y ystyryawd, dyuynnu
kennat attei a'e anuon at yr amherawdyr ac erchi idaw dyuot
yn oet dyd teruynedic y fforest ynyal a oed yn y iarllaeth Giwn
yn gyuagos y'r kastell yd oedynt yn presswylyaw yndaw, a
niuer mawr o varchogyon aruawc gyt ac ef, ac ymdirgelu yno,
50   a dywedut y parei hitheu y'r iarll vynet yn oet y dyd hwnnw a
niuer yskyuala gyt ac ef heb arueu, megys y gallei llad y iarll
a chyflenwi eu damunedic serch o hynny allan. Ac uuudhau a
oruc yr amherawdyr y hynny oll.

A ffan gigleu y iarlles hynny, sef a wnaeth hitheu, kymryt
55   arnei y bot yn glaf o orthrwm heint a dywedut na bydei vyw ony
damweinei idi gaffel y chwant o gic baed koet a oed yn y fforest
racdywededic. Ac yn oet y dyd y gwydat hi vot yr amherawdyr
yn ymdirgelu yn y fforest honno, annoc a wnaeth hitheu y'r
iarll vynet y hela y baed koet.

*In the forest the emperor Don is already lying in ambush with
his men. Giwn defends himself bravely but cannot fend off
the superior forces and is killed. His head is sent as a present*

*to his former wife, who welcomes the emperor and announces
that they will get married the next day. Bown laments his
father's death and chastises his mother. She strikes him, and
Bown falls to the ground.*

YBH 211–361 (= *BdH* 223–363)

Sef a wnaeth datmaeth[19] y mab (Sabaoth oed y enw, a marchawc   60
dewr kyuoethawc oed), kyuodi y vyny[20] ac achub y mab a'e
dyrchauel y vyny rwng y ddwylyaw,[21] a thu a'e lys mynnu
mynet[22] a'r mab. 'Sebaoth,' heb hitheu, 'reit vyd it tyngu yr
awr honn y pery hediw llad[23] y mab hwnn, neu ditheu a
grocker neu a vlinger yn vyw.' 'A mineu, arglwydes, a wnaf   65
hynny yn llawen.'

   Y mab a gymerth Saboth[24] ac a aeth ac ef tu a'e lys e hun.
A chyt ac y deuth adref, peri llad hwch a wnaeth Saboth a
chymryt dillat y mab a'e wlychu y gwaet[25] yr hwch. A gwedy
hynny y rwymaw y gyt a'e bwrw mywn dwfyr mawr. Ac yna   70
y dywawt Saboth wrth y mab, 'Mi a'th caraf[26] yn vawr o achos
dy dat. Ac wrth hynny byd di wrth vy ghyghor i, ac ef a ddaw
lles yt o hynny.' 'Mi a wnaf,' heb y mab, 'yn llawen.' 'Reit vyd
yt,' heb Saboth, 'cadw vy wyn i yn y weirglawd obry a chymryt
gwisc wgeileid[27] drwc ymdanat hyny el y pymthec niwarnawt   75
hyn heibyaw. Ac gwedy hynny mi a'th anuonaf y wlad[28] arall at
iarll kyuoethawc yssyd gyueillt a chedymdeith gwahanredawl
ymi. A phan ellych dwyn arueu a marchogaeth, dabre attaf ui,
a mi a thi a ryuelwn yn gadarn-wychyr ar yr amherawdyr.'
'Arglwyd dat, Duw a dalo yt, a minneu a wnaf hynny yn   80
llawen.'

   Trannoeth y bore y mab a aeth y gyt a'r wyn y'r weirglawd.
Sef a wnaeth ef, edrych ychydic ar y llaw deheu.[29] A ffan edrych,
ef a glywei yn y[30] llys a ry fuassei llys y dat y sawl gerdeu a
glodest a sarllach ar neithawr y vam ar nys clywssei kyn no   85
hynny y kyfelybrwyd. Sef a wnaeth y mab, anryuedu yn vawr
beth oed hynny a dywedut, 'Oi a arglwyd nef, truan a beth yw
hyn, vy mot i doe yn vab iarll kyuoethawc a hediw yn wugeil
wyn, ac eissoes mi a af y holi tref 'ynhat[31] y'r amherawdyr.' A
chymryt y wugeilffon[32] gadarn yn y law a cherdet tu a'r llys a   90
wnaeth ef. Ac y'r porth y doeth, a chywarch gwell y'r porthawr

a wnaeth ef ac adolwyn idaw y ellwg y mywn y ymwelet a'r
amherawdyr a'e gedymdeithon. Ac anheilwg uu gan y porthawr
ymadrodyon y mab, a dywedut a wnaeth drwy dicyouein, 'Ffo
95 ymdeith, herlot rubalt truant, bychan wyti a mawr yw dy
druansayth, a mab y butein wyt.' 'Gwir a dywedy ti,[33] vy mot i
yn vab y butein. Kelwyd a dywedy ditheu am vy mot i yn druawnt
neu yn rubalt.' A dyrchaf llaw ac a'y ffon y daraw ar warthaf
y ben yny eheta y emennyd yghylch y glusteu a'y ysgwydeu.
100   A cherdet racdaw a wnaeth y mab yny vyd yghynted y neuad
rac bronn yr amherawdyr a'e gedymdeithon. Ac yn ehofyn-
wychyr gofyn y'r amherawdyr pwy a royssei gennat idaw ef y
dodi y dwylaw am vynwgyl y wreic a oed ar y neillaw neu o'e
chussanu, kanys royssei ef, canys y vam ef oed hi. 'A chanys
105 kymereisti vy mam i y dreis, a llad vy nhat o'e hachos hi, mi a
wnaf uot yn ediuar y'th gallon di hynny etwa.' 'Taw, herlot
ffol,' heb yr amherawdyr. Sef a wnaeth y mab yna, llidyaw a
sorri, ac rac llit tardu y gwaet drwy y eneu a'e dwy ffroen. Ac
eissoes dyrchauel y ffon a wnaeth y mab a dyrchaf llaw ar benn
110 yr amherawdyr a'e daraw teirgweith ar y ben yny dygwydawd
ynteu a llewygu. Sef a wnaeth hithe,[34] y iarlles, dodi llef uchel
ac erchi dala y traytur. Sef a wnaeth rei o'r marchogyon,
kyuodi y vyny, a thrwy vn a thrwy arall diagk y mab a ffo at y
datmayth a wnaeth.
115   Sef a wnaeth Sabot, gouyn idaw pa ffo a oed arnaw. 'O lad vy
llystat,' heb y mab, 'vy galw yn herlot truawnt a wnaeth, ac o
achos hynny mi a rodeis tri dyrnawt idaw ar y ben, ac o'm tebic
i nys goruyd.' 'Cam a wnaethost,' heb y Sebaot, 'a cherydus
wyt. A bei[35] buassut wrth vy ghyghor i, ny chyuaruydei a thi na
120 thrallawt na gofit. Ac ar hynt ef a daw dy vam di, a hi a beir
vy llad i neu vy grogi.' Sef a wnaeth y mab yna, ofnocau[36] rac
kyuaruot trallawt a'e datmaeth a gellwg dagreu ac wylaw. Ac
yna kyuodi Sebaot y vyny a chymryt y mab a mynet o'e gudyaw
y'r celerdy.[37]
125   Ar hynny, nachaf yr iarlles yn dyuot yn vn o'r gwraged
kyweiraf a gwisgocaf a theckaf ry welsei[38] neb eiroet. A thrwy
y llit gouyn Bown y mab y Sebaot a wnaeth. 'Beth a ovynny di
imi o'r mab? Mi a'y lledeis megys y hercheisti ddoe ac a
rwymeis linin am y vynwgyl ef ac am vayn mawr ac a'y byryeis
130 y mywn dwfyr mawr anodyfyn.' 'Kelwyd, dwyllwr, a geny.[39]
Mi a baraf dy wligaw a'th losgi ony rody ym y mab.'

Sef a wnaeth Bown rac kyuaruot gofut a'y datmaeth, kyuodi o'e lechua a dyuot rac bron y vam. 'Llyma viui. Osit yt a holych, hawl. Nyt oes dim a dylyych y holi y'm datmaeth.'[40] Kymryt idi hithe y mab a galw deu varchawc attei a rodi y mab   135 yn eu llaw ac erchi udunt mynet ac ef y'r borthua, ac o cheynt neb a'y prynei y werthu, onys keynt y lad. Wynt a gerdyssant rocdun[41] tu a'r borthua a'r mab gantu,[42] ac yn y borthua yd oed dromwnt (sef yw hynny, llog diruawr y meint), a honno a oed lawn o Sarasinieit kreulawn. Y Sarasinieit a brynyssant y   140 mab yn drut, nyt amgen yr y petwarpwys o eur coeth. A guedy prynu y mab hwyl a dyrchafyssant, a hwylaw a wnaethant yny doethant hyt yn Egipt.

In Egypt Bown is presented to king Ermin, who is pleased with the boy and asks him where he comes from. Bown replies that he was born in England, and that his father was unlawfully killed and he himself exiled, but that he hopes to avenge his father's death as soon as he is grown up.

YBH 390–414 (= BdH 392–410)

Sef a wnaeth y brenhin yna, truanhau wrth y mab a gofyn idaw pwy oed y enw. 'Arglwyd,' heb ynte, 'Bown yw vy enw.' 'Bei   145 crettuti y Mahom,[43] vyn dyw i, ys da wr vydut ti. Ac nyt oes imi etiued namyn vn verch, a honno a'm brenhinaeth i a rodaf it yr ymadaw[44] a'th Gristonogayth.'[45] 'Arglwyd,' heb y mab, 'na daly adlo am hynny. Yr yssyd o dir a dayar a da gan y Sarassinieit a'r paganieit nac yr dy verch ditheu yn ygwanec, nyt ymadawn   150 i a'm Gristonogaeth[46] nac a Iessu Grist. Ac nys gorffo[47] a amdireto neu a gretto y Vahom.' 'A vab,' heb y brenhin, 'guastat iawn yw dy gallon ac anawd[48] yw dy drossi. A chyny wediych di Vahom, mi a vynnaf itti wassanaethu o'm ffiol arnaf i pob amser, a ffan elych yn oetran gwr, mi a'th vrdaf yn varchawc   155 vrdawl ac a'th wnaf yn synsgal[49] ar vy holl gyuoeth ac yn ben ystondardwr im.'

Bown grows up at king Ermin's court, and the knights are envious of the high regard the king shows for the fair and valiant boy. They devise a plan to kill him. One day when Bown has gone

to hunt an exceedingly dangerous wild boar, ten armed foresters
attack him, and although Bown has no weapon except the
shaft of his lance, he kills six of them and the others flee. From
a tower of the castle Iosian, the king's daughter, witnesses Bown's
bravery and falls in love with him. However, Bradmund, the
king of Damascus, arrives with a large host at Ermin's castle
and demands Iosian as his wife. Iosian suggests dubbing Bown a
knight so that he can lead the armies against king Bradmund.
Bown is dubbed a knight and dressed in armour and Iosian equips
him with a sword named Morgley and the horse Arwndel.

YBH 567–800 (= BdH 559–772)

Yna y kymerth Bown corn mawr ac y cant y gadarn. Sef a
wnaeth pawb o'r dinas yna, gwiscaw ymdanunt. A guedy
160 guiscaw dyuot y gyt a wnaethant. Yna y dywawt Ermin wrth
Bown, 'Kymer vy ystonder[50] i a cherda o'r blaen. A chwitheu,
ewch pawb gyt ac ef vegys yd elewch[51] gyt a mi pei elwn vy hun
y'r gyfranc.' Edrych eu niuer a wnaethant. Sef yd oedynt,
deugein mil o berchein meirych.
165   Adaw y dref a wnaythant, ac yn y[52] herbyn y doeth Bradmwnd
a chan mil o berchein[53] meirych gyt ac ef, a Rodefon oed yn
arwein y ystonderd[54] ef o'r blaen, ac ny charawd hwnnw duw
namyn Mahom. A blewogach oed a garwach y vlew no'r hwch
arwaf y gwrych neu yr[55] draenawc. Sef a wnaeth Bown yna,
170 ymgywreinyaw yn y gyfrwy ac ystynnu y draet yn y warthafleu
a brathu Arwndel ac ysparduneu a chyrchu Rodefon a gossot
arnaw a'y wayw a'y vrathu ymherued y daryan yny dyr y daryan
yn drylleu ac yny aeth y gwayw trwydaw ynteu a thrwy y holl
arueu yny dygwyd[56] Rodefon yn varw dan draet y varch, ac y
175 dywot Bown wrthaw, 'Gwell fuassei itt trigyaw gartref no dyuot
yma.' Ac ymchoelut at y gedymdeithon a dywedut wrthunt,
'Arglwydi, bydwn da, kanys ni a gawssam dechreu da ac nyt
oes na ffrwyth na nerth yn y bopyl a welwch racco.' A hwynteu,
nifer Bradmwnd, a fu argysswr mawr arnunt o welet llad eu
180 hystondardwr rac eu bron, a'r glewaf onadunt a fynnei y uot
gartref.
        Yna ymgyrchu a wnaethant, ac ar yr ymgyuaruot kyntaf ef
a las petwarcant o wyr Bradmwnd. A guedy hynny Bown a

dynnawd Morglei[57] y gledyf ac ysgathru ac ef, vegys paladurwr
yn llad y weirglawd, penneu y alon ac eu dwylaw a'e breicheu　185
a fob kyfryw aylawt o'r a gyuarfei ac ef, a'e gedymdeithon
ynteu yn vychyr-lew yn llad pawb o'r a gyfarfei ac wynteu. Ac
yna y dywot Bradmwnd yn vchel wrth y wyr, 'Lledwch ini niuer
Ermin yn ebrwyd, ac onys lledwch, ny chewch o'm da vyth werth
vn notwyd.' Sef a wnaeth Bown yna, glaschwerthin a dywedut,　190
'Bradmwnd, beth a vynneisti y'r wlat hon? Ae tybyeit kael
Iosian? Byd kynt[58] y key dy grogi wrth y iubet. Pony wely dy
daruot llad canmwyaf dy holl allu?'

　　Beth a dreithir yghwanec? Kyn hanner dyd neu ry daroed
llad holl allu Bradmwnd, ac ynteu e hunan ac ychydic o niuer y　195
gyt ac ef yn oledrat ar hyt dyfryn a ffoyssant, a deu o wyr Ermin
yn garcharoryon ganthun.[59] A darpar oed gan Bradmwnd peri
eu blingaw yn vyw, a gwaethiroed Duw na blingwyt kanys
trallawt braf a baryssant y Bown wedy hynny.

　　A guedy gwybot o Bown ry ffo Bradmwnd brathu Arwndel　200
a'r ysparduneu, a chynt y redawd y danaw noc yd ehettei y
llamysten neu yr walch pan ehettynt gyntaf. Ac ar hynt
ymordiwes a wnaeth a Bradmwnd a rodi dyrnawt idaw yny
dygwydawd ynteu y'r llawr, ac yna disgynnu y[60] Bown a'e achub
ar vessur llad y ben. Sef a wnaeth Bradmwnd, dygwydaw ar　205
ben y lin ac erchi nawd a thrugared a chynnic y wrogaeth idaw
a daly y danaw petwarcant cited a their mil y rwg kestyll a
thyroed a'e holl gyfoeth y am hynny. 'Na vynaf,' heb y Bown,
'namyn gwra ohonot y Ermin a chynnal dy gyuoeth y danaw
ef o hyn allan.' 'A minneu a wnaf hynny yn llawen.' A rodi y　210
wrogaeth a'e gywirdeb yn llaw Bown y dallei[61] o hynny allan y
dan Ermin. Ac yna y gellygawd Bown ef o'y wlat, a guaethiroed
nas lladawd, a Bown a rydhaawd y ddeu varchawc a oydynt
ygharchar,[62] a cham a wnaeth.

　　A guedy hynny ymhoylut dracheuyn a wnaeth Bown a'e　215
gedymdeithon yn ryd gyt ac ef, a dyuot a wnaethant hyt rac
bron Ermin. Ac yna y dywot Ermin,[63] 'Mawr a beth y dylywn
i dy garu di, Bown.' A galw y verch a wnaeth ac erchi idi mynet
y dynnu arueu Bown y ymdanaw a gwedy hynny mynet y'r
ystauell y vwytta a gwassanaythu arnaw yn didlawt. A hynny　220
a wnaeth hitheu yn llawen.

　　A guedy bwyta Iosian a dywot wrth Bown, 'Arglwyd tec,' heb
hi, 'ny chelaf ragot, ac ny allaf y gelu bei ys mynnwn, llawer

deigyr a wyleis i a llawer nos y colleis vy ghysgu o'th garyat, ac
225 ymhwyth na wrthot titheu vy gharyat i. Ac os gwrthody, ny
byd ym na hoydyl na bywyt, namyn o dicyouein mi a vydaf
varw.' 'A unbennes dec, na dala adlo am hynny canny weda.
Nyt oes nac amherawdyr na brenhin na iarll o'r a'th welei neu
a'th wypei ny bei dda ganthaw y wreica arnat. A Bratmwnd
230 vrenhin gwr arbennic kyfoethawc a ry fu y'th geissaw, ac ny
thygawd idaw. A minneu, gwr gwlat arall wyf heb na chastell
na thref na thy y'm helw, ac wrth hynny hwyrach y tycyei a
gwaeth y gwedei ym ymgyffelybu a thydi.'⁶⁴ 'A unben tec
bonhedic, na wrthot vi, kanys gwell yw genhyf tydi vnben o'th
235 vnbeis no bei kawn brenhin a uei eidaw dec vrenhinaeth.'⁶⁵
'Gwrthodaf, y rof a Duw,' heb y Bown.
    Sef a wnaeth hitheu yna, diliwaw a duaw vegys glo a
dygwydaw y'r llawr a llewygu. A guedy y chyuodi⁶⁶ y vyny,
gellwg y dagreu a wnaeth ac wylaw, a thrwy y llit y dywot hi,
240 'Gwir a dywedeisti nat oed nac amherawdyr na brenhin ny bei
dda ganthaw wreicca arnaf, a thitheu a'm gwrthodeisti vegys
bilein profadwy. A guell y gueduti yn glawdwr yn cladu clodyeu
ac yn kerdet ar dy draet yn anurdedic vegys pedestyr noc yn
varchawc vrdawl anrydedus yn llys arbennic. A dos y'th wlat,
245 uilein truawnt.' 'A unbennes,' heb y Bown, 'kelwyd a geny⁶⁷ am
'y mot⁶⁸ i yn vilein truawnt. Ny henwyf o'r bileineit. Ac amws⁶⁹
a royssosti imi, kymer ef, ny mynaf dy uacrayth yrdaw. A mi a
debygasswn ry daruot im y brynu yn drut pan enilleis y'th dat
ti vrenhinaeth arall hediw y arnaw ef.' Sef a wnaeth hitheu
250 yna, dygwydaw y'r llawr a llewygu, a breid na holltes y challon
rac llit a blwg.
    Kyuodi idaw ynteu yna y vyny ac adaw yr ystauell a mynet
y dy porthmon o'r dref a chyrchu vn o'r guelyeu a wnaeth a
mynet y orwed yndaw. A llitiawc oed ef am ymadrodyon Iosian.
255 Sef a wnaeth hitheu y gyt ac y kyuodes o'e llewygua, kymryt
ediuarwch am ry dywedut ohonei ymor⁷⁰ serth ac y dywot
wrth Bown a galw ar vrawtwayth idi ac erchi idaw mynet at
Bown ac adolwyn idaw dyuot dracheuyn y ymdidan a hi, ac o
ry dywedyssei hitheu dim a uei wrthwyneb ganthaw ef, hi a
260 wnaei iawn idaw wrth y varn a'e ewyllus e hun. Y gennat a aeth
at Bown ac a dygwydawd ar ben y lin rac bron Bown, a menegi
y gennadwri idaw a wnaeth ac adolwyn idaw mynet y ymwelet
a Iosian. 'Nac af, y rof a Duw,' heb ynteu, 'ac o achos dy dyfot

ti ar y gennadwri honno, kymer 'y gwisc[71] las racco, brethyn
odidawc yw o'r parth draw y'r mor.' Y wisc a gymerth y gennat,   265
a thrachefyn at Iosian y doeth a menegi idi na ddoi ef y ymwelet
a hi. Gofyn idi hitheu pwy a royssei y wisc odidawc honno
idaw ef. 'Bown,' heb ynteu. 'Myn Mahom vyn duw i, kelwyd
oed dywedut y vot ef yn vilein, a channy daw ef y ymwelet a
miui, miui a af y ymwelet ac ef.'   270

A rocddi y kerddawd hi yny ddoeth y'r ty yd oed Bown
yndaw. Ac y gyt ac y guyl èf hihi yn dyuot, kymryt idaw ynteu
y vot yn kysgu a chwrnu[72] yn vchel a wnaeth ef. Dyuot idi hi[73]
rocdi yny doeth hyt y guely, ac eisted ar erchwyn y gwely a
wnaeth hi a dywedut wrthaw, 'Arglwyd tec, duhun, yd oed im   275
ychydic ymdidan a vynnwn y dywedut wrthyt pei da gan dy
anryded di y warandaw.' 'A unbenes,' heb y Bown, 'lludedic a
briwedic wyf i, ac ymhwyth taw a sson[74] wrthyf a gat ym
orfowys, ac ys drwc a beth y diolcheisti imi vy llafur.' Sef a
wnaeth hitheu yna, ellwg y dagreu yn hidleit yny wlychawd y   280
hwyneb hi oll gan y dagreu. A gyt ac y gwyl ef hi yn y
drycyruerth hwnnw, truanhau yn y gallon a wnaeth wrthi. Ac
yna y dywot hi drwy y hwylaw wrthaw ef, 'Arglwyd,' heb hi,
'trugarhaa di wrthyf, ac o dywedeis eireu cam wrthyt, mi a
wnaf iawn it wrth dy vod, ac yn ygchwanec mi a ymadawaf[75]   285
a Mahom ac a gredaf y Iessu Grist, y gwr a diodefawd agheu
ymhren crok, ac a gymeraf Gristonogaeth yr dy garyat ti.' Sef
a wnaeth ynteu yna, kyuodi yn y eiste[76] a dodi y dwylaw am y
mynwgyl hi a rodi kussan idi.

*The kiss is witnessed by the two knights of Bradmund whom
Bown had released after the battle. They tell king Ermin that
Bown is treating his daughter dishonourably, sleeping with her
in broad daylight. Ermin, enraged but afraid to accuse Bown
openly, sends him with a letter, which Bown is on no account
to open, to king Bradmund. Bown leaves for Damascus without
his horse and his sword, unaware that the letter contains his
death warrant. On his way to Damascus Bown meets Sabaot's
son Terry, who has come to seek Bown. Bown however does
not reveal his identity but tells Terry that the person he is
seeking has been killed. Terry asks to read the letter but Bown
refuses to show it to him. When Bown reaches Damascus, he
hears the chanting of the heathen priests. Offended in his*

Christian piety he destroys an idol of their god Mahom and kills a priest. Bown delivers the letter to Bradmund who, following king Ermin's instructions, has Bown thrown into jail.

YBH 982–1016 (= BdH 940–70)

290 Ac yn llwrw y benn y byrywyt y waelot yr eol, a ffei nas differei Duw, ef a dorrassei[77] y vynwgyl kyn y vot hanner y fford.

Yn yr eol honno yd oed amylder o nadred a cholubyr a ffryuet ereill gwenwynic, a'r pryuet hynny oedynt yn y ofalu ac yn y vrathu yn vynych. Sef y cauas ynteu dan y dwylaw trossawl 295 petrogyl cadarn, ac a hwnnw ymdiffin rac y pryfet ac eu llad oll hayach. A hyt tra fu ef yn yr eol honno, ny chafas ef vn dyd trayan y wala o vara; a dwfyr, o mynnei ynteu, dan y draet y kaei. A deu varchawc a ossodet o'y warchadw ynteu.

A dydgweith y dywot Bown, 'Oi a arglwyd Duw, llawer 300 trallawt a gofut yd wyf i yn y gael yn yr eol hon. Ac myn Pedyr, pei diagwn odyma, mi a ddygwn y goron rac Ermin, a mi a rodwn idaw dyrnawt yn yghwanec hyt na dywettei vyth wedy hynny vn geir wrth arall. Ny haydysswn arnaw peri vym phoini vel[78] hyn, canys o'm cledeu i yd enilleis idaw brenhinaeth arall.' 305 A thrwy wylaw y dywot Bown yr ymadrodyon hynny.

A nosweith yd oed ef yn kysgu, y doeth pryf gwenwynic, a cholubyr oed y enw, a'y vrathu ygnhewillin[79] y tal. Sef a wnaeth ynteu, duhunaw a chael y pryf ac a'y drossawl y dyffust a'y lad.

In the meantime Iosian, unaware of Bown's imprisonment, asks her father where he is. King Ermin tells her that Bown has returned to England to avenge his father's death. Iosian, who has sworn to be true to Bown, is given against her will in marriage to Iuor of Mombraunt. She makes herself a silken chastity belt in order to be able to protect herself from Iuor. She takes Bown's horse and his sword with her to Mombraunt. Iuor attempts to mount Bown's horse and is seriously injured, but survives. Iosian remains in Mombraunt for six years, while Bown is still in prison.

YBH 1081–1149 (= *BdH* 1038–97)

A gwedy bot Bown chue blyned yn gwbyl ygharchar y dechreuis   310
ef ymdifregu a Iessu Grist a dywedut, 'Oi a arglwyd, vrenhin
nef a dayar, y gwr a'm gwnaeth ac a'm ffuruawd ar y delw ac
a'm prynawd yn ddrut ym bren crog[80] yr creu y gallon, yd
archaf it na'm gettych yn y poeneu hyn[81] a uo hwy, namwyn vy
grogi neu vy mligaw neu vy rydhau inheu odyma.' Sef yd oydynt   315
yn gwarandaw arnaw y ddeuwr a oedynt yn y warchadw, ac y
dywetyssant hwy, 'Ef a'th grogir di traytur auory.' A disgynnu
y[82] vn onadunt ar hyt raf y'r gwayret ar uessur dwyn Bown y'r
llawr uchaf.

   Y gyt ac y gwyl Bown ef yn disgynnu, sef a wnaeth ynteu,   320
kyuodi yn y seuyll yn y erbyn, a chyt ac y daw y gwr y'r llawr
ar ogyfuch a Bown, dyrchaf[83] llaw a'y ddwrn yn gayat a tharaw
Bown ar uon y glust yny dygwydawd ynteu y'r llawr. 'Oi a
arglwyd nef,' heb y Bown, 'praf a beth y gwanheeis i, kanys pan
ym byrywyt i yma gyntaf a bot 'yg cledeu[84] y'm llaw a chant   325
pagan o'r parth arall,[85] ny rodwn i geinawc erdunt hwy yll cant.
Ac[86] yr vn dyrnawt bychan y pagan hwn y dygwydeis inheu y'r
llawr, ac ony ddialaf ineu y dyrnawt, ny rodwn yrof wy piliedic.'
A dyrchauel y drossawl y vyny a wnaeth a tharaw y pagan ac ef
ar y ben yny vyd y emennyd yghylch y trossawl ac ynteu yn varw   330
y'r llawr. A chael cledeu y pagan o Bown[87] yna a'y dynnu allan.

   Ar hynny galw o'r marchawc arall ar y gedymdeith ac erchi
idaw ffrystaw a Bown y vyny wrth y diuetha. Sef a wnaeth
Bown yna, dachymygu[88] kelwyd a dywedut, 'Rydrwm wyf i,
ac ny digawn e hunan 'yn[89] dwyn, a dabre ditheu o'e gymorth   335
ef.'[90] 'Mi a wnaf hynny yn llawen.' A disgynnu a wnaeth ef ar
hyt y raf y'r gwaeret. Sef a wnaeth Bown yna, torri y raf a'r
cledeu yn vchaf y[91] gallei od uch y benn, a dygwydaw y gwr ar
vlaen y cledeu yny aeth y cledeu trwy y gallon ac ynteu yn
uarw y'r llawr. A thri diwarnawt kyn no hynny ny chawssei ef   340
dim bwyt. Ac yna guediaw a wnaeth ac ymdifregu a Duw y[92]
rydhau odyno. A guedy gwediaw ohonaw, trwy nerth yr arglwyd
Duw torri yr holl kadwyneu[93] heyrn a oedynt arnaw. Ac ny bu
lawenach ynteu eiroet noc yna, ac o lewenyd y neidawd uch y
benn pymthec troedued, at y uot[94] y neidawd, ac nyt oed un   345
ofyn yno arnaw. A fford ehag oed honno,[95] ar hyt y fford honno
y kerdawd yny doeth y berued y dinas.

*Bown reaches the centre of the city. In a stable he finds a horse
and armour. He mounts the horse, dons the armour and escapes
through the gates of the city. When Bradmund learns that Bown
has escaped, he is so enraged that he almost breaks the image
of his god Mahom. Together with his nephew Grandon and a
host of three thousand men he sets out to pursue Bown and
finally overtakes Bown on a river bank.*

YBH 1260–1434 (= *BdH* 1195–1347)

Sef a wnaeth Bratmwnd yna, brathu y march ac achub Bown
a thynnu y gledyf a'e daraw yny hyllt y daryan. Ynteu Bown
350 trwy y lit a dynnawd gledyf ac a'e trewis ar y benn trwy y
helym a'y arueu yny aeth ffiol y benn a thalym o'r emennyd
yndi hyt yn eitha⁹⁶ y maes ac ynteu yn varw y'r llawr. Ac yna
y dywot Bown wrthaw, 'Y rof a Duw, Bratmwnd, da yd
ymgyfarfuwyt⁹⁷ a thi, canys kefeist dy vrdaw yn effeirat gan
355 esgob kystal ac y kefeist, kanys tebic wyt y effeirat yr awr hon.'
      Ar hynny, nachaf Grandon y nei ar varch⁹⁸ da yn dyuot
attaw, ac ef a dywot wrth Bown yn vchel, 'Kyn mynet na bwyt
na diawt y'm penn i, ti a vydy yg groc.' 'A vackwy,' heb y Bown,
'o gwney 'y gyghor,⁹⁹ ti a ymhoyly dra'th gefyn ac a dygy dy
360 ewythyr atref, kanys effeirat yw newyd vrdaw, ac ym kyffes, o
doy a uo nes, mi a'th wnaf a'm cledeu yn diagon idaw.'
      Ac yna medylyaw y¹⁰⁰ Bown bei kaei y march a oed y danaw
na bydei arnaw wedy hynny ofyn neb. Ac yna kymryt gwayw
Bratmwnd a wnaeth a gossot ar Grandon ac ef a'e vedru yn y
365 daryan yny dorres y daryan ac yny aeth y gwaew trwydaw
ynteu a thrwy y holl arueu yny dygwyd ynteu yn varw y'r llawr.
Ac yna y disgynnawd ef y ar y varch ac y kymerth y march da,
ac yn amysgafyn yd ysgynnawd arnaw, ac heb vn ofyn yna
arnaw y kerdawd racdaw a ffawb yn y ymlit ynteu.
370   Ar hynny y doeth ef y lan dwfyr mawr, a haner milltir oed
yn llet y dwfyr, ac ny safei pont yn y dwfyr. Ny allei na llong nac
ysgraf arnaw ynteu. Sef a wnaeth Bown, dodi arllost y wayw
yn y dwfyr y edrych a oed dwfyn, ac yn diannot y dwfyr a duc y
gwaew gantaw o law Bown, kyn gadarnet oed y dwfyr a hynny.
375 Ac yna yd ofnocaawd Bown yn vawr ac y dechreuis wediaw a
dywedut, 'Oi a arglwyd Duw, vrenhin paradwys, a anet o'r

vorwyn wyry ym Bethlem a[101] diodefawd agheu ym phren croc
yr yn prynu ni, a'y gladu, ac odyno[102] yd aeth y anreithaw
uffern ac y torres y drysseu, ac a uadeuawd y Veir Vadlen y[103]
houered a'e ffechodeu, ac yn nawr[104] y mae yn eiste[105] ar ddeheu   380
y tat, a Dydbrawt a daw y varnu ar vyw a marw[106] herwyd eu
gweithret,[107] ac y gorchymynnaf it, Iessu Grist, vy eneit a'm corff
kanys gwell genhyf vy modi yn y dwfyr no'm kael o'r pagannieit
raco y'm verthyru[108] wrth y hewyllus.' Ac y gyt ac y darfu idaw
y wedi brathu y march ac ysparduneu a'e lityaw[109] a'e gymhell   385
y'r dwfyr. A'r march ar y neit kyntaf a vyryawd dec troetued ar
hugein yn y dwfyr. A thrwy nerth y wedi, a chedernyt y march,
drwy drallawt a gofut drwod yd aythant.

A gwedy eu dyuot drwod, nyt oed o'r byt wr lawenach noc
ef. Sef a wnaeth y march yna, ymysgytweit yny dygwydawd   390
Bown pedeir troytued y wrthaw. Eilweith ysgynnu ohonaw ar
y march a thygu, 'Myn y gwr a'm prynawd ym pren croc, yn
llawen mi a rodwn vy march a'm holl arueu yr haner vn dorth
o vara gwenith peilleit.'[110] Ac yna guedy diangk Bown drwod
hwynteu y paganneit y[111] trist-aflawen a ymhoylyssant drachefyn.   395

Ynteu Bown a gerdawd racdaw yny doeth y emyl castell o
vein marmor, ac ar ffenestyr o'r castell y gwelei wreicyangk
dec yn gogwydaw. 'Oi a arglwydes dec, yr y duw y credy di
idaw, dyro ym vn walyeit o fwyt.' 'A varchawc,' heb hitheu,
'ouer yw it dy ymbil a mi am vwyt, kanys Cristawn wyt ti, a'm   400
arglwyd inheu ysy[112] gawr dewr dihafarch, a mi a af ar hynt y
erchi idaw rodi yt dy giniaw a'e[113] drossawl heyernnyn.' 'Myn
Duw,' heb y Bown, 'ony chaf vwyt, wreicda, mi a vydaf varw.'

Sef a wnaeth hitheu, mynet at y cawr a menegi idaw ry dyuot
marchawc attei a begythyaw dwyn bwyt y dreis arnei. 'Mi a af   405
y ymwelet ac ef.' A'e drossawl heyernyn a gaflach a gymerth,
ac at Bown y daw[114] a gofyn idaw[115] o ba le y ducsei y march yn
lledrat. 'Tebic yw y'r march oed[116] gan Bratmwnd vy mrawt.'
'Gwir a dywedy,' heb y Bown, 'mi a'e hurdeis ddoe o'r tu yma
y Damascyl a'm cledeu yn effeirat, ac o'm tebic ny digawn   410
ganu[117] efferen vyth.' Sef a wnaeth y cawr yna, dyrchauel y
drossawl y vyny a cheissaw taraw Bown ac ef, ac nys metrawd
namwyn y march yny ddygwyd yn varw y'r llawr, a Bown yn
ehwybyr[118] a gyuodes y vyny ac a dynnawd y gledyf ac yn llitiawc
a ossodes ar y cawr, a fei metrassei, ef a'y trawssei trwydaw. Sef   415
a wnaeth y cawr yna, y vwrw a'r gaflach a'e vedru yn y uordwyt

yny aeth y gaflach trwy y vordwyt ac elchwyl dyrchauel y drossawl
a cheissaw taraw Bown ac ef, ac nys metrawd namwyn gan y
ystlys y'r llawr. Yna y gossodes Bown arnaw ynteu a'e vedru ar
420 ben y ysgwyd yny aeth y vreich ddeheu idaw ymdeith ac yn gyflym
y trewis y freich asseu[119] ymdeith ac yn ol hynny y benn a'e
deudroet, a'e eneit a gymerth y kythreuleit yn ddidadleu.

Ac yna yd aeth Bown y mywn y'r castell ac[120] yd erchis y'r
wreic dwyn bwyt idaw. A hitheu a dywot y cai ddigawn, ac nyt
425 oed uawr y diolchei idi yr hynny. Yna y duc y wreic idaw bara[121]
peilleit da, yr hyn a oed reit idaw, a chic gwarthec ac yn ol
hynny kic garanot a hwyeit a guedy hynny amylder o gic man
adar a gwin claret digawn y gadarnet. Ac ynteu a fwytaawd
yn rawth megys dyn disynwyr, a ffeth diryued oed hynny, hir
430 y buassei heb vwyt.

A guedy bwyta digawn ohonaw ac yuet kymedrolder, y gryfder
oll a'e lewder a gafas drachefyn. Ac yna y dywot wrth y wreic,
'Moes[122] im varch.' A march a rodes hitheu idaw, ac ysgynnu a
wnaeth ynteu ar y march a cherdet racdaw hyt yGharusalem[123]
435 at y Padriarch.

*Bown comes to the patriarch in Jerusalem, confesses and
informs him of what has happened to him so far. The patriarch
pities him and provides him with money. However, before he
returns to England, Bown decides to see Iosian one more time.
At Ermin's court he learns that Iosian has been married to Iuor
of Mombraunt. He asks for the way and proceeds towards
Mombraunt.*

YBH 1481–1617 (= *BdH* 1381–1490)

A gwedy dyuot Bown y Mamwrawnt[124] y klywei dywedut ry
vynet Iuor a'e holl nifer y gyt ac ef y hela ac na thriciassei neb
yn y llys a'r castell onyt Iosian a'e brawtwaeth. A diruawr
lewenyd a gymerth ynteu o glybot hynny. A thu a'r llys yd aeth
440 ef, a chyseuyll yn emyl y llys a wnaeth heb vynet y mywn.

Sef y clywei Iosian yn wylaw yn vchel ac yn dywedut, 'Oi a
Bown de Hamtwn, mawr a beth y'th gereis ac y'th caraf,[125] a ffa
wed y bydaf vyw inheu canys colleis i didi?' Sef a wnaeth ynteu
yna, truanhau wrthi. Ac yna yn niwycyat palmer yd aeth y mywn

y'r llys ac erchi y giniaw y Iosian. 'Ti a'e key yn llawen,' heb   445
hitheu, 'a chroyssaw wrthyt.' A dyuot ohonei e hunan a rodi
dwfyr idaw y ymolchi,[126] a hitheu a wassnaethawd[127] ac a rodes
idaw yn didlawt bwyt a llyn.

A gwedy bwyta hi a dechreuis ymddidan ac ef a gouyn o ba le
pan hanoed a ffa le y ganydoed. 'O Loygyr pan hanwyf, ac yno   450
y'm ganet.' Sef a wnaeth hitheu yna, kymryt diruawr lewenyd
yndi a gofyn y'r palmer a atwaynat marchawc o Loygyr a elwit
Bown de Hamtwn. 'Atwen yn hyspys,' heb ynteu, 'car imi oed
y tat,[128] vegys y dywetpwyt imi, ac nyt oes wlwydyn etto yr pan y
gueleis i ef yn llad cawr dewr a brenhin kyfoethawc yn ygwanec.   455
Ac y may ef yn y wlat yn iach-lawen ac yn dial y dat yn ffenedic,
wedy ry gymryt gwreic dec vonhedic kyfoethawc a'e ffriodi.'
'Gwreic?' heb Iosian. 'Ie, ys gwir,' heb ynteu. Sef a wnaeth
hitheu yna, dygwydaw y'r llawr a llewygu, a ryued fu na bu
uarw.   460

A gwedy y chyfodi o'r llewycua, lleuein a wnaeth yn vchel a
dywedut, 'Ys truan a amser y'm ganet i ac ys drwc a dyn y
thyghetuen wyf i kanys colleis i Bown.' Ac nyt oed yn y byt
dyn druanach y chyssyr no hi na mwy y drycyruerth. Ac yna
edrych yn graf a wnaeth hi yn wyneb y palmer a dywedut, 'Y   465
palmer,' heb hi, 'bei na'th welwn yn y diwygyat hwn, mi a
gredwn ac a dywedwn y taw[129] ti oed Bown.' 'Na vi,' heb ynteu,
'a mi a'e kicleu ef yn dywedut yn vyneich[130] am y march, ac a
ydiw hwnnw genhyt ti?' 'Och,' heb hi, 'y mae y march yna, ac
nyt oes neb o'r llys yma a veido mynet yn y gyfyl yr pan golles   470
Bown y arglwyd.'

Ar hynny y doeth y brawtuaeth hi attei ac y gofynnawd
hitheu idaw beth a dybygei ef am y palmer, ae Bown oed ef ae
nyt ef,[131] ac erchi idaw mynet oe y[132] edrych. Ac ynteu a aeth ac
ar hynt a doeth etti drachefyn ac a ddywot wrthi y mae Bown   475
oed y palmer. Y gyt ac y cicleu y march enwi Bown, kymryt
llewenyd a ryfic yndaw a wnaeth, a gweryru yn vchel-orawenus
a wnaeth. A hitheu a doeth at y palmer ac a dywot wrthaw,[133]
'Pony chlywy di y ryw ryfic ac ynni y mae y march yn y gymryt
yndaw o achos clybot enwi Bown vnweith?' 'Clywaf,' heb ynteu,   480
'a mi a af o'e[134] edrych ac a wybydaf a atto im y varchogaeth.'

Ac at y march yd aeth, ac ar hynt ysgynnu[135] arnaw a oruc.
A'r march yna, wedy cael y arglwyd, a fu ryfugus llamsachus,
a cherdet gwalop y danaw ar hyt y kwrt a wnaeth yny doeth

485 at Iosian. A hitheu drwy y hwylaw a dywot yna wrth y palmer,
'Yn awr y gwn i yn wir y mae tydi yw y gwr mwyaf a gereis ac
a garaf, ac yd oedwn ys llawer o amser yn damunaw y welet;
ar yr Iessu Grist,[136] disgyn y'r llawr a llyma dy varch yt, a'th
gledyf, ti a'e key.' 'Arglwydes,'[137] heb ynteu, 'y cledyf dyro ym,
490 ac ragof y kerdaf inheu tu a Lloegyr.' 'Nyt y uelly y byd,[138]
namyn pan elych di, minheu a af gyt a thi.' 'Arglwydes,' heb
ynteu, 'gat e hunan, brenhines gyuoethawc wyt ti, a minheu
gwr tlawt wyf. Ac myn[139] Iessu Grist, iawnach oed ym dy
gassau no'th garu, kanys dy dat a beris 'y gharcharu[140] yg
495 charchar drwc llawer[141] o amser. A ffeth arall heuyt, y nos arall
y kyffesseis i wrth y Padriarch, ac ynteu a orchymynnawd im
na chymerwn ym gwreica onyt morwyn, a thitheu, yd vyt seith
mlyned yn gwbyl gyt ac Iuor dy wr, ac o beut vorwyn yr hyt
honno, ryuedawt mawr yw.'[142] 'A unben tec,' heb hitheu, 'myn
500 y gwr a dylyaf i y wediaw, yn wir mi a dywedaf na bu kytknawt
hyt hyn eto y rof i ac Iuor, ac awn y gyt y Loygyr. A gwedy
darffo vy medydyaw, ony'm key yn vorwyn, o'm vncrys gyr vi
ymdeith.' 'Yn llawen,' heb ynteu. Ac yna disgynnu a wnaeth ef,
a mynet dwylaw mynwgyl a wnaethant, a mawr yd ymgerynt
505 a llewenyd praf a gymerth pawb onadunt, vegys y digawn
pawb y wybot.

*Before Iosian and Bown can flee together, Iuor returns from the
hunt. By a ruse they succeed in sending Iuor away, intoxicate the
remaining knights and escape together with Iosian's foster
brother Boniface, taking with them some gold and silver, but
no food. The next day they find themselves pursued by Iuor's
men and decide to hide in a cave until the men return to the
castle. While Bown is hunting, Iosian and Boniface are attacked
by two lions; they kill Boniface, but leave Iosian unharmed,
since it is against their nature to harm a person of kingly
descent.*

YBH 1852–2056 (= *BdH* 1678–1840)

Ar hynny, nachaf Bown yn dyuot y'r lle yd adawssei Bonfei a
Iosian wedy ry lad danys ohonaw. A ffan edrych, ef a wyl
breich Bonyfei yno, ac o'r parth arall ef a wyl y droet, o'r tu arall

ef a welei mordwyt y varch a'e droet wedy ry biliaw hyt y'r 510
esgyrn. Sef a wnaeth ynteu yna, galw ar Iosian ac erchi idi dyuot
y ymddidan ac ef. A gwedy nas gwyl ac nas kigleu, y
dygwyddawd ynteu y ar y march y'r llawr ac y llewygawd. Ac os
drwc oed drycyruerth Bown, gwaeth oed, bei gallei,[143]
drycyruerth y march herwyd y ssynwyr ef, yn gweryru ac yn 515
cladu y ddayar a'e draet. A ffwy bynnac a vei yn edrych arnadunt,
truan vydei yn y gallon, yr kadarnet vei, gwelet eu drycyruerth.

Yna kyuodi Bown y vynyd a dyuot yn y ansawd e hun a'e
lewder, ac ysgynnu ar Arwndel y varch a cherdet racdaw ac
edrych ar y gwreic[144] a wnaeth. A ffan edrych, ef a wyl y llewot 520
a Iosian y rygthunt yg charchar. Sef a wnaeth Iosian, llefein y
gyt ac y gwyl Bown, ac erchi idaw dial agheu Bonfei y ysgwier.
'Mi a wnaf hynny,' heb y Bown, 'a thi a allut y wybot yn
hyspys y dialaf. Ef a vyd reit y'r llewot vynet drwy vy nwylaw
i.'   525

Y gyt ac y clyw y llewot ynteu yn dywedut kyuodi udunt
hwynteu y vynyd. Sef a wnaeth Iosian, dodi y dwylaw am
vynwgyl y neill a'e attal herwyd y gallei oreu. Sef a wnaeth
Bown, erchi idi y ellwg. 'Na ellygaf,' heb hitheu, 'hyny darffo
yt llad y llall.' 'Myn Duw,[145] reit vyd it y ellwg. Sef achos yw, 530
pan uof i y'm gwlat ac ymplith 'y gwyrda,[146] o dywettwn[147] i
neu o bocsachun ry daruot im llad deu lew, titheu a dywedut
y mae ti a dalyssei y neill hyt tra fum inheu yn llad y llall, a
hynny nys mynnwn inheu yr yr holl Gristonogaeth. Ac wrth
hynny ellwg ef. Ac onys gellygy, ym kyffes, miui a af ymdeith, 535
a thitheu a drigye[148] yna.' 'Gellygaf, arglwyd,[149] a Iessu Grist
a'thiffero[150] rac eu drwc.'

Yna disgynnu Bown y ar y varch rac kyuaruot drwc a'r
march. A chywreinyaw y daryan ar y ysgwyd asseu a thynnu y
gledeu. Sef a wnaeth y neill o'r llewot o'r blaen, y achub a 540
dyrchauel y ddeudroet vlayn a gossot ar Bown a'e vedru ar y
daryan yny dorres y daryan yn drylleu. Sef a wnaeth ynteu
Bown, gossot ar y llew a'e gledeu a'e vedru ar y ben, ac ny
wnaeth[151] y dyrnawt hwnnw dim argywed y'r llew rac calettet
croen y ben. Yna agori y safyn y'r[152] llew ar vessur tagu Bown. 545
Sef a wnaeth ynteu Bown drwy y lit a'e angerd, gossot ar y
llew a'e vedru yn y safyn yny aeth y cledeu ar y hyt a thrwy y
gallon, ac heb olud tynnu y gledyf a wnaeth ef, a'r llew a
dygwydawd yn varw.

550 Y llew arall a'e achubawd yn llitiawc-wenwynic ac a rwygawd
lluruc Bown hyt nat oed well hi no henbeis lom doll dreuledic.
A dyrchafel y deudroet ulaen a wnaeth ef a cheissaw gossot ar
Bown. Sef a wnaeth Bown yn drebelit yna, gossot arnaw ynteu
a'e vedru ar y ddeudroet yny aeth y draet a thalym o'r breicheu
555 y wrth y corff ac yny dygwyd ynteu y'r llawr. A gwedy hynny
y cwplaawd Bown wassanaeth y llew yn dda digawn.

A gwedy daruot idaw llad y ddeu lew, ysgynnu ar Arwndel
a wnaeth, ac edrych ychydic o'e vlaen a wnaeth. A ffan edrych,
ef a wyl ar diwycyat dyn ryw aniueil gobraff y veint ar nys
560 gwelsei eiroet y gyffelyb. A ffon hayarn braff oed yn y law, ac
ny allei degwyr cryf y dwyn un cam rac y thrymet. Ar y ystlys
yd oed yspodyl drom vnuiniawc. Y rwg y deu lygat yd oed teir
troetued ehalaeth a thal mawr amhyl, a duach oed no'r muchyd.
A thrwyn praff-froenuoll oed idaw a choesseu hir-lymyon
565 yscyrnic. Gwallt y ben oed vegys rawn meirych gre. Y lygeit
oedynt gymeint a'r dwy sawsser vwyaf ry welsei neb eiroet.
Hwy oed y ddanned noc ysgithred y baed coet hwyaf[153] y
ysgithred, a geneu gobraf oed idaw. A ffan dywettei dan agori
y safyn vegys hen ellgi bwn, aneglur agharueid y dywedei. A
570 breicheu hirion cadarn ac ewined calet-lym, a chyn galettet
oed y ewined yn wir ac nat oed mur maen yn y Gristonogaeth
nys diwreidei ef yn gwbyl yn vn dyd.

A'r gwr hagyr aflunyeid hwnnw, y gyt ac y gwyl ef Bown y
dywot yn vchel, 'Reit vyd it, twyllwr bradwr, ymhoylut dra'th
575 gefyn a rodi Iosian vy arglwydes im a dugost yn llathrut.' Sef a
wnaeth Bown, anryuedu yn vawr prafder y gwr[154] a'e afluneidet
a chwerthin a dywedut, 'Tydi vilein,' heb y Bown, 'yr y duw y
credy di idaw, dywet ym ae kymeint pawb y'th wlat i[155] a thidi.'
'Kymeint, myn vyn duw i Teruygawnt.[156] A ffan[157] fum i y'm
580 gwlat, hwynt a dywedynt na bydei ohonaf inheu dim meint
byth. Ac rac kewilid yd edeweis 'y gwlat[158] ac y deuthum y'r
wlat hon ac y gwrheeis y Iuor o Mwmbrawnt ac y guesneitheis
yn gywir. A thitheu a dugost y wreic ef yn llathrut, ac myn
Mahom vy nuw i, mi a vriwaf dy ben di yn drylleu a'm ffon i y
585 drom.' 'Taw, pagan,[159] a'th son,' heb y Bown, 'a gormod yw dy
vocsach oll. A ffan ymladom, ony ladaf i dy benn di yr mawr
a'm cledeu, ny volaf fu hunan werth vn uanec.'

Ac heb olud brathu Arwndel ac ysparduneu a gossot ar y
gwr du, a Chopart oed y enw, a'e vedru yg cledyr y dwyuron

a'e wayw hyny dyrr y paladyr yn drylleu. Ac ny chyffroes vn   590
aylawt ar Gopart yr y vedru mwy noc yr na metrit. Ac yna
dyrchafel y ffon idaw ynteu a bwrw Bown a hi, ac rac daet y
diuachellawd Bown. Ny medrawd namyn derwen, a honno a
diwreidawd ac a dygwydawd y'r llawr gan y dyrnawt. Ac ar
hynt dodi y law ar dwrn y yspodol a wnaeth ef ar uessur taraw   595
Bown. Sef a wnaeth y march yna, dyrchauel y ddeudroet ol a
gossot ar y gwr du yg cledyr y ddwyfron a'e daraw yghyueir y
gallon yny dygwyddawd ynteu y'r llawr. A'r march yna a'e
duludawd yn gadarn-gryf y ryddaw a'r dayr hyt na allei
Copart yn vnwed kyuodi yn y seuyll.   600

   Yna disgynnu Bown y ar y march a thynnu y gledeu ar
uessur llad penn Copart. Sef a wnaeth Iosian yna, dywedut ac
erchi y Copart gwrhau y Bown a chymryt Cristonogaeth.[160]
'Ny wna ef hynny,' heb y Bown, 'a channys gwna, myn y gwr
y credaf inheu idaw,' heb y Bown, 'mi a ladaf y benn a'm   605
cledeu yn ddiannot.' Sef a wnaeth Copart yna, dywedut yn
vchel yny datseinawd y coydyd o pob parth, ac adolwyn y
Bown nas lladei a dywedut y bydei wr idaw ac y kymerei
Cristonogaeth yn llawen. 'Ny allaf credu it,' heb y Bown.
'Gelly, ys gwir,' heb y Iosian, 'mi a vydaf warant y byd gwr   610
fydlawn it.' 'Yn llawen, 'heb y Bown, 'a minneu a gymeraf y
wrogaeth ef.' Yna cyuodi Copart y vyny ac heb olud rodi y
wrogaeth y Bown a wnaeth.

Together with Copart they reach a port, enter a ship and sail
to Cologne. At the harbour Bown is met by his uncle, the
bishop of Cologne. Bown and Iosian are made welcome.

YBH 2147–2241(= *BdH* 1916–1979)

Ar hynny, nachaf Copart[161] yn dyuot ac yn gyrru y meirych a
oed arnunt eu pynneu o eur ac aryant o'e vlaen.   615

   Y gyt ac y gwyl yr esgob Copart mor anfurueid a hynny,
dyrchauel y law y vyny ac rac y ofyn degweith yd ymswynawd,
a gofyn y Bown pa ryw gythreul oed hwnnw. 'Ny chelaf[162]
ragot, arglwyd ewythyr, gwas ym yw, ac vn o'r gwyr dewraf o'r
byt oll yw.' 'Gwas?' heb yr esgob, 'Nyt ef a wnel Duw y dyuot   620
ef y'm llys a miui[163] yn dragywyd.' 'Daw, or byd da genhyti,

arglwyd, a ni a vynnwn y vedydyaw ef hediw.' 'Pa wed, anwylnei,
y bedydjit ef? Canys pei delynt holl wyr y dinas y gyt, ny ellynt
hwy y dyrchauel ef o'r bedydlestyr.'

625   A ffan wyl Copart yr esgob, ef a dybygassei may bugeil oed yr
esgob am y welet yn newyd eillaw a gwedy torri y wallt. Ac yna
ymdidan a wnaeth yr esgob a'e nei [. . .]. A gwedy yr ymddidan
hwnnw hwynt a gerdyssant racdun[164] tu a'r llys, ac y eglwys y
Drindawt yd aethant. A Iosian yn diannot a vedydywyt, ac ar
630   Copart[165] y gelwit. Ac ny ellit y dodi ef yn y betydlestyr[166] rac
y veint, namwyn kerwyn uawr a gyrchwyt a'e llenwi o dwfyr.
     Sef a wnaeth y dynnyon a'e delynt wrth vedyd, keissaw y
dyrchauel. Ac yna y dywot ynteu, 'Ofer yw ywch wch[167] lafur,
gedwch ym vy hunan mynet y mywn a dowch chwitheu a
635   dodwch wch[168] dwylaw arnaf.' 'Ni a wnawn hynny yn llawen,'
heb y dynyon, 'ac nyt oes kyghor well no hwnnw.' Yna y
byryawd ef neit yn y gerwyn yn llwrwf y deudroet, ac oer iawn
oed y dwfyr. Ac yna yd ymgeinawd ef a'r esgob ac y dywot,
'Beth a vynny di, fugeil bilein, ae vy modi i yn y dwfyr hwnn?
640   Ryhir yd wyf Gristawn, gellwg vi ymdeith!' Ac ar hynt y
kyfodes ef yn y seuyll ac y byryawd neit y maes o'r gerwyn yn
hoeth-lumun.[169] A ffwy bynhac a'e gwelei ef yna, ny welas
eiroet delw ar dyn kyn hacret na chyn dybrytet a honno, ac nyt
oed debic y dim onyt y gythreul yn keissaw eneideu wrth eu
645   poeni. Ac achub y dillat a wnaeth ef ar hynt ac eu gwisgaw. A
gwedy hynny y'r neuad yd aethant oc[170] eu bwyt.

*Bown learns from the bishop that his foster father Sabaot has
begun to wage war upon the emperor Don, who had killed his
father. He leaves Iosian under Copart's protection and, provided
with a troop of five-hundred men, sets out towards England. He
comes to Hamtwn and, pretending to be a French mercenary and
offering Don his services in his war against Sabaot, succeeds in
getting provisions from him. He takes them to Sabaot, who is
overjoyed to see Bown, who was believed to have been killed by
the Saracens. Meanwhile Iosian, who has remained in Cologne,
is courted by earl Milys. She rejects his advances and tells him
that she will never accept him as long as she is protected against
his threats by Copart. As soon as Milys hears that, he lures
Copart to a castle in the sea and locks him up there. Copart tears
down the walls with his nails and jumps into the sea, but Milys*

has already sailed back to Cologne and married Iosian. News of this reach Bown, who sets out for Cologne at once.

YBH 2413–2458 (= BdH 2099–2133)

A gwedy daruot y Milys priodi Iosian o'e hanuod, y nos honno y peris ef y dwyn hitheu y ystafell. A guedy y dyuot hi y mywn yd erchis ef cau drws yr ystauell ody vaes, a hynny a wnaethpwyt. A guely mawr ehalaeth uchel wedy y[171] dyrchauel ar pedeir 650 fforch oed idaw, ac y hwnnw y kymhellawd ef arnei vynet. Ynteu ar eistedfa oed[172] ar ogyfuwch hayach a'r erchwyn.

Y gwr a eistedawd y ymdiarchenu, a mawr iawn oed y ffrwst y gwplau y ewyllys ar Iosian. Y gyt ac y gwyl hi y ffrwst ef, ucheneidaw idi hitheu yn uchel. Ac eissoes dyuot cof idi y 655 gwregis, a'e gymryt a'e wneuthur yn redecuagyl, ac yn ehuthwimwth y dodes dros y ben am y vynwgyl. Ac heb olud y'r parth arall y'r gwely y byryawd neit y'r llawr a ffen y gwregis yn y llaw, ac y velly y delis y gwregis yn gryf-fenedic yn y dwylaw yny dagawd y gwr ac yny dorres asgwrn y vynwgyl. 660

Trannoeth y bore y doethant y varchogyon a'e vaccwyeit yghylch drws yr ystauell ac erchi y Milys kyfodi y vyny canys talym o'r dyd oed. Hitheu a dywot, 'Ofer yw wch[173] son, mi a'e tegeis yr neithwyr.' Yna y torryssant drws yr ystauell ac y kymeryssant Iosian ac y rwymyssant y dwylaw yn galet ac 665 yd aethant a hi maes o'r dinas wrth y llosgi. A than mawr a gyneuwyt. Ac y gyt ac y gwyl hi hynny, ymdifregu a'r arglwyd Duw a wnaeth ac adolwyn y vot yn drugarawc wrth y heneit kan daroed barnu y chorff. A[174] wylaw a lleuein a wnaeth.

Bown and Copart arrive just in time to save Iosian from being burned in the fire. All three of them then return to Sabaot's castle and are made welcome. Preparations for battle are made. A messenger is sent to the emperor, telling him that Bown has come to avenge his father's death. The emperor asks for the support of the king of Britain. With their combined forces they march against Bown. Bown defeats the emperor and his army is put to flight. Copart takes the emperor in chains to the castle. Don pleads for mercy, but Bown has him killed in a vat of boiling lead. When Bown's mother is informed of her husband's death, she kills the messenger and commits suicide. Bown now takes possession of his estates and marries Iosian. He travels to the court of London to meet the king of Britain.

YBH 2801–2815 (= *BdH* 2408–19)

670 Ac yna y kyuarchassant well idaw yn y mod hwnn, 'Duw yr hwnn
a anet o'r vorwyn wyry yrom ni pechaduryeit, ac a uu teir blyned
ar dec ar ugeint[175] ar y dayar yn diodef penyt, ac a drywestawd
deugein niwarnawt yr amdiffyn[176] y bobyl, ac y gwerthawd
Iudas y'r Idewon yr dec ar ugeint aryant y poeni[177] a'e ffrowy-
675 llaw, ac a diodefawd agheu ym phren croc, ac a uu varw ac a
gladwyt, a'r trydyt[178] dyd y kyuodes o veirw, ac y daw Dydbrawt
y varnu arnam[179] ni oll, boet ef a'th iachao di a'th varwneit.'

The king restores his dominion and lands to Bown. The next day a horse-race is held, in which Bown is asked to participate. Bown overtakes the other knights on his horse Arwndel, and Arwndel runs so fast that they reach the borders of his patrimony. Bown vows to build a castle at this place and to name it after Arwndel. He then returns to the king's court in London. The king's son is impressed by Arwndel's speed and tries to obtain the horse from Bown. When Bown refuses, he attempts to steal Arwndel at night but is killed when the horse strikes him with its hooves. Bown is made liable for the king's son's death and is again expelled from the country. His land is given to Sabaot. Bown, Iosian – who is pregnant by now – and Sabaot's son Terry return to Egypt. Copart stealthily escapes to Mombraunt and betrays Bown and Iosian to Iuor. Meanwhile Iosian's time has come. As she lies alone in a forest, Copart arrives with a number of Saracens and abducts her. Bown and Terry return and find the newborn infants, but there is no trace of Iosian. They begin to seek her all over the country.

YBH 3162–3220 (= *BdH* 2729–81)

Tewi weithon a wnawn am Bown a dywedut am Sabaot. Mal
yd yttoed yn y ystauell yn kyscu, ef a welei breudwyt mal nat

oed hof ganthaw. Sef ryw vreudwyt a welei, kant o lewot yn 680
achub Bown ac yn dwyn y varch rac Bown, ac odyna ef a welei
y vynet y Seint Gilys y geissaw trugared. A duhunaw a oruc a
menegi y wreic yr hynn a welsei. A hitheu a erchis idaw nas
kymerei yn drwc arnaw a dywedut daruot y Bown colli Iosian
a geni deu vab idi.   685
    Ac yna Sabaot a gymerth gwisc pererin ymdanaw ac a gauas
llong vawr a elwit dromwnd. Ac yn honno yd aeth trwy'r mor,
ac ny orffwysawd hyny deuth y Seint Gilys. A phan deuth y'r
dywededic le, yr eglwys a gyrchawd ac y offrwm yd aeth ac
vgein o gydymdeithon gyt ac ef o'e wlat. Ac yn dyuot udunt 690
o'r eglwys y kyhyrdawd ac wynt Iosian. A phan y gwelas
Sabaot, llawen uu. 'Arglwydes,' heb ef, 'mae Bown a Therri?'
'Syr,' heb hitheu, 'ymwarandaw a mi. Ef a damchweinawd geni
deu vab ym mywn fforest, a thra yttoydwn yn y damwein
hwnnw, mynet a orugant Bown a Therri y'r coet y droi, ac yn 695
hynny dyuot[180] o'r Sarassinyeit racco a'm dwyn ganthunt.' 'Ae
Sarascinyeit ynt, arglwydes?' 'Ie,' heb hitheu, 'wely di y twyllwr
a beris Bown y vedydyaw.'
    Sef a oruc Sabaot, dyrchauel y ffonn a tharaw y traytwr ar
y benn yny dygwydawd[181] yn varw. Ac o lef vchel erchi a oruc 700
Sabaot y'r pererinyon taraw y Sarascinyeit. Ac yna y pererinyon
ac eu ffynn a drawssant y Sarascinyeit, a porthmyn y dref a
deuthont, ac y llas y Sarascinyeit oll.
    Ac heb ohir y kymerth Sabaot Iosian. Heb yr hitheu, 'Yn
digelwyd dywet ym pa wed yd arwedy ui trwy y gwledi[182] 705
hynn.' Heb y Sabaot, 'Na vit arnat vn offyn. Ti a wisky wisc
gwr ymdanat, ac yn aruer gwr ti a gerdy.' Heb hitheu, 'Nyt
affreit ym ymoglyt.' Ac yna Sabaot a gymerth gwisc pererin[183]
ymdanaw ac ymdanei hitheu gwisc adfwyn gwrawl. Ac yna yd
aeth Iosian y rodyaw y varchnat, a phroui a oruc[184] hi llysewyn, 710
ac ny welas hi erroyt[185] llysewyn well, kanys a hwnnw y[186] gallei
wneuthur y llyw y mynhei[187] ar y hwyneb a'e chorff. Ac racdunt
y kerdassant heb orffowys y geissaw Bown a Therri.

Sabaot and Iosian come to Bradford, where Sabaot is taken ill.
They remain there for seven years because of Sabaot's illness.
Meanwhile Bown and Terry continue to look for Iosian. Bown
has his sons, Miles and Gi, baptized and gives them into fosterage
with a forester and a fisherman. Then Bown and Terry travel on.

YBH 3250–3458 (= *BdH* 2817–3006)

Ac yskynnu ar eu meirch a orugant ac ymiachau, ac ny
715 orffwyssassant hyny deuthant y dref a oed gyfagos. A chymryt
eu lletty a orugant ynhy[188] Garsi, porthman o'r dref, ac yn
esmwyth y kawsant. A phan daruu vdunt bwyta ac yuet dogyn
ac eu meirch dogyn, eu gwelyeu a oydynt barawt, y gysgu yd
aethant.
720   A'r bore pan uu eglur y dyd, edrych a wnaeth Bown allan, a
gwelet a oruc ef penyadur ac amkan y vil o wyr gyt ac ef yn
arfawc. Ac yna yd achubawd Bown vdunt yn gyntaf ar
Arwndel[189] y varch clotuorus, ac yn gyntaf y trewys ef yr hwn
a oed yn dwyn y maner. A hyt tra barhaawd y wayw, ef a'e
725 troes wynt y agheu. A Therri vegys marchawc da a ladawd arall
ac a gymerth y amws herwyd y afwyneu ac a'e rodes y lettywr
yn hur y letty. A phei na damchweinei dyuot Bown, ef a
yspeilyssit y dref ac a'e lloscyssit.
Pann deuth Bown ac[190] eu hymlit, o lef vchel dywedut wrth
730 wyr y dref, 'Ef a'ch[191] anreithir ony bydwch ffenedic yn awch
ymdiffyn trwy dewrder hyt na cheffwch[192] byth werth vn
geinawc oc yssyd yn y dref.' Ac yna ymwan a oruc Bown ac
Armiger, ac ymhoylut a orugant oll at y trywyr, a'r trywyr
hynny a orugant, ac ny wydynt o py le pan hanoydynt na pha
735 le y genyssit. A digyaw a oruc Bown wrth y bobyl hynny a tharaw
penn y iarll y ergyt y arnaw a'e anuon yn anrec y'r vnbennes
bioed y dreff. A gwelet a oruc hitheu y dyrnodeu a rodes Bown,
a hof uu genthi, a bwrw y charyat arnaw ef a oruc hi. Ac ar
hynny y teruynawd[193] y gyfrageu,[194] a chyrchu eu llettyeu a
740 orugant Bown a Therri, a pharawt oed eu bwyt gan eu llettywr.
A gwedy daruot vdunt vwyta ac yuet dogyn, ef a athoed y
rei ereill y'r llys, a diolwch mawr a oruc hi y'r marchogyon a'e
hanregawd. A gwell uuassei genthi pei kawssoedei y trywyr
racdywededic. Yr arglwydes a anuones y synyscal y erchi idaw
745 vynet[195] yn ebrwyd y gyrchu y marchogyon, ac ynteu a aeth ac
ny ffynnyawd racdaw. A phan gigleu hi na doent, hi a aeth e
hunan hyt attunt.
A phan y gwelas Bown hi yn dyuot, ymgymhwyssaw a oruc.
A hitheu a gyuarchawd well idaw val hynn, 'Duw yr hwnn a'n
750 kreawd a'th iachao[196] di, vy gharedic. Mi a anuoneis attat y
adolwc yt dyuot attaf, a thitheu a diogeist.' 'Arglwydes, nys

medylyeis. Namyn os gallaf, yn vore[197] mi a gychwynnaf odyma
y geissaw Iosian vy gwreic a golleis kyn echdoe y bore, ac y
Duw y diolchaf deu vab a edewis ymi.' Heb yr vnbennes,
'Ryued yw hynny. A thitheu, kymer vi yn wreic it os mynhy.' 755
'Vyg chwaer[198] dec,' heb Bown, 'peit a hynny. Yr yssyd ytti, ny
wnawn i hynny a bot yn dwyllwr.'

A thrwy hynny tyfu kynhen y rydunt hyt pann digiawd
bob[199] vn ohonunt ac y begythyawd y vrenhines peri llad y
ben. 'Arglwydes,' heb Bown, 'gwarandaw arnaf vi: trwy yr 760
amot hwnn yma mi a'th gymerhaf yn wreic ym, ony chaffaf
gyuot ar Iosian ody vywn y seith mlyned hynn a petwar[200]
mis.' 'Ac yn llawen,' heb hi, 'da y dywedy.' Ac ar hynny y
teruynwys yr amrysson rygthunt, ac y gyscu y nos honno yd
aethant. 765

A thranoeth y bore y kyuodes y iarlles, a thros y bont y'r
eglwys yd aethant, ac archescob Gris a gant yr efferen ac a
wnaeth eu priodas. A phann daruu yr efferen, y llys a
gyrchassant. Dwuyr·y ymolchi a gymerassant, ac eu[201] bwyt
yd aethant, a marchogyon vrdolyon advwyn yn gwasanaethu 770
arnunt. A gwedy bwyt yd erchis[202] Bown y'r ieirll vynet ar
lleilltu[203] y rodi vdunt rydideu, a dyuot ohonunt hwynteu y
rodi gwrogaeth idaw ynteu. A gwedy daruot udunt talu
teyrnget a gwrogaeth idaw, y dyd a ediw a'r nos a dyuu.[204] Y
gyscu yd aethant ody vywn paleis brenhinawl. 775

A thrannoeth pan dwyrhaawd y dyd yd aeth duc Uascal a'y
wyr ac a gyhyrdassant[205] a duc Dostris, ac y gyt[206] yd aethant
y ryuelu ar arglwydes y dref, ac y gyt ac wynt yd oed pymptheg
mil o wyr aruawc. A gyrru eu meirch a orugant megys gwyr
kyndeirawc, ac ny orffwyssassant hynny[207] doethant y'r dref 780
trwy distryw y wlat heb trugarhau wrthunt o dim.

Ac yn vore y kyuodes Bown a chlybot a oruc y sson, a phan
vwybu ef yr ystyr, ef a orchymynwys y wyr gwiscaw eu
harueu. A gwelet a oruc y llurugeu a'r helmeu yn discleiraw.
Ac y gwiscawd ynteu y gledyf, ac yscynnu a orugant ar eu 785
meirch, ac yscynnu yn gyntaf a oruc Bown ar Arwndel a chyt
ac ef Terri y marchawc clotuorus, ac ymlaen y rei ereill achub
y Sore a'e daraw yny holltes y daryan ac yny ballwys idaw y
luruc ac yny aeth ynteu y'r llawr yn varw. Ac yna Terri a
achubawd Lancelin a thrwy vawred y daraw yny dygwydawd 790
yn varw y'r llawr.

Ac yna y dodes Bown kri ac yd[208] erchis y varchogyon clotuorus
ac eu cledyfeu awchus taraw dyrnodeu da. A phob vn yn mynet
dros y gilid, a mawr uu yr ymlad gan y kadeu trymyon. Niuer y
795   dref a enillawd y maes, a'r[209] rei ereill a gilyassant y ystlys brynn.
Ac o vlaen y niuer y marchocaawd Bown. A Therri, ny bu hwyra,
ef a ladawd agos y deugein. Ac yna Bown a ymlidyawd duc
Uascal, a phan ymhoelawd penn y varch at Bown, ef a dorres
Bown y wayw yndaw heb odric ac yny aeth ynteu y'r llawr. Ac
800   yna tynnu Morglei y gledyf a oruc ar vessur llad y benn. Ac yna
erchi trugared a oruc ac ystynnu y gledyf at Bown, ac ynteu
a'e kymerth.

Ac odyna yd ymlidiawd ef duc Dostris ac a'e trewis ar y
luruc dyrnawt mawr braf, ac ar yr helym yr eil dyrnawt yny
805   dorres yn deu ac yny dygwydawd ynteu yn varw. Tec oedynt y
bydinoed a orchyuygawd Bown, ac ar hynny y teruynawd y
vrwydyr. Ac yna yd aethant y'r llys, ac eu bwyt a gymerassant.

A mawr y karei Bown yr vnbennes uonhedic, a seith mlyned
y buant y gyt, ac ny bu kytknawt rygthunt mwy no chynt. A
810   dydgweith mal yd oedynt velly, galw a oruc yr vnbennes ar
Bown. 'A dybygy di caffel vy holl ewyllus i ual hynn?' 'Ef a'r
allei ymi y gaffel,' heb y Bown.

Weithon tewi a wnawn am Bown a menegi am Sabaot, nyt
amgen no dyuot gwaret idaw o'e gleuyt, diolwch y Duw, a galw
815   ar Iosian a oruc, 'Ni a awn y geissaw vy arglwyd.' 'Iawn a[210]
dywedy,' heb hitheu. Ac yna yskynnu a orugant ar eu meirch,
a'r fford a gerdassant.

A dyuot a orugant diwarnawt am awr osper y dinas vrdedic
a elwit Amulis, gwedy keissaw eu harglwyd ar draws yr holl
820   vrenhinyaeth. Ac ynhy[211] vrda o'r dinas kymryt lletty a orugant.
Ac yna yd aeth Sabaot y'r llys, a phan deuth y mywn, kyntaf
dyn a welas Bown yn eisted ar veinc, a chyr y law y wreic vwyaf
a garei yn yr[212] amser hwnnw, kany wydat dim y wrth Iosian.
A chyrchu attaw ef a oruc a chyfarch gwell idaw yn y mod
825   hwnn, 'Arglwyd, Duw a'th iachao di ac a gerych.' Ac yna y
gouynnawd Bown wrth Sabaot, 'Py le y'th anet?' 'Arglwyd,'
heb ef, 'pererin o vrenhinyaeth arall wyf i, ac yn y dinas[213] yd
wyf ys dydyeu, a dyuot attat ti y erchi nerth[214] yr Duw.' 'A thitheu,
vy gharedic,' heb y Bown, 'a geffy digawn.'

830   A galw a oruc ar Terri a dywedut wrthaw, 'A wely di y tybycket
ef[215] y Sabaot? A dyro vwyt idaw.' 'Mi a rodaf digawn it, gann

debyccet wyt y'm tat.' 'Duw a diolcho yt,' heb Sabaot. 'Ef a
dywedit y'm gwlat dy uot ti yn vab y mi.' Ac yna y diolches
Terri y Duw welet y dat, a redec at Bown a dywedut wrthaw y
mae Sabaot oed y pererin. Ac yn gyflym yd achubassant attaw   835
ac yd amouynassant ac ef am Iosian. Ac ynteu a dywawt y
gwydat chwedleu y wrthi a menegi y bot ynhy[216] wrda yn lletty.
      Ac yna mynet a oruc Bown a Therri a Sabaot tu a'e lletty hi.
A hitheu a ymolches o'r lliw a oed erni hyny ydoed[217] yn y lliw e
hunan. A phan doeth Bown a Therri etti, y chymryt a orugant a'e   840
harwein gyt ac wynt hyt at y duces. A phan y gwelas y dukes
hi mor dec ac y gwelas a mor adfwyn, gouyn a oruc y Bown ae
y wreic briawt ef oed honno. 'Ie, arglwydes,' heb ef. 'Kymer di
dy wreic,' heb hi, 'a dyro y minheu Terri.' 'Mi a wnaf hynny yn
llawen.' Ac yna y[218] llawenhaawd pob vn o'r gwraged wrth y   845
gilid.

*At this moment the foster fathers, having heard that Bown is in
the city, arrive with the two sons of Iosian and Bown. They all
rejoice in their meeting. The duchess of Amulis marries Terry.
A son is born to Terry and named after Bown, and Iosian gives
birth to a daughter. Bown is told that Iuor is warring upon
king Ermin in Mombraunt. He assembles a host and comes to
Ermin's aid. Ermin begs Bown's forgiveness for the imprison-
ment Bown has had to suffer on his account. Iuor assembles his
army outside king Ermin's castle. Bown defeats Iuor's army,
which retreats, but Iuor sends for new troops. Bown sends for
Terry. In the following battle Iuor is captured but afterwards
set free for a large ransom. King Ermin falls ill and, having
confessed his sins, dies. Gi is crowned king of Bradford. Sabaot
takes his leave and returns to Hamtwn. One day Sabaot sees in
a dream that Iuor has stolen Bown's horse by means of magic.
He returns to Iuor's capital in the guise of a pilgrim, frees
Arwndel and takes the horse back to Bown. Bown decides to
prepare for a final battle against Iuor and the pagans.*

YBH 4031–4182 (= *BdH* 3551–3684)

Bellach y dywedwn am Iuor ffalst prouadwy. Pan gyuodes y
bore drannoeth, anuon kenhadeu yn ol vgein admirales a

phymthec brenhin, ac wynteu a doethant wrth y ewyllus ef. Ac
850 y gyt y marchoccaassant tu a Bratmwnd[219] megys kyndeirawc.[220]
Eu son a gigleu niuer y dinas, a gwiscaw a oruc y brenhin a
niuer y dinas ymdanunt, ac yscynnu yn gyflym ar eu meirch
ac y'r porth allan yd aeth y marchogyon grymussaf o'r dyrnas.
Ac yna y gelwis Ifor ar Iudas o Machabes y erchi idaw rodi
855 kyghor, 'canys os mi a gymer arnaf vrwydyr yn erbyn Bown,
y gyffelyb varchawc ny bu eiroet,[221] a goreu wyf inheu o'm holl
kenedyl,[222] ac wrth hynny ni a ymgyhyrdwn.' 'Jawn a[223] dywedy,'
heb y brenhin Damaskyl. Ac yna yscynnu ar eu meirch, ac y
ymwan yd aethant.
860   A Bown a yscynnawd ar y varch yn gyflym, a galw a oruc Iuor
yn vchel ar Bown ac erchi idaw aros ychydic a dywedut wrthaw,
'Syr,' heb ef, 'y mae gyt a thi kynulleitua vawr o varwneit y dinas,
ac y mae gyt a minheu brenhined ac[224] admiralys. A mawr vyd
hynny gwedy ymgymyscant, ac wrth hynny ymgyhyrdwn,
865 myn duw, os mynhwn.[225] Ac os mi a ledir neu a oruydir, ef a
vyd tyghedic it pymthec brenhin a'm tir a'm dayar yn ryd y
titheu, a minheu ym Mwmbrawnt.' A gwrtheb a oruc Bown idaw
a dywedut mae da oed gantaw hynny. Ac ar hynny dyrchauel
eu dwylaw ac ymgadarnhau hyt pan oed diogel gantunt.
870   Ac yn gyflym yd aeth y marchogyon y wiscaw aruei ymdanunt
hwynteu ac eu meirch. Ac yna y kerdassant ar lleilltu, a gwedyaw
a oruc Bown ar Duw yr hwnn ny dywawt kelwyd, ac Iuor a
oed yn gwediaw ar Mahwn[226] ac Apolin. Ac yscynnu a orugant
ar eu meirch a rodi dyrnodeu mawr mynych ar eu taryaneu, a
875 chedeirn oedynt eu llurugeu na thorassant, ac ny dygwydawd
un onadunt.
       Ac yna tynnu a oruc Bown Morglei y gledyf a tharaw Iuor ac
ef ar y helym dyrnawt mawr yny dygwydwys y blodeu a'r mein[227]
ac yny aeth y dyrnawt ar y march yny dygwydawd y march yn
880 varw y'r llawr. A gwedy dygwydaw y march ynteu[228] a gyuodes,
a Bown a discynnawd rac kyhwrd drwc a'e varch. A phan welas
Iuor Bown yn discyn, tynnu cledyf a oruc a rodi dyrnawt mawr
y Bown[229] yny dygwydawd y blodeu a'r mein gan y dyrnawt. A
blyghau a oruc Bown a gwneuthur chwaen Ffragheid ffrwyth-
885 lawn, yssigaw y vwnwgyl a llad y benn, a dygwydaw a wnaeth
y korff ar y dayar, a Belsabub a aeth a'r eneit.
       Ac yna yd ymhoyles Gi urenhin ar y varch at Bown, a Milys a
deuth attunt, ac ar yr hynt honno yd ouynoccaawd y bydinoed.

Ac yna y brathawd Gi y varch at Abraham a'e daraw, a da y traweint[230] y Ffreinc a ffrwythlawn. A Milys a gyrchawd arall o'r 890 Sarassinyeit ac a'e lladawd, nyt amgen no brenhin Damascyl, mab y Abraham. A Bown vab Terri a ladawd arall, a Sabaot a vyryawd arall, a Therri duc Ciuil a ladawd admiral, a Bown o Hamtwn a ladawd arall, ac enkyt un awr y teruynwyt[231] y vrwydyr.   895

Ac yna ar lann[232] auon yd ymgynullassant y Sarascinyeit, ac yna y delit dec admiral ar hugeint a dec mrenhin ac a'e dugassant ganthunt y Vratmwnd.[233] Ac yna y dywawt y barwn penhaf ohonunt, 'O mynwch chwi caffel tir Mwmbrawnt, reit vyd ywch caffel arueu y pauwneit, canys clotuorus yw marchogyon 900 Ffreinc mywn arueu. A mi a gytunaf a chwi ac a gredaf, os mynwch, y Duw creawdyr ac a wrthodaf Mahwn[234] vyn duw a Theruagawnt.' Ac y velly y dywawt heuet y pympthec mrenhin.

Ac ar y geir hwnnw y brathassant eu meirch tu a'r llys, ac yn gyntaf y barwn penhaf yMwmbrawnt[235] ac yn y ol ynteu Gi 905 vrenhin a chyt ac ef pymtheg mil yn y ganlyn. Ac ody vaes yd oed Bown yn gwneuthur marthyrolyaeth mawr. A phan welas y pauwneit hynny, trist uuant. A'r porthcwlis a ystygassant, a Gi ody vywn a chyt ac ef mil o varchogyon clotuorus. A phan welas y pauwneit wynt yn dyuot y lys Iuor, ffo a orugant, ac 910 nyt arbedassant na mawr na bychan. Eithyr a alwei ar vedit[236] onadunt[237] ny welei na mam na mab.

A heb ohir, nachaf hen Bown yn dyuot attaw a'e niuer gyt ac ef. Ac yna yd aeth Gi vrenhin yn erbyn Bown a dywedut wrthaw. 'Syr,' heb y[238] Bown, 'Duw a dalo it.' Ac yna anuon a orugant yn 915 ol Iosian y Vratmwnd,[239] ac yn ol escyb ac yscolheigion gwybydus hyt na thrigyei neb heb dyuot, ac yn ol brenhin Damascyl heuyt ac a vynhei gret ar gyhoed ac a vynhei[240] heb ohir y vedydyaw. Heb y brenhin Damascyl, 'Mi a vydaf Gristawn ac a wrthodaf[241] Teruygawnt.' Ac y velly y dywawt pawb y gyt ac ef.   920

Yna y dywawt Bown, 'Dygwch yma Teruagawnt.' Ac y gossodassant[242] yn y seuyll rac bron Bown. 'Mahwn,' heb y Bown, 'ti a uuost mawrhydic[243] eiroet, gwna hediw ffrwytheu mawr.' Ac yna y kymerth Bown ffon bres ac a[244] trewis Teruagawnt ac ef, a'r escob a vyrywys dwfyr sswyn arnunt, 925 ac yna y neidawd kostawcki koch ohonaw ac a[245] ffoawd. 'Edrychwch,' heb y Bown, 'y pydiw yd oedewch yn credu.' Heb y brenhin Damascyl, 'Drwc yd oedem yn credu, ac y velly y

gwnaeth yn tadeu kyn no ni. Y neb a gredawd mywn kelwydeu,
930   madeuit Duw vdunt.' 'A ninheu,' heb y brenhined a heb y[246]
petwar admirales, 'ny chredwn ni yn yn bywyt vdunt.' Ac
anuon a orugant yn ol y gwraged ac eu meibon, ac ereill yn ol
eu tadeu ac eu kyfnesseuieit, ac wynteu a deuthant yn llawen.
Ny bu eiroet yscolheic, yr daet darlleawdyr vei, a allei enwi eu
935   riuedi gan veint y gynulleitua. A mawr[247] uu y ryuedawt meint
a vedydywyt, kanys petwar mis y parhaawd y bedyt.[248] Ac
escob yn pregethu udunt, ac wylaw a orugant o ediuarwch a
ffustaw cledyr eu dwyuron yr gogonyant y Duw ac yr tristwch
y'r diawl.

*The pope is sent for and crowns Bown and Iosian. Messengers
arrive and relate that the king of England has disinherited
Sabaot's son Roboant, who had been appointed guardian of
Bown's dominions. Bown and Terry travel to England with a
great army. At their arrival the frightened king surrenders and
offers his daughter to Bown's son Miles, together with his
kingdom.*

YBH 4301–4373 (= *BdH* 3787–3850)

940   Weithon y mae Bown o Hamtwn yn vrenhin coronawc a'e deu
vab yn vrenhined, diolwch y Duw.
[. . .] Ac yna y kerdawd Bown vrenhin racdaw hyt yn
Hamtwn, ac y'r borthua y doeth[249] ac y eu llogheu. Ac yna y
kymerth Terri gennat y vynet y wlat. A'r nos honno yd aeth
945   Bown y dinas Cwlwyn. A thrannoeth y bore kymryt y genhat
a oruc Bown a cherdet dros amryuaylon gwledi[250] hyny deuthant
hyt yn Ruuein y dinas da. Ac yno[251] yd oed archescob o'e
vrenhinaeth ef a'e vab. Ac yn drebelit y doeth y vab attaw, ac
y'r mor yd aethant, ac ny orffwyssassant yny deuthant hyt yn
950   Mwnbrawnt.[252]
A phan deuthant y'r llys, yd oed y vrenhines yn glaf-
gorweidawc.[253] A phan welas hi y harglwyd, galw arnaw a
oruc. 'Arglwyd,' heb hi, 'claf iawn wyf, ac ny pharhaaf nepell.'
A phan gigleu y brenhin hynny, ynuydu hayach a oruc a dywedut,
955   'Arglwydes, or bydy varw di, minheu a vydaf uarw gyt a thi.'
'Arglwyd,' heb hi, 'pwy a gynheil dy gyfoetheu urdedic?'

'Arglwydes,' heb ef, 'ny'm tawr[254] ohonunt. Eisswys diolchaf[255]
y Duw y mae im tri meib a allant kynhal vy ghyfoetheu.'
　　Ac yna y peris galw ar yr archescob ac a[256] dywawt wrthaw,
'Gwna orchymyn vy arglwydes.' 'Mi a wnaf, arglwyd, yn vfyd.'　960
Ac yna y kyffessawd[257] ac y dywawt y ewyllus.[258] A thra yttoydyn[259]
yn hynny, ef a athoed Bown y edrych y varch, a phan doeth yr
ystabyl, ef a welei y varch yn varw, ac yna yd ymhoelawd dan
wylaw. Ac yna y doeth y vab attaw y hyfrydu,[260] ac val kynt
abreid na cholles y synwyr, ac y deuth y mab at y vam a dywedut　965
wrthi, 'Vy mam,' heb ef, 'yd wyt yn llad vy nhat, kanys kymeint
yw y duchan ac na bu eiroet y gymeint.' 'Vy mab y tec,' heb yr
hi, 'galw ar Bown yma.'
　　Ac yna y redawd y mab yn ol y tat,[261] 'Vyn that y tec,' heb ef,
'bryssya att vy mam.' A phan welas Bown hi, y kymerth ef hi　970
rwg y vreicheu, a gorchymyn a orugant Gi eu mab y Duw, ac
ar hynny y teruynassant wyll deu[262] ac y doeth yn yghwanec y
gant o egylyon y dwyn eu heneideu y'r nef at Duw. Eu gwylaw
a orugant y nos honno hyt trannoeth, ac nyd[263] oed da gan Gi
urenhin eu cladu wynt ymplith dynyon ereill. Ef a beris　975
wneuthur ysgrin o vein marmor a pheri y urenhined vrdedic ac
escyb dwyn y kyrff y'r eglwys a barassei ef e hun y wneuthur
yn enw Seint Lawrens, ac yna y coronawyt Gi a goron
Mwmbrawnt. Ac y velly y teruyna ystorya Bown.[264]

Manuscript readings and variants

[1] gwreic *R*, wreic *W*, gwreic *W* l. 6.
[2] o'r racdywededic *R*, o racdywededic *W*, o'r vn dywededic *E*.
[3] deuth *R*, rydyuu *W* l. 13.
[4] att *R*.
[5] dremygu] dremygu a oruc *R*.
[6] amherawdyr *R*, amheradyr *W*.
[7] ychydic *R*.
[8] yscyuala] ysgaelusaf *R*.
[9] yna *R*, ynna *W*.
[10] elwir *E*, elwit *W*, *R*.
[11] *corrected in the MS from* archyssei *W*, archyssei *R*.
[12] oet *R*.
[13] glaf *R*.
[14] doluryawd] doluryawd y iarll *R*.

15 itt *R*.
16 an *R*.
17 fforestwr *R*.
18 bedwyryd *R*.
19 tatmaeth *R*.
20 uynyd *R*.
21 dwylaw *R*.
22 mynet *R*, mynyt *W*.
23 hediw llad] dihenydyaw *R*.
24 Y mab a gymerth Saboth] Sabaoth a gymherth y mab *R*.
25 ae gwlychu yggwaet *R*.
26 garaf *R*.
27 uugeileid *R*.
28 wlat *R*.
29 deheu] deheu idaw *R*.
30 yn y llys *R*, yn llys *W*.
31 vyntat *R*.
32 uugeilffonn *R*.
33 di *R*.
34 hitheu *R*.
35 phei *R*.
36 ofnocau] ofynhau *R*.
37 selerdy *R*.
38 gwiscgocaf a theckaf ry welsei] gwisgocaf or a welsei *R*.
39 geny] dywedy di *R*.
40 tatmaeth *R*.
41 gerdyssant rocdun] gerdassant racdunt *R*.
42 gantunt *R*.
43 uahumet *R*.
44 ymadaw] ymadaw ohona[t] *R*.
45 cristonogaeth *R*.
46 cristonogaeth *R*.
47 gorffo *R*, gorsfo *W* (perhaps a scribal mistake).
48 anawd] anawd iawn *R*.
49 synysgal *R*.
50 ystondard *R*.
51 elewch *R*, yleech *W*.
52 eu *R*.
53 berchein *R*, berchen *W*.
54 ystondard *R*.
55 neur *R*.
56 dygwydod *R*.
57 Morglei *R*, moglei *W*.

58 Byd kynt] Ys byd gynt *R.*
59 gantunt *R.*
60 awnaeth *R.*
61 dalhei *R.*
62 a rydhaawd . . . ygharchar] a ellyngawd y deu garcharawr a oedynt ygkarchar gan bratmwnt *R.*
63 dywot ~~bown wrth~~ ermin] dywawt ermin wrth bown *R.*
64 ath thydi *W.*
65 brenhinyaeth *R.*
66 y chyuodi *R,* ychkyuodi *W.*
67 geny] dywedy *R.*
68 vy mot yn *R.*
69 amws] amws da *R.*
70 mor *R.*
71 wisc *R.*
72 chwyrnu *R.*
73 Dyuot idi hi / dyuot a oruc hi *R.*
74 a sson] ath son *R.*
75 ymwadaf *R.*
76 eisted *R.*
77 dorrassei *R,* dorrei *W.*
78 ual *R.*
79 ygknewillin *R.*
80 croc *R.*
81 poeneu hyn] poen hwnn *R.*
82 o *R.*
83 dyrchauel *R.*
84 vygcledyf *R.*
85 arall] arall im *R.*
86 ar *W,* Ac *R.*
87 vown *R.*
88 dechymygu *R.*
89 vyn *R.*
90 o'e gymorth ef] y gymorth dy gedymdeith *R.*
91 y] ac y *R.*
92 y] ar y *R.*
93 gadwyneu *R.*
94 uot *R,* not *W.*
95 yno *R.*
96 eithaf *R.*
97 ymgaruuwyt *R,* ymgarfuwyt *W.*
98 y ar varch *R,* ar march *W.*
99 vygkyghor *R.*

[100] medylyaw y Bown] medylyaw a wnaeth bown*R*.

[101] a] ac a *R*.

[102] odyna *R*.

[103] y *R*, y | y *W*.

[104] awr *R*.

[105] eisted *R*.

[106] ar vyw a marw] ar vyw ac ar veirw *R*.

[107] gweithretoed *R*.

[108] merthyru *R*.

[109] lidyaw *R*.

[110] peilleit *R*, peillit *W*.

[111] y trist] yn drist *R*.

[112] yssyd *R*.

[113] a'e *R*, a *W*.

[114] deuth *R*.

[115] idaw] idaw or kawr *R*.

[116] oed] a oed *R*.

[117] canu *R*.

[118] ehwybyr *R*, ehwydyr *W*.

[119] asseu] asseu idaw *R*.

[120] yr castell ac *R*, yr ac *W*.

[121] bara] bara gwenith *R*.

[122] Moes] a wreicda moes *R*.

[123] ygkaerussalem *R*.

[124] y Mamwrawnt] hyt ymwbrawnt *R*.

[125] garaf *R*.

[126] ymolchi *R*, ymochi *W*.

[127] *corrected from* wassanaethawd.

[128] y tat] y dat ef *R*.

[129] y taw] panyw *R*.

[130] uynych *R*.

[131] beth . . . nyt ef] Beth a debygy di heb hi am y palmer ae bown yw ef ae nat ef *R*.

[132] oe y] oe *R*.

[133] wrthaw *R*, wrtha *W*.

[134] y *R*.

[135] ysgynnu *R*, ygynnu *W*.

[136] Grist] grist y welet *R*.

[137] Arglwydes *R*, argwydes *W*.

[138] byd] byd heb y iosian *R*.

[139] myn *R*, my *W*.

[140] vygkarcharu *R*.

[141] lawer *R*.

[142] oed *R.*

[143] bei gall[?] *W,* – *R.*

[144] greic *W, R.*

[145] Duw] duw heb ynteu *R.*

[146] vyggwyrda *R.*

[147] dywedwn *R.*

[148] drigyy *R.*

[149] arglwyd] arglwyd heb hitheu *R.*

[150] ath differo *R.*

[151] ac ny wnaeth *R,* ac wnaeth *W.*

[152] or *R.*

[153] hwyaf *R,* hwyf *W.*

[154] gwr *R,* gw *W.*

[155] ti *R.*

[156] Teruygawnt] teruygawnt heb ynteu *R.*

[157] ffam *W,* phan *R.*

[158] vyg gwlat *R.*

[159] bagan *R.*

[160] Sef . . . Cristonogaeth] Ac yna y dywawt Josian. kopart gwrhaa y bown. a chymer gristonogaeth *R.*

[161] gopart *R.*

[162] Nyskelaf *R.*

[163] miui] miui yn vyw *R.*

[164] racdunt *R.*

[165] gopart *R.*

[166] bedydlestyr R.

[167] awch *R.*

[168] awch *R.*

[169] noeth lumyn *R.*

[170] y *R.*

[171] y *R;* eu *W.*

[172] oed] a oed a oed *R.*

[173] awch *R.*

[174] Ac *R.*

[175] hugeint *R.*

[176] amdiffyn *R,* amdiffim *W.*

[177] boeni *R.*

[178] trydyd *R.*

[179] arnam *R,* arnā *W.*

[180] dyuot *R,* dyuor *W.*

[181] dygwyd *R.*

[182] gwladoed *R.*

[183] perein *W,* – *R.*

[184] oruc *R*, oru *W*.
[185] eiryoet *R*.
[186] y *R*, a *W*.
[187] y mynhei] a uynnei *R*.
[188] ynty *R*.
[189] arwndel *R*, awndel *W*.
[190] oc *R*.
[191] Ef a'ch *R*, ef ac *W*.
[192] chaffoch *R*.
[193] teruynawd *R*, teuynawd *W*.
[194] kyfrangeu *R*.
[195] ac erchi idaw mynet *R*, y erchi vynet *W*.
[196] iachao *R*, iacha *W*.
[197] yn vore] auory *R*.
[198] vy chwaer *R*.
[199] pob *R*.
[200] phedwar *R*.
[201] ac eu] Ac y eu *R*.
[202] erchis *R*, erchi *W*.
[203] neilltu *R*.
[204] doeth *R*.
[205] gyhyrdassant *R*, gyhyrassant *W*.
[206] y gyt *R*, y gyt ac *W*.
[207] yny *R*.
[208] ac yd erchis *R*, ac erchis *W*.
[209] a'r *R*, a *W*.
[210] y *R*.
[211] ynty *R*.
[212] yn yr amser *R*, yny yr amser *W*.
[213] y dinas hwnn *R*.
[214] nerth *R*, nerch *W*.
[215] ef] y pererin *R*.
[216] ynty *R*.
[217] hyny ydoed] yny ytoed *R*.
[218] yn *R*, yn *W*.
[219] bratfwrt *R*.
[220] megys kyndeirawc] megys kwn kyndeirawc *R*.
[221] eiryoet *R*.
[222] genedyl *R*.
[223] y *R*.
[224] ac *R*, ad *W*.
[225] mynnwn *R*.
[226] Mahwn] vahumet. atheruagawnt. *R*.

[227] mein] mein y arnei *R*.

[228] ynteu] ynteu iuor *R*.

[229] Bown] bown ar y helym *R*.

[230] trewynt *R*.

[231] teruynwyt *R*, teuynwyt *W*.

[232] lann *R*, llann *W*.

[233] vratfwrt *R*.

[234] uabumet *R*.

[235] ym mwmbrawnt *R*.

[236] vedit] vedic *W*.

[237] Eithyr . . . onadunt] eithyr a welynt ar ureint medygon onadunt *R*.

[238] heb **ef** y bown *W*, heb y bown *R*.

[239] uratfwrt *R*.

[240] uynnei *R*.

[241] wrthodaf *R*, orthodaf *W*.

[242] gossodassant] gossodassant ef *R*.

[243] uawrhydic *R*.

[244] y *R*.

[245] y *R*.

[246] y *R*, y̲ *W*.

[247] mawr *R*, maẇ *W*.

[248] bedyd *R*.

[249] doethant *R*.

[250] wladoed *R*.

[251] yno *R*, yna *W*.

[252] ymmwmbrawnt *R*.

[253] orweidawc *R*.

[254] dawr *R*.

[255] diolchaf *R*, diochaf *W*.

[256] y *R*.

[257] kyffessawd] kyffessawd hi *R*.

[258] hewyllys *R*.

[259] yttoedynt *R*.

[260] y hyfrydu] oe hyfryttau *R*.

[261] dat *R*.

[262] wyll deu] wy elldeu *R*.

[263] nyt *R*.

[264] Bown] bown o hamtwn *R*.

Notes on the text

In the text of the following notes, l(l). plus number refers to the lines of our selections, W plus number to the lines of the text of *YBH* in the White Book of Rhydderch in Watkin's edition.

3 **Sef gwreic**: W *sef wreic*; *Sef gwreic* is the reading of R and also of W in the parallel sentence in the first beginning of *YBH* in W 6. Since lenition of a noun after adjectival *sef* is unexpected, Watkin (1958: cvi) suggests that <w> is used for <gw> here. For the uses of *sef* see *GMW* § 55 (f), Evans (1958–60), and Watkins (1997).

3–4 **gwreic ieuanc tu draw y vor** 'a young woman from overseas': *tu draw y vor* without article before *mor* presumably means 'overseas'. Compare *BT* 38: *y kyffnessauyon genedloed, nyt amgen, Saesson a Freinc a chenedloed ereill o'r tu draw y vor* 'the neighbouring peoples, that is, Saxons and French and other peoples from overseas', and contrast ll. 264–5: *brethyn odidawc yw o'r parth draw y'r mor* 'it is fine cloth from beyond the sea'. Watkin (1958: 70) suggests emendation to *[o'r] tu draw y vor*, which is closer to the reading of E, *o'r tv draw y'r mor*.

7 **dyfu**: the older by-form of the pret. 3 sg. of *dyuot* (*GMW* § 143, Morris-Jones (1913: 368), Bromwich and Evans (1992: xvi)). The form *dyfu* is used twice in W; R has *deuth* in both these instances. The second example is l. 774, *y dyd a ediw a'r nos a dyuu* 'the day went and the night came'. Contrast W 3090–1, *y dyd a ediw a'r nos a deuth*.

7 **mab a anet a elwit Bown** 'a boy was born who was called Bown': we take *gelwit* as an impersonal preterite, referring to the single act of christening in contrast to l. 1 *Yn Hamtwn yd oed iarll a elwit Giwn* 'In Hamtwn was an earl who was called Giwn', where *gelwit* denotes the habitual past and is thus in the imperfect tense. However, in the case of *gelwit* it is not possible to distinguish

orthographically betwen the impersonal preterite and the impersonal imperfect. Watkin (1958: 209) takes both forms as impersonal imperfect. W 2780–82 would appear to be a parallel passage: *deu vab a enillawd yna y rei a uuont glotuorus pan deuthant mywn oetran, a'r neill a elwit Gi, a'r llall Miles* 'two sons she conceived then who were famous when they came of age, and the one was called Gi and the other Miles'. In this case Watkin agrees with our interpretation of *gelwit* as an impersonal preterite.

7–9 **A'r mab hwnnw a rodet ar uaeth ar varchawc kyuoethawc a elwit Sabaoth** 'and this boy was given in fosterage to a powerful knight who was called Sabaoth'. R uses the preposition *att* for W's *ar* in *ar varchawc*; there were originally two homophonous prepositions *ar* in Middle Welsh, *ar* 'to', with the conjugated forms *attaf* etc., and *ar* 'on', with the conjugated forms *arnaf* etc., see GMW § 205. R's *att* is the later abstraction from the conjugated forms of *ar* 'to'.

10–11 **gwelet o'r iarlles y iarll yn llithraw parth ac amdrymder heneint, y dremygu** 'the countess saw the count slipping towards the feebleness of old age [and] she despised him': the juxtaposition of two non-finite clauses is somewhat awkward; R has *y dremygu a oruc*. For the use of the forms *y* and *yr* of the article before /j/, as in *y iarll*, see GMW § 27. Watkin (1958: cxvii) notes eighteen examples of *y* and two examples of *yr* as forms of the article before /j/ of *iarll* and *iarlles* in W.

11–12 **o garyat y racdywededic amherawdyr** 'out of love for the afore-mentioned emperor': *o garyat* here governs an objective genitive as in l. 13 *yr y charyat* 'out of love for her' and l. 224 *o'th garyat* 'out of love for you'.

15 **achydic**: R *ychydic*; R has the more common form. According to GMW § 3, an alternation of *a* and *y* before *ch*, as in W's *achydic*, is rare, but it is also attested in one other word in l. 334, *dachymygu* versus R *dechymygu* (with *e* for *y*, compare GMW § 1); see GPC s.v. *dychmygaf* and also Rodway (2004: 114).

16 **yscyuala**: for the meaning of *yscyuala* see GPC s.v. *ysgafala*; both 'unarmed' or 'small (of number)' would suit the context here. *BdH* 90 has *desarmez* 'unarmed'. Note that in l. 51 Giwn's host is

characterized as both *yskyuala* and *heb arueu*. R has *ysgaelusaf*, superlative of *ysgaelus/esgeulus* 'negligible, insignificant'.

19 *ac a ouynnawd yr amherawdyr* 'and asked for the emperor': the direct object of *gouyn* denotes the person or thing asked for; compare *BdH* 74 *si lui demaunde ou est le emperur* 'and he asked him [i.e., *un vavasur* 'a vassal'] where the emperor was' and W 1464–5 *Ac o'r diwed Bown a ofynnawd Josian idaw* 'And finally Bown asked him about Josian', with a prepositional phrase with *y* 'to' to denote the person asked. Compare also l. 127 *gouyn Bown y mab y Sebaot a wnaeth* 'she asked Sebaot about Bown, her son', but contrast below on l. 267. In ll. 127–8, *Beth a ovynny di imi o'r mab* 'Why do you ask me about the boy', the person asked for is exceptionally denoted by a prepositional phrase with *o*.

20 *yn llys idaw* 'in a court of his': for the construction see *GMW* § 221 (d) and Morris-Jones (1931: 20–1, 161). Compare also l. 257 *a galw ar vrawtwayth idi* 'and she called one of her foster brothers' and l. 361 *diagon idaw* 'a deacon of his'.

20 *a elwir Calys*: both W and R have imperfect impersonal *a elwit* here, whereas E has present impersonal *a elwir*; the sense seems to require a present tense, provided the relative clause is still to be considered part of the answer; the emendation is also suggested by Watkin (1958: 74). *Calys* is Calais in France, but according to *BdH* 75 and 77 the emperor is in unidentified *Retefor*, presumably in Germany. Watkin (1958: 74) notes that W 2120 reads *Bwlwyn* 'Boulogne' in France, whereas *BdH* 1895 has *Colonie* 'Cologne' in Germany, but in all other instances where *BdH* mentions Cologne, *YBH* has *Cwlwyn* or a related form.

25 *erchi idaw mynet*: the indirect semantic object of *erchi* precedes its direct semantic object; compare *GMW* § 221 (b).

25–6 *y wreic vwyaf a garei* 'the woman he loved most': *mwyaf* is lenited after the fem. noun *gwreic* – contrast l. 486 *y gwr mwyaf a gereis* 'the man I loved most' – and functions as an adverb within the relative clause which it precedes; for the construction of such compared forms of adjectives as adverbs, see *GMW* § 251 (d); in *Pwyll*, p. 33, this construction is described as adjectival.

26 **o'r a archassei** *lit.* 'of that which she would ask': for the use of the demonstrative *ar* with the preposition *o* 'of' as the antecedent of a relative clause, see *GMW* § 75.

archassei is corrected in W from *archyssei*, which is also the form in R. For the variation between <-ass-> and <-yss-> in the pluperfect, see *GMW* § 136. Watkin (1958: cxxix) notes that the distribution of <-ass-> and <-yss-> in W is fairly even, but see below on l. 137 for the distribution of <-ass-> and <-yss-> in the plural forms of the preterite. The pluperfect is here used as a subjunctive.

30 **llawen uu hitheu orawenus** 'she was joyous and joyful': this phrase corresponds to *BdH* 118 *grant joie ad demené* 'she displayed great joy'; the collocation *llawen-orawenus* occurs in other Middle Welsh texts as a loose compound; see *PKM* 73.23–4, *YSG* 1886, *SDR* 53–4, 1082. On similar loose compounds in *YBH* compare below on l. 79.

30 **oed**: final <d> for /d/ is unusual in Middle Welsh orthography; note R *oet* and W 105 *oet*. According to Watkin (1958: cvii), there are altogether eleven examples of <-d> for /-d/ in W. See also below on ll. 44–59.

34 **it**: W prefers, with very few exceptions, the forms *it* and *yt* of the preposition *y* 'to' with suffixed pronoun 2 sg., where R has, again with few exceptions, *itt* and *ytt*. These variants are not noted in the manuscript readings and variants. For the same variation in the texts of *Culhwch ac Olwen* in the White Book and the Red Book, see Rodway (2004: 103).

35 **yr a gosto** 'whatever it may cost' (*lit.* 'despite that which it may cost'): a relative clause without an expressed antecedent and governed by a preposition, here *yr* meaning 'despite, notwithstanding'; compare *GMW* §§ 77 (d) and 246. For another example, see ll. 149–50 *Yr yssyd o dir a dayar a da gan y Sarassinieit a'r paganieit* 'whatever the Saracens and the pagans own of land and ground and goods' and below on l. 732.

43 **ar y petwyryd marchawc** (*lit.* 'on his fourth knight') 'he and three knights': for the number of Giwn's companions, see *BdH* 141

treis compainons sunt ov lui muntez 'three companions mounted with him'. The construction of the preposition *ar* with possessive pronoun, ordinal and noun and its possible interpretations with regard to the number of people involved are discussed in *GMW* § 52. The plural form of the verb *yd aethant* indicates that all four knights, and not Giwn alone, are the subject. The lenition after the possessive pronoun masc. 3 sg. *y* is not shown in W, but compare R *bedwyryd*. Watkin (1958: cxv) notes that lenition frequently remains unmarked orthographically in W; see similarly for the texts of *Culhwch ac Olwen* in the White Book and the Red Book Rodway (2004: 110).

44–59 W is the only manuscript of *YBH* which has two beginnings; see above, pp. xx, and Poppe and Reck (2006: 145–50). The first, W 1–49, breaks up in the middle of the second column of folio 118, the rest of which is then left blank. The second beginning then starts anew on folio 119. The first twenty-one lines of the first beginning closely agree with the text of the second beginning, W 50–73; the remaining lines, which are given here (W 21–49 = ll. 44–59), are different in style and narrative structure. The narrative is more condensed and, in contrast to the Anglo-Norman original and the second beginning, does not employ direct speech. A striking orthographic feature of the first fourteen lines is a preference of <d> for /d/, W 2, 14 *elwid* (versus W 51, 65 *elwit*), W 3–4 *ieueingtid* (versus W 53 *ieueigtit*), W 13 *priawd* (versus W 63–4 *priawt*), but note W14 *anet*; from line 14 onwards the first beginning follows the normal conventions of <-t> for /-d/, compare W 16 *elwit*. Watkin (1958: cvii) notes altogether eleven examples of <-d> for /-d/ in W, of which four cluster in these first fourteen lines. Thomas (2000: 30) notes a similar small cluster of three examples of <-d> for /-d/ at the beginning of *Peredur* in the same manuscript W and suggests that this could be due to more careful copying of a source which used <-d> for /-d/.

44–5 *y serchawl damunedic ywyllus* 'her amorous desired wish': the adjectives here precede the noun which they qualify. Compare similarly l. 52 *eu damunedic serch* 'their desired love', l. 6 *o'r racdywededic Giwn* 'from the afore-mentioned Giwn' and ll. 11–12 *y racdywededic amherawdyr ieuanc* 'to the afore-mentioned young emperor', as well as W 3180, 3778–9 and 4279, but contrast ll. 56–7 *yn y fforest racdywededic* 'in the afore-mentioned forest', as well as ll. 743–4 and W 3768.

45–6 *Sef y mod y ystyryawd, dyuynnu kennat [attei a'e anuon] at yr amherawdyr* 'This is the way she devised it, she summoned a messenger to her and sent him to the emperor': for the insertion of *attei a'e anuon*, compare Watkin (1958: 72); for the meaning and construction of *dyuynnu* 'to summon, order to appear', compare *PKM* 21.18–19 (= *Pwyll* 499-500) *Hitheu Riannon a dyuynnwys attei athrawon a doethon* 'And she, Rhiannon, summoned to her wise and learned men'. Alternatively, the sentence could possibly be understood as 'she summoned a messenger to the emperor', without the insertion of *attei a'e anuon*.

If *ystyryawd* is transitive here, then the *y* preceding it conflates the relative particle and an object pronoun 3 sg.; for the absence of sandhi-*h* after an object pronoun 3 sg. in this case, see Morgan (1952: 154–5).

47 *yn y iarllaeth Giwn* 'in Giwn's earldom': the article is not normally used with a definite noun qualified by another definite noun; see *GMW* § 28 (d). Perhaps this is a scribal mistake, but compare W 415: *Sef a wnaeth rei o'r marchgoyon y llys* 'some of the knights of the court did this', where R has *rei o uarchogyon*. See also Watkin (1958: cxlviii), and *GMW* § 28 (d) for further examples from other Middle Welsh texts, and the discussion in Ó Gealbháin (1991: 139–40), who notes that examples of this usage mostly 'occur in translation literature and probably result from this fact'.

57–8 *Ac yn oet y dyd y gwydat hi vot yr amherawdyr yn ymdirgelu*: 'And on the appointed day when she knew the emperor was lying in ambush'. For the construction of an adverbial relative clause with an antecedent denoting time, see *GMW* § 71.

60 *Sef a wnaeth datmaeth*: R *tatmaeth*; lenition of the subject after *gwnaeth* is irregular (see Morgan 1952: 221–2). However, the distinction between voiced and voiceless stops (*t-d*, *p-b*, *c-g*) after spirants (*s*, *th*, *ff*, *ch*, *ll*) is generally lost phonetically (see Jones 1984: 42–3); this makes, for instance, *th + d* and *th + t* sound identical and allows for <-th t-> to be wrongly spelt <-th d->.

61 **kyuodi y vyny**: W prefers the form *y vyny* whereas R uses *y vynyd*. This variant is not noted in the manuscript readings and variants. On the loss of final /ð/, see *GMW* § 11 and compare l. 274 *eisted* versus l. 288 *eiste*, R *eisted*.

62 **y ddwylyaw**: R *dwylaw*; this is the only instance of *dwylaw* spelt with /j/ in W, against twenty-six examples of *dwylaw*, compare Watkin (1958: cxxxix); /j/ appears to have no phonological justification here, compare *GMW* § 8 N. <dd> for /ð/ is common in W in initial and word-internal position, see Watkin (1958: cviii).

63 **reit vyd it tyngu** 'you will have to promise' (*lit.* 'promising will be a necessity for you'): this is the idiom to express necessity, compare *GMW* § 221 (c); the verbal noun *tyngu* is the subject of the sentence and the prepositional phrase *it* specifies *reit* 'necessity'.

67 **Y mab a gymerth Saboth ac a aeth ac ef tu a'e lys e hun** 'Saboth took the boy and went with him to his own court': Y *mab* here selects the particle *a* before *aeth* although it is neither the subject nor the object of the second clause. Note that R has straight-forward *Sabaoth a gymherth* [sic] *y mab*.

69 **a'e wlychu**: the possessive pronoun refers to *dillat* 'clothes', and the lenition points to *dillat* being used here as a masculine singular noun with collective meaning, but note R *gwlychu* and, in the next sentence, l. 70 *a'e bwrw* without lenition marked, with the possessive pronoun again referring to *dillat*. Watkin (1958: 79) gives examples of *dillat* used both as a singular collective and a plural in Middle Welsh. On p. 80 he notes examples of a confusion of <w> and <gw> in spelling and suggests that the scribe may have taken <w> as <gw>; in this case no marking of lenition was intended and *dillat* is used as a plural noun.

71 **Mi a'th caraf**: R *garaf*. W shows devoicing, or delenition, of /g/ after *'th*. For the devoicing of /g/, /b/ and /d/ after *'th* compare Morgan (1952: 156–8), also *GMW* § 20 N.1 and Watkin (1958: cxv). See similarly l. 442 *y'th caraf*, R *garaf*, but also l. 148 *a'th Gristonogayth*, R *Cristonogaeth*.

72–3 **ef a ddaw lles yt** 'there will come benefit to you': for the standard account of *ef* as preverbal particle see *GMW* § 191; for the detailed discussion of an alternative explanation as an expletive subject compare Willis (1998: 149–53). According to Willis, such expletive subjects occur most frequently with intransitive verbs denoting change of state, as in this example, or with impersonal forms of verbs, as in ll. 182–3: *ef a las petwarcant o wyr Bradmwnd* 'four hundred of Bradmwnd's men were killed'. For a further subgroup see below on ll. 524–5 and ll. 620–1.

75 **wgeileid**: R has *uugeileid*. This is the only example of <w> for <uu>/<vu> in W, see Watkin (1958: cix), who notes a few further examples of this spelling in other Middle Welsh texts. He also draws attention to the spelling <w> for <vu> in Anglo-Norman manuscripts with reference to Stimming (1899: 220), where the latter notes occasional examples such as *wlt* for *vult*. The spelling <wu> for <uu>/<vu> is also used in W, compare below on l. 88.

75–6 **hyny el y pymthec niwarnawt hyn heibyaw** 'until these fifteen days have passed': *BdH* 246 *taunt ke ceo quinze jours seient passé* 'until these fifteen days are passed'. The use of the demonstrative pronoun in both texts is curious as the fifteen days have not been mentioned before. Watkin (1958: 80) notes that in medieval French romances fifteen days are given as the usual duration of a wedding feast.

The numeral is here, as expected, followed by a singular, *diwrnawt*, but the demonstrative pronoun is plural, following semantic rather than grammatical conventions.

The conjunction *hyny* meaning 'until' is spelt both with and without initial <h->, compare Morris-Jones (1913: 446).

79 **yn gadarn-wychyr** 'strongly and bravely': this compound adverb corresponds to *BdH* 252 *com pruz e hardi* 'like a brave and bold one', *pace* Watkin (1958: clxiii). A number of such adverbs occur in *YBH* (see Watkin 1958: clxiii–clxiv), and in the case of l. 456 *yn iach-lawen* 'safely and soundly' and ll. 641–2 *yn hoeth-lumun* 'stark-naked' respectively these predate the first attestations given in *GPC*. In contrast to *Ger.*, where similar compounds are used mainly adjectively (but compare *Ger.* 1106–7 *yn llidiawcdrut gyflymwychyr greulanfyryf* 'furiously and valiantly, swiftly and

ardently, bloodily and resolutely'), adjectival use appears to be very rare in *YBH* (but compare l. *570 ewined calet-lym* 'hard and sharp nails'). Compare *Ger. yn llidiawcdrut gyflymwychyr* with semantically similar compounds in *YBH*, l. *550 yn llitiawc-wenwynic* 'angrily and furiously', l. *79 yn gadarn-wychyr* 'strongly and bravely', and ll. *101–2 yn ehofyn-wychyr* 'boldly and bravely'.

83 **A *ffan edrych*** 'And when he looks': the narrative present is rare in Middle Welsh prose and mainly confined to subordinate clauses (see Poppe 1995, 1999).

85–6 ***ar nys clywssei kyn no hynny y kyfelybrwyd*** 'the like of which he had not heard before': a genitival relative clause in which the possessive pronoun 3 pl. refers back to the demonstrative *ar* which serves as antecedent (see *GMW* § 75). *Ar* may refer to singular or plural nouns; here it refers to plural *y sawl gerdeu a glodest a sarllach* 'so many songs and revelry and mirth'. The negative particle *nys* contains a redundant infixed pronoun which refers to *y kyfelybrwyd*. For a parallel example, see ll. 559–60: *ar nys gwelsei eiroet y gyffelyb* 'the like of which he had never seen'.

87 ***truan a beth*** 'a sad thing': for the use of the preposition *a* 'of' between an adjective and a noun qualified by it, see *GMW* § 39 (c) and Manning (2002: 418–25, 435–6).

88 ***yn wugeil***: <w> stands for /v/ here; compare Watkin (1958: cviii) and l. 90 *y wugeilffon* (R *uugeilffonn*, but l. 639 *fugeil*), l. 131 *dy wligaw*, and l. 454 *wlwydyn*.

89 ***tref 'ynhat*** 'my patrimony': in the laws and elsewhere, the collocation *tref tat* means 'patrimony'; see Jenkins (1986: 387) and *HGvK*, p. 60. For the position of the possessive pronoun compare, for example, *Ior* § 102 *ac ny dele nep e wadu o'r a deleho tref e tat ef guedy henne* 'no one is entitled to deny him who will be entitled to his patrimony after that' (Jenkins 1986: 136) and *y geissyav tref y dat* 'to seek his patrimony' (*HGvK* 6.17). R has *vyntat*, and Watkin (1958: cxx) suggests that the <f> of *tref* may have 'double value' here and in W 390 *mi a dialaf 'ynhat* 'I shall revenge my father', R *vyntat*. The form *'y* for *vy* also occurs in other phonetic contexts, see Watkin (1958: cxx) and below on l. 246.

95 ***wyti***: one of the frequent examples in the text in which an affixed pronoun 2 sg. (*di, ti*) is assimilated to the ending of the preceding verb, here to *wyt*, present indicative 2 sg. of *bot*.

96 ***mab y butein wyt*** 'you are a whore's son': no 'whore' is mentioned in the immediately preceding context and *y* is therefore not the article, but the preposition 'to', denoting possession, similar to l. 20 *yn llys idaw* 'in one of his courts'. Compare further the immediately following rejoinder ll. 96–7 *Gwir a dywedy ti, vy mot i yn vab y butein* 'you say the truth that I am a whore's son', with predicative *yn*, which is used with indefinite nominal phrases only.

100 ***A cherdet racdaw a wnaeth y mab*** 'and the boy went ahead/on his way': for the use of the preposition *rac* with verbs of motion and a reflexive suffixed pronoun, see *GMW* § 235.

104 ***kanys royssei ef, canys y vam ef oed hi*** 'because he had not given it [i.e., the permission], since she was his mother': the first example of *canys* here contains the negation and an infixed pronoun, whereas the second example combines the conjunction with the 3 sg. of the copula and is followed by the 'mixed order'; compare *GMW* § 261 (b). In ll.104–5, *A chanys kymereisti vy mam i y dreis* 'And since you took my mother by force', *canys* is the simple conjunction followed by a finite verb; compare *GMW* § 261 (c).

105 ***y dreis 'by force'***: *y* here is the preposition orginally meaning 'from', not 'to', compare *GMW* § 223 N.2, *GPC* s.v. *i*[4], and Williams (1995: 311–5).

105–6 ***mi a wnaf uot yn ediuar y'th gallon di hynny*** 'I will cause that you will be sorry for this': *lit.* 'I will cause that this will be regrettable to your heart'; for the construction of *ediuar* in a copular clause with the preposition *y* to introduce the experiencer of regret and the cause of regret as the subject, compare W 2102–3 *ef a vyd ediuar it y twyll hwn* 'you will be sorry for this treason'.

111 ***hithe***: a reflex of the reduction in the spoken register of *-eu* > *-e* in final unaccented syllables; compare *GMW* § 6 N.1.

There are three examples of this form in W, against 53 of *hitheu*, and similarly four examples of *ynte*, against 132 examples of *ynteu* (compare Watkin (1958: cxx), all between columns 10 and 15 of altogether 134 columns. There is a further example of *gynne* for *gynnev* (R) in column 29 of W = W 977.

115 **gouyn idaw pa ffo a oed arnaw** 'he asked him what he was fleeing': *lit.* 'which flight was on him', for the construction of the interrogative with a prepositional relative clause see *GMW* § 84 (b).

116 **vy galw**: R *vyg galw*; nasalization of *galw* after *vy* 'my' is left unmarked only apparently in W, since <g-> represents /ŋ/; see Morris-Jones (1913: 173) and Rodway (2004: 109, 112).

118 **heb y Sebaot**: in phrases with *heb* and a personal name or a personal pronoun, such as W 3205 *Heb yr hitheu* 'she said', *y/yr* is not the definite article, but part of the original verbal form, compare *GMW* § 170.

119 **A bei** 'and if': R *a phei*; Morgan (1952: 325) notes that *bei* and *pei* were felt to be basic forms of the conjunction meaning 'if' and that therefore both *bei* and *phei* are attested after the aspirating conjunction *a* 'and'. W uses both forms; see, for example, W 165 *A ffei*. This also happenend in the case of the prepositions *gan* 'with' (*gan/can/chan*) and *gyda* 'together with' (*gyda/cyda/chyda*); compare Ball (1989–90). On the origin of the conjunction *bei/pei* as imperfect subjunctive 3 sg. of *bot* 'were it (that)', see Morris-Jones (1913: 349) and *GMW* § 274.

123 **o'e** 'to his': R *y*; for the forms of the combination of the preposition *y* 'to' with the possessive pronouns of the 3. person, see *GMW* § 56 N.2 and 3 and the glossary s.v. o^3.

124 **celerdy**: <c> represents /s/ here, and in l. 207 *cited* 'city', compare R *selerdy* and Anglo-Norman *celer* 'cellar' and *cité* 'city' respectively.

127–8 **Beth a ovynny di imi o'r mab** 'Why do you ask me about the boy': *beth* means 'why' here; compare *GMW* § 82 N. and *GPC* s.v. *beth*. For the construction, see above on l. 19.

128 *megys y hercheisti* 'as you ordered it': *erchi* is probably used transitively here and *y* conflates both the subordinating particle and the object pronoun 3 sg., with sandhi-*h* following the pronoun (contrast above on ll. 45–6); if it is used intransitively, 'as you ordered', then this is an example of *h*- before a verb beginning with a vowel after the particle *y*, see *GMW* § 26 N.1.

130 *Kelwyd [. . .] a geny* 'you are lying (*lit.* you say falsehood)': for a meaning 'to say, utter' of *canu* 'to sing', compare *GPC* s.v. The phrase is repeated l. 245; R has *a dywedy* in both instances instead. Compare, however, l. 96 *Gwir a ~~geny~~ dywedy* 'You say the truth', with *geny* changed to *dywedy*, and l. 97 *Kelwyd a dywedy*. Examples of the idiom *canu gwir* from other texts are given by Watkin (1958: 82–3), who suggests that the meaning 'to say' for *canu* was transferred from Old French *chanter*, which can also mean 'to say'. *BdH* 338 has *"Sabaot, vus mentez"* '"Sabaot, you are lying"'.

131 *ony rody ym y mab* 'unless you give me the (*or* my?) boy/son': Watkin (1958: cxx) suggests that *y* is a form of the possessive pronoun 1 sg., but R does not prefer the standard form *vy* here, in contrast to other examples in W of *'y* for *vy*. Morris-Jones (1913: 179, 274) suggests that the variant *'y* for *vy* only occurs when the initial of the following noun can be nasalized. Compare below on l. 246.

132 *rac kyuaruot gofut a'y datmaeth* 'for fear that his foster father would meet with affliction': for the meaning 'lest, for fear that' of *rac* with verbal nouns, compare *GMW* § 235.

133–4 *Osit yt a holych* 'If there is anything that you might demand' (Watkin 1958: 81, 'if you have a charge to lay'): for *os(s)it*, see *GMW* § 272 (b) (1); for the relative clause without expressed antecedent, see *GMW* § 77. Compare similarly ll. 151–2: *nys gorffo a amdireto neu a gretto y Vahom* 'may he not prevail who trusts and believes in Mahom'.

134 *Nyt oes dim a dylyych y holi y'm datmaeth* 'There is not anything that you should demand of my foster father': a genitival relative clause in which the possessive pronoun *y* (before *holi*) refers back to the antecedent *dim*; see *GMW* § 69.

y'm datmaeth 'to my foster father': R *y'm tatmaeth*; no lenition is expected after the possessive pronoun 1 sg. *'m*. Watkin (1958: cxiv) suggests that W made a mistake in copying, but note similarly l. 151 *a'm Gristonogaeth*, R *a'm Cristonogaeth*, and l. 384 *y'm verthyru*, R *merthyru*, and see below on l. 235.

135 **Kymryt idi hithe y mab** 'She took her son': the preposition *y* introduces the agent of a verbal noun here. This construction appears to be rarely used in Middle Welsh texts except in *YBH*; see *GMW* § 181 (c) and Watkin (1958: clxxi–clxxii) for further examples from the text.

137 **a gerdyssant**: R *a gerdassant*; for the variation between <-ass-> and <-yss-> in the plural forms of the preterite, see *GMW* § 134. Watkin (1958: cxxviii) notes that in W <-yss-> is the dominant form up to p. 41, with thirty-nine occurrences against five occurrences of <-ass->, whereas <-ass-> is the preferred form from p. 42 onwards, with seventy-five occurrences against two occurrences of <-yss->. This is one indication for the existence of two linguistically different parts within the text of *YBH* in W. A similar distribution is displayed by other verbal forms (compare Watkin 1958: cxxvii), by the two forms *onadunt/ohonunt* of the preposition *o* with the suffixed pronoun 3 pl. (see below on l. 180), and by some stylistic features (compare Poppe 1999: 311–2, Reck 1999: 293, and Poppe and Reck 2008: 155–9).

138 **rocdun**: *roc(-)* is a by-form of *rac(-)*, compare also l. 271, *rocddi*, and Watkin (1958: cxxiv–cxxxv). Watkin (1958: xlvii) draws attention to the existence of the form *roc(-)* in southern dialects of Modern Welsh. For *-nt > -n(n)* in the suffixed pronoun 3 pl. and in the endings 3 pl. of verbs, see *GMW* §§ 63 and 130 N.2 and compare Watkin (1958: cxxxiv–cxxxv) for further examples of the same development in suffixed pronouns.

138 **gantu**: R *gantunt*; W has the earlier form of the suffixed pronoun 3 pl.; compare *GMW* § 63 N.1 and Rodway (2004: 119–20).

139 **llog diruawr y meint** 'a ship of very great size': see *GMW* § 40 and Mac Cana (1966) for the construction in which a noun is qualified by a phrase consisting of an adjective, a possessive pronoun

which refers back to the qualified noun, and a noun 'which pertains
to or is a part of the person or object denoted by the first noun'
(Mac Cana 1966: 91). Compare also ll. 168–9 *no'r hwch arwaf y
gwrych* 'than the sow with roughest bristles' and l. 428 *gwin claret
digawn y gadarnet* 'claret wine of sufficient strength'.

143 **Egipt**: this is an unassimilated loan word from Anglo-Norman,
corresponding to *BdH* 363 *Egipte*, but in W 1455 the usual form *Eift*
derived from Latin (compare Lewis 1943: 32) is used.

146 **da wr** 'a good man': this is probably an example of the loss of
the preposition *a* 'of' in the partitive expressive structure; compare
Manning (2002: 420): 'Another MW deviation from partitive expres-
sive structure involves cases of omission of the preposition *a* entirely,
as in examples like *da varchawc* "good knight" (W.SG. 294), as
opposed to the expected *"da a varchawc"*. This occurs only after
the adjective *da* "good", which might be explained plausibly by a
contraction (*da a* N → *da:* N → *da* N). The covert presence of the
preposition *a* is secured by the lenition (*marchawc* → *varchawc*) that
it triggers'.

149 **dir a dayar a da** 'land and earth and goods': *BdH* 400 has *pur
tut la tere* 'for all the land'; *tir a dayar* is an expression which
occurs in *PKM* and *YSG* (698, 4113) and which is common in the
laws; compare Davies (1995: 182) and Jenkins (1986: 386). The
phrase *tir a dayar* reoccurs in W 3837 and l. 866.

151–2 **Ac nys gorffo a amdireto neu a gretto y Vahom** 'And may he
not prevail who trusts or believes in Mahom': the scribe of W may
have written <-sf-> or, slightly indistinctly, <-ff->. *gorffo* is in any
case easier than Watkin's suggested emendation to *(h)onys y gors
fo a amdireto* 'disgraced be his body who trusts', with otherwise
unattested Old French loan words *honys* 'disgraced, shamed' and
cors 'body'; see Watkin (1958: 86) and Watkin (1939: 376–7).
Watkin's reading is based on *BdH* 405 *Honi seit de son cors ki en
Mahun se afie* 'Shame on (*lit.* the body of) him who trusts in
Mahomet'.

154 **mi a vynnaf itti wassanaethu o'm ffiol arnaf i** 'I want you to
serve me from my cup': this is probably not yet the construction in

which a prepositional phrase with *y* introduces the agent of a following verbal noun in a subordinate clause – which is rare in Middle Welsh, see *GMW* § 181 (d) – but an example of the ordinary syntax of *mynnu* with a prepositional phrase with *y*, denoting the addressee of the wish, and a direct object, denoting the object desired; compare l. 191 *beth a vynneisti y'r wlat hon?* 'what did you want from this country?'. However, this construction of *mynnu*, with the direct object realized as a verbal noun and similar uses of *erchi* – compare l. 25 *erchi idaw mynet* 'asking him to go' and below on ll. 744–5 – may have provided a springboard for the later construction by reanalysis: [*mynnu* + (*y* + N/PRON)] + VN > *mynnu* + [(*y* + N/PRON) + VN], see Lewis (1927–9: 183–4), Schumacher (2000: 17) and Borsley, Tallermann and Willis (2007: 330–3).

158 *y gadarn*: *y* is a variant of the adverbializing particle *yn*, see *GMW* §§ 250 and 222.

158–9 *Sef a wnaeth pawb o'r dinas yna, gwiscaw ymdanunt* 'This everyone from the city did then, he armed himself (*lit*. they armed themselves)': *pawb* can be used with singular or plural reference, see *GMW* § 106.

164 *meirych*: R *meirch*; for epenthetic *y* in the consonantal group *-rch* see Morris-Jones (1913: 17) and *GMW* § 16. W uses *meirych* – where R regularly has *meirch* – up to column 71, but *meirch* from the next example in column 81 onwards.

168–9 *no'r hwch arwaf y gwrych* 'than the sow with roughest bristles': see above on l. 139. The superlative *garwaf* is used here as an elative, expressing a very high degree.

169 *neu yr draenawc*: for *yr* as an occasional variant of the article when the preceding word ends in a vowel, compare *GMW* § 27 N.1.

174–5 *ac y dywot Bown wrthaw* 'and Bown said to him': one of the infrequent instances of a sentence-initial finite verb in a positive main clause in Middle Welsh prose; the dominant order has the finite verb in second position, i.e., constituent + particle + verb, traditionally called 'abnormal order' (see *GMW* § 199; for other approaches see Willis 1998: 50–101 and Poppe 2000). Willis (1998: 129) suggests that with verbs other than *bot* 'verb-initial ordering is highly marked, occurring only in contexts of narrative continuity'. See also Borsley, Tallermann and Willis (2007: 299–302).

177 **bydwn da**: Watkin (1958: 200) suggests a meaning 'valiant' for *da* here, 'let us be valiant (*or* fight valiantly)', parallel to *BdH* 585 *Ferez, compaignouns!* 'Strike, friends!'

178–9 **A hwynteu, nifer Bradmwnd, a fu argysswr mawr arnunt** 'And on them, Bradmwnd's host, was great fear': the construction appears to be that of an originally mixed sentence (*GMW* § 146) with a prepositional relative clause (*lit.* '(it was) they, Bradmwnd's host, on whom was great fear') which became a device for the fronting of a noun extracted from a prepositional phrase; compare Willis (1998: 88–9). Parallel examples are *BR* 1–2 *Madawc uab Maredud a oed idaw Powys yn y theruyneu* 'To Madawc uab Maredud belonged Powys from one end to the other' and *PKM* 48.2–3 (= Bran. 466–7) *A'r pump wraged hynny, yn yr un kyfnot, a anet udunt pum meib* 'And to these five women, at the same moment, five sons were born'.

180 **onadunt**: Watkin (1958: cxxxiv) notes that up to p. 43 in W *onadunt* is the preferred form of the preposition *o* with a suffixed personal pronoun 3 pl., with thirteen examples against one example of *ohonunt*, whereas *ohonunt* is more frequent from p. 43 to p. 67, with eleven examples against six examples of *onadunt*. See above on l. 137 for another example of similar morphological differences.

184–5 **vegys paladurwr yn llad y weirglawd**: *BdH*'s courtly comparison of Boeve with a falcon (*BdH* 593, 602) is replaced here by the more homely image of a man with a scythe. A similar image, which does not occur in the French original, is also found in *Cân Rolant* (*CR* 238.6–8), *a llyweo y varch parth a'e elyn – val dyn yn llad a phaladur – ac ar y estlys drwy y arueu y daraw* 'and he steered his horse toward the enemy – like a man cutting with a scythe – and he struck him in the side through his armour'; see also Rejhon (1984: 90). The French text has *Sun ceval brochet, si li curt ad esforz. / Tient Durendal, qui plus valt que fin or; / Vait le ferir li bers, quanque il* *pout,* / *Desur sun elme* (*CdR* 1582–5) 'He spurs his horse and speeds to smite the foe / with Durendal, more worth than finest gold. / By might and main the baron deals the stroke / full on the helm' (Sayers 1957: 112).

187 **yn vychyr-lew** 'bravely and courageously': <v> is used for /w/ here and also in W 160–1, *yn vychyr*; compare Watkin (1958: cxiv) and contrast l. 79 *yn gadarn-wychyr*.

188–9 **Lledwch ini niuer Ermin yn ebrwyd** 'Kill for us Ermin's host swiftly': the prepositional phrase indicates the persons affected by the verbal action. Similarly l. 191 *beth a vynneisti y'r wlat hon?* 'what did you want from this country?', and compare above on l. 154.

189–90 **ny chewch o'm da vyth werth vn notwyd** 'you will never obtain anything (*lit.* the value of a single needle) from my goods': compare *BdH* 608 *jammés ne averez de moi le vailaunt d'un parsis* 'you will never receive anything (*lit.* the value of a Parisian penny) from me' and *GPC* s.v. *nodwydd* for further examples of *nodwydd* denoting a worthless object in emphatic negations. The phrase is repeated in W 1228–9. For further examples of emphatic negations in *YBH* and their Anglo-Norman models, compare Poppe and Reck (2008: 147–9).

193 **canmwyaf dy holl allu** 'the majority of your whole force': 'majority', the nominal meaning of *canmwyaf, ganmwyaf*, is a development of 'for the most part', the original adverbial meaning of the phrase *gan mwyaf, can mwyaf*; compare *YSG*, p. 248.

194 **Beth a dreithir yghwanec?** 'What more shall be said?': the rhetorical question is an auctorial intrusion and corresponds to *BdH* 618 *Que vus en dirrai plus?* 'What more can I tell you about this?'. This type of formula does not occur in native Middle Welsh prose; for similar phrases in works based on Latin originals, compare *HGvK* 30.17 *Pa beth hefyt* 'What more now' and *BD* 86.8–9 *Pa beth wedy hynny?* 'What more afterwards?'.

195–6 **ynteu e hunan ac ychydic o niuer y gyt ac ef yn oledrat ar hyt dyfryn a ffoyssant**: here two adverbial phrases are interposed between the subject, which selects the preverbal particle *a*, and the finite verb. For other examples compare ll. 349–50, l. 386, l. 395 and ll. 413–14; for further discussion of this word order see Willis (1998: 60–72).

198 **gwaethiroed Duw** 'alas God': We follow Watkin (1958: 93) and Williams (1968), who translate *Duw* as 'God'. Another possibility is to read *gwaethiroed duw* 'woe worth the day', with *duw* as a form of *dydd* 'day'; see *GPC* s.v. *gwaethiroedd*.

204 **disgynnu y Bown** 'Bown dismounted': R *disgynnu a wnaeth Bown*. Whereas W uses the rare construction with the preposition *y* to introduce the agent of a verbal noun (see above on l. 135), R has the common periphrastic construction with a finite form of *gwneuthur*. Compare also l. 273 *Dyuot idi hi* 'She came' versus R *Dyuot a oruc hi* and l. 362 *medylyaw y Bown* 'Bown thought' versus R *medylyaw a wnaeth Bown*.

211 **dallei**: imperfect indicative 3 sg. of *dala*, with geminated *l* for /l/ after short /a/; compare Watkin (1958: cxi). R has *dalhei*. For further forms with <-ll-> for /l/, see W 1035 *dellynt* (imperfect indicative 3 pl., R *delhynt*), W 2631 *dallwn* (present indicative 1 pl.), and l. 153 *gallon* 'heart'. R's forms *dalhei* and *delhynt* are probably indicative, despite the spelling with <-h->, since in 1035–6 *delhynt* is co-ordinated with imperfect indicative *oedynt*.

212 **yna y gellygawd Bown ef o'y wlat** 'then Bown let him go to his country': *o'y* here is the combination of the preposition *y* 'to' with the possessive pronoun 3 sg.; compare also l. 298 *deu varchawc a ossodet o'y warchadw ynteu* 'two knights were appointed to guard him', Watkin (1958: cxxi), and *GMW* § 56 N. 2.

217–18 **Mawr a beth y dylywn i dy garu di** 'I should love you greatly': for the use of adjective + *a* + *beth* as an adverbial phrase in sentence-initial position, with or without a preceding finite form of the copula, see *GMW* §§ 39 (c) N. and 251 (a), Morris-Jones (1931: 178), and Watkin (1958: clxiii). See also on l. 87. For an example with a form of the copula, see l. 279, *ys drwc a beth y diolcheisti imi vy llafur* 'you thanked me ill for my labour'; for the form of the copula compare *GMW* § 146.

222 *Arglwyd tec*: for *tec* 'fair, dear' as term of address see Watkin (1958: 94).

225 *ymhwyth* 'please': this secondary meaning of *ym pwyth* 'in return' appears to be rare; see *GMW*, § 245 (p) and Watkin (1958: 92).

230–1 *ny thygawd idaw*: 'it did not avail him'; compare l. 788 and *GMW* § 176.

232 *y'm helw* 'in my possession': with the possessive pronouns 1 and 2 sg., the preposition *yn* 'in' has the form *y*; see *GMW* § 222.

234–5 *o'th vnbeis* 'with a (*lit.* your) single shirt': *GPC* s.v. *o*^{1} (19) gives a number of examples of the preposition *o* used with the meaning 'with' (i.e., 'wearing)'. Compare also l. 502 *o'm vncrys* 'with a single shirt' and *YSG* 3420–1 *yn gyrru Lionel y vrawt o'e vnbeis yng karchar* 'sending his brother Lionel with a single shirt into prison'.

235 *bei kawn brenhin a uei eidaw dec vrenhinaeth* 'if I found a king who owned ten kingdoms': for parallel examples compare *MIG* 195.29 *y gwr a oed eidaw berffeith wybot* 'the man who has perfect knowledge' and, from the text of *Brut y Brenhinedd* in Llanstephan MS. 1, quoted by Lewis, *BD*, p. 234, *kanys ve hentadev am gorhentadev a wu eydunt er enys* 'since (it were) my grandfathers and my great-grandfathers (who) owned this island'. This is an extension in relative clauses of a special 'reversed' usage of *eidaw* (the stressed possessive pronoun 3 sg. 'his', see *GPC* s.v. *eiddo*^{1}) noted by Lewis, *BD*, p. 234, and *GPC* s.v. *eiddo*^{1}(4), in which *yn eidaw* is 'virtually given the meaning "owning or possessing"', as in *BD* 192.25 *a Chaduan [. . .] yn eidav coron Lundein* 'and Cadfan owning the crown of London'.

Nasalization of <b-> would be expected after *dec* 'ten' (see Morgan 1952: 138–9) R has *brenhinyaeth*. Watkin (1958: 80) suggests that <v> is written for <b> here, as also in W 3616 *y vydinoed* 'the hosts', R *bydinoed*. The expected nasalization is marked in l. 897, *dec mrenhin*.

245 *kelwyd a geny*: present indicative 2 sg. *geny* is corrected from *gene* in W, compare below on l. 536. Watkin (1958: ciii) takes the final -*e* in the uncorrected form to be an example of *e* for *y*, with reference to Morris-Jones (1913: 16).

246 **'y mot i**: R *vy mot*; *'y* is a variant of the possessive pronoun 1 sg. which occurs only when the initial of the following noun can be nasalized, compare Morris-Jones (1913: 179, 274) and the note on l. 131 above. See also l. 494 *'y gharcharu*, R *vyg karcharu* and l. 531 *ymplith 'y gwyrda*, R *vyg gwyrda* and Watkin (1958: cxx).

256–7 **ymor serth ac y dywot wrth Bown** 'as insulting as she had spoken to Bown': R *mor*; unless the *y-* is simply a scribal mistake it could be prosthetic here, as suggested by Watkin (1958: 96). For the equative followed by a clause expressing result, see *GMW* § 44.

264 **'y gwisc las**: R *y wisc*; in view of *BdH* 738, *mon bliaunt* 'my robe', it is probably best to understand this phrase as meaning 'my green robe', with *'y* for *vy* 'my' (compare above on l. 246) and <g> for /ŋ/. l. 267 *y wisc odidawc honno* 'this fine robe' shows that *gwisc* is treated as a feminine noun, and this is also reflected in R's *wisc*, with lenition following the article, i.e. 'the green robe'. For the range of colours covered by *glas*, see *GPC* s.v. *glas*[1].

267 **Gofyn idi hitheu** 'She asked [him]': for the construction see above on l. 135; the preposition *y* here introduces the agent of the verbal noun, not the person asked, as is the usual construction with *gofyn*; see above on l. 19.

272 **Ac y gyt ac y guyl ef hihi** 'And as soon as he sees her': *hihi* is perhaps more likely to be an independent pronoun functioning as the object than an affixed pronoun supporting an infixed pronoun contained in *y*. For similar examples see l. 281, W 934–5, l. 320, W 2319, l. 970.

278 **taw a sson** 'be silent (with noise)': R *a'th son*, compare also W 930–1 *Tewch a sson* versus R *a'ch*, but l. 585 *Taw, pagan, a'th son*.

292 **[o nadred]**: this insertion is suggested by Watkin (1958: 101); it is required by the sense and supported by *BdH* 945–6 B *En cele prisoun out vermin a plentez: / serpens e coluvers e granz verms*

cuez 'The prison was full of vermin: snakes and adders and large reptiles with tails'.

292 **colubyr**: a loan-word from Anglo-Norman *coluvre* 'colubrid, viper' which is only attested in this text. Note that in ll. 306–7, *pryf gwenwynic, a cholubyr oed y enw* 'a venomous worm, and *colubyr* ['viper'] was its name', the word is explained and glossed.

304 **vel**: R *ual*; this is a very early example of the form *vel*; see Watkin (1958: 101, 169) for references to other instances in Middle Welsh manuscripts.

304 **o'm cledeu** 'with my sword' (?): Watkin (1958: xlvii) suggests that *o* is used for *a* 'with' here and that this is a southern dialectal feature. *cledeu* is a variant of *cledyf*, the form used in R; there are 16 examples of *cledeu* in W, against 36 of *cledyf*.

313 **ym bren**: R *ym prenn* and compare l. 377 *ym phren*; Watkin (1958: xlvii) suggests that *ym bren* represents an isolated southern (Pembroke) dialectal realization of the nasal mutation, see also below on l. 756.

314 **na'm gettych yn y poeneu hyn a uo hwy** 'do not leave me in these pains any longer': the relative clause *a uo hwy* serves as an adverbial phrase; compare ll. 360–1 *o doy a uo nes* 'if you come closer', *GMW* § 251 (c) and Watkin (1958: clxiii).

316 **y ddeuwr a oedynt yn y warchadw** 'the two men who were guarding him': the dual *deuwr* is lenited after the article, see Morgan (1952: 17–18).

   In relative clauses the verb is usually in the 3 sg. with plural antecedents, but agreement is sometimes found. Watkin (1958: clxviii) and Evans (1971: 54) note two further instances in l. 343 *yr holl kadwyrneu heyrn a oedynt arnaw* 'all the iron chains which were on him' and W 1208–9 *y'r gwyr a oedynt yn cadw Bown* 'to the men who were keeping Bown'; contrast W 2517–8 *y rwymeu a oed ar y dwylaw* 'the fetters which were on her hands'. Evans (1971: 49, 56) suggests that the use of concord is due to French influence in works translated from French.

324–5 **pan ym byrywyt i yma gyntaf a bot 'yg cledeu y'm llaw** 'when I was thrown here first and my sword was in my hand': this appears to be one of the rare instances of the coordination of the finite verb and a verbal noun in a subordinate clause, to avoid repetition of the conjunction; compare l. 729 and *PKM* 16.23–4 (= *Pwyll* 381–2) *ony chyuyt dyleydauc [. . .] a ssenghi a'y deudroet* 'unless you find a noble [. . .] and he treads down with his feet', as well as Morgan (1937–39: 201). *ym* is a syllabic form of the object pronoun 1 sg., compare *GMW* § 59.

327 **Ac yr vn dyrnawt bychan y pagan hwn** 'And because of the single small blow of this pagan': this is the reading of R which is also favoured by Watkin (1958: 103); W has *Ar yr vn dyrnawt bychan*.

328 **wy piliedic** 'a peeled egg': compare *BdH* 1060 B *vailaunt un oef pilé* 'value of a peeled egg'.

333–6 The Anglo-Norman version states that Boeve is speaking in jest, *BdH* 1072 *Boefs le oi si prent a degaber* 'Boeve heard him [i.e., the other guard upstairs] and began to fool him'.

343 **yr holl kadwyneu**: R *gadwyneu*; a noun following *holl* is normally lenited, and W shows unvoicing of /g/ after /ʎ/; see *GMW* § 20 (and N. 1.) and compare W 2937 *vy holl kenedel* and W 4049 *o'm holl kenedyl*; R has *genedyl* in both instances.

345 **at y uot y neidawd** 'he jumped to the vault': both W and R have *y not*, i.e. 'he jumped to the mark'; Watkin (1958: 103) suggests that *y not* is confused with *y uot* in their exemplar(s) and refers to *BdH* 1093 *en une voute saili* 'he jumped into a vault'. Surridge (1985: 72) considers the etymological connection proposed by Watkin unproven but both etymology and emendation are accepted by *GPC* s.v. *fowt*, variant *fôt*.

346 **A fford ehag oed honno** 'And this was a wide road': the reading of R with *yno* 'there' instead of *honno* would appear to be better, since no road has been mentioned before.

353–5 **da yd ymgyfarfuwyt a thi, canys kefeist dy vrdaw yn effeirat gan esgob kystal ac y kefeist, kanys tebic wyt y effeirat yr awr hon** 'well did it befall you, since you were ordained a priest by as good a bishop as you could find, because you are like a priest now': Bown's highly sarcastic comment which compares Bradmwnd's loss of his skull-cap (*ffiol y benn*) to a priest's tonsure. Both W and R have *ymgarfuwyt*; the emendation to *ymgyfarfuwyt*, impers. pret. of *ymgyuaruot* 'to meet (together), encounter', is suggested by Watkin (1958: 106). Compare *BdH* 1210–11: *"Par deu!" dyt a Bradmund, "bien vus est encontré, / quant de si bon evesque estes ordiné* '"By God!", he said to Bradmund, "it's turned out well for you that you've been ordained by such a good bishop"'.

356 **ar varch da** 'on a good horse': this is the reading of R, W has *ar march*, without the expected lenition after *ar* orthographically expressed on *m-*, as is normally the case (exceptions are found with personal names, e.g., l. 873 *ar Mahwn* versus W 1181 *ar Vahom* and l. 436 *y Mamwrawnt* versus W 3682 *y Vwmbrawnd*). For the phrase compare l. 367 *ac y kymerth y march da* 'and he took the good horse' and W 4018–9 *yna yd yskynnawd y duc ar varch da* 'then the duke mounted a good horse'. Watkin (1958: 106) suggests that *m-* could be read as *i u-*, but also notes that this would be the only example in W of a form *i* of the possessive pronoun 3 sg.

359 **dra'th gefyn**: compare *GMW* § 238.

360 **newyd vrdaw** 'newly ordained': compare *GMW* § 251 N. and W 2170–1 *yn newyd eillaw* 'newly shaved'.

371–2 **Ny allei na llong nac ysgraf arnaw ynteu** 'Neither ship nor boat could (be) on it [i.e., the water]': This property of the river is not mentioned in the Anglo-Norman version; see *BdH* 1246–7, but compare *PKM* 40.21 (= *Bran.* 287–8) *ny eill na long na llestyr arnei* 'neither ship nor vessel can (be) on it [i.e., the river]' and *Bran.*, p. 33.

376–84 The syntax of this reworking of the Creed is fairly complex; *arglwyd Duw* serves as the subject and object respectively of *a anet*, *a* (R *ac a*) *diodefawd*, *ac a uadeuawd* and *a daw*; into this sentence are inserted a verbal noun expression (*a'y gladu*) and two sentences with adverbial phrases preceding the verb (*odyno yd aeth [. . .] ac y torres* and *yn nawr y mae yn eiste*). GPC gives both 'from there' and 'then' as possible meanings of *odyno* and only the meaning 'then' allows the coordination of *aeth* and *torres* (see also Watkin 1958: 108). Compare below on ll. 670–7 for another reworking of the Creed with similar syntactic complexities.

385 *a'e lityaw*: R *lidyaw*; the form in W probably shows unvoicing of a media before /j/, see *GMW* § 17 (3).

386–9 We follow Watkin's completion from R of parts of words illegible in W.

394 **peilleit** 'flour': this is the form in R, W has *peillit*. GPC s.v. *peilliaid* suggests that the word contains a suffix -*(i)aid*; on this basis R's form is preferable to W's otherwise unattested *peillit*. *gwenith peilleit* 'wheat flour' is probably a loose compound here.

397 **ar ffenestyr o'r castell** 'on a crenel of the castle': the meaning 'crenel' is suggested by Watkin (1958: 208), because *ffenestyr* here corresponds to *kernel* in the Anglo-Norman text, see *BdH* 1279. The use of the preposition *o* shows that *ffenestyr* is indefinite, since a definite genitive would make the noun it depends on definite, **ar ffenestyr y castell* 'on the cernel of the castle'.

400–1 **a'm arglwyd inheu ysy gawr dewr dihafarch** 'and my master is a brave and fierce giant': R *yssyd*; this is an example of a copular clause with the order subject plus copula plus indefinite predicate. Compare *PKM* 49.10 *Dy geuynderw yssyd urenhin yn Ynys y Kedyrn* 'Your cousin is king in the Island of the Mighty' and *YSG* 2080 *Myvi yssyd vugail da* 'I am a good shepherd' and also Early Modern Welsh *Y groes sydd obaith i'r Cristnoniog* 'The Cross is hope for the Christians' (quoted Evans 1966–8: 318).

410–1 **ny digawn ganu**: R *canu*; lenition of an object after suffixless forms of the present indicative 3 sg. is rare, see Morgan (1952: 207–8), but compare W 2549 *y digawn wisgaw*.

411 We follow Watkin's completion from R of parts of words torn off in W.

412–3 *ac nys metrawd namwyn y march*: 'but he did not strike him [i.e., Bown], but the horse', with an object pronoun; contrast l. 593 *Ny medrawd namyn derwen* 'he only struck an oak-tree', without an object pronoun. The conjunction *a(c)* here would appear to have adversative force, as also in l. 418 *ac nys metrawd*; compare *GMW* § 252 N.1 and Watkin (1958: clxiv) for further examples.

426 We follow Watkin's insertion of *da* from R.

429–34 We follow Watkin's completion from R of parts of words illegible in W.

447 *ymolchi*: this is the reading of R, W *ymochi*; Watkin (1958: cxi) notes a few more examples of <l> being omitted in W, including l. 489 *Argwydes*, R *Arglwydes*.

447 *hitheu a wassnaethawd*: W has *wassanaethawd* with two dots under the second *a*. Watkin (1958: 110) suggests that *arnaw* should be inserted after *wassnaethawd*.

449–50 *o ba le pan hanoed* 'from where he came': for *pan* as an interrogative 'whence' and as a relative in indirect questions compare *GMW* § 87 and l. 734. It is repeated in the answer l. 450 *O Loygyr pan hanwyf* 'I come from England'.

453–4 *car imi oed y tat* 'a friend of mine was his father': R *y dat ef*; *GMW* § 28 (b) notes other examples of the article apparently used for a possessive pronoun, but also notes that *y* could be a possessive pronoun 3 sg. masc. with the expected lenition left unmarked.

454–5 *yr pan y gueleis i ef* 'since I saw him': *y* is the form of the object pronoun 3 sg. used after *pan*; see *GMW* § 59.

462–3 *drwc a dyn y thyghetuen* 'a woman with a sad fate': this is a conflation of the construction underlying *truan a beth* 'a sad thing' (see above, l. 87, i.e., *drwc a dyn*) with the construction underlying *no'r hwch arwaf y gwrych* 'than the pig with very rough bristles' (see above, ll. 168–9, i.e., **dyn drwc y thyghetuen*). For a further example see W 1766–7 *drwc a wyr eu dihenyd* 'men with sad deaths'. Compare Manning (2002: 423–4) and Mac Cana (1966: 92–3) for a discussion with further examples, among them *PKM* 7.22 (= *Pwyll* 161) *cadarn a ungwr y gydymdeithas* 'a man steadfast in his fellowship'.

465–6 **Y *palmer***: for the use of the article with a vocative see *GMW* § 28 (c).

467 **y *taw* ti *oed Bown*** 'that it is you who is Bown': for the use of *y taw* to emphasize the immediately following constituent in a noun clause, compare *GMW* § 148 (b) (3); *y taw* is rare in Middle Welsh and Thomas (1993: 22) suggests that it was non-standard. In Modern Welsh it is confined to southern dialects. Wmffre (2003: 366) suggests that '[a]nother word that seems to be shunned by the medieval Welsh written tradition [. . .] is [adverbial] *maes* 'out', found throughout southern Wales [. . .]' (again it is first found in *Ystorya Bown de Hamtwn*)'; compare l. 666 *yd aethant a hi maes o'r dinas* 'they went with her out of the town'.

467 ***Na vi*** 'No': for the use of *na(c)* plus pronoun to signal disagreement see *GMW* § 197 N.

468 ***vyneich***: R *uynych*; *GPC* s.v. *mynych* accepts *myneich* as a variant of *mynych*.

473–4 ***beth a dybygei ef am y palmer, ae Bown oed ef ae nyt ef*** 'what he thought about the pilgrim, whether he was Bown or not': this indirect question in W is transformed in R into a direct question. Compare also ll. 602–3.

474 ***oe y edrych*** 'to look at him': R *oe*; for the various forms which the combination of the preposition *y* 'to' and the possessive pronoun 3 sg. can have, see *GMW* § 56 N.2, where, however, a form *oe y* is not noted; Watkin (1958: cxxi) gives some further examples of this form from other manuscripts.

475–6 ***y mae Bown oed y palmer*** 'that the pilgrim was Bown (*lit.* that it is Bown who was the pilgrim)': *(y) mae* is used here to emphasise the immediately following constituent in a noun clause which refers to the past; see *GMW* § 148 (b) (3) and compare ll. 834–5 *y mae Sabaot oed y pererin* 'that the pilgrim was Sabaot', l. 868 *mae da oed gantaw hynny* 'that he would agree with this'.

479–80 **y ryw ryfic ac ynni y mae y march yn y gymryt yndaw** 'the kind of boldness and vigour which the horse is taking upon itself': in addition to the uses of *y mae* listed in *GMW* § 148 (b), it is also employed relatively in improper relative clauses; compare examples in *GMW* § 70 N. 1 and 2, and further W 2904–5 *meint y kam y mae yn y wneuthur y'r march* 'the amount of injury he is inflicting on the horse', W 3101–2 *yn y lle y mae tir mawr idaw* 'in the place where he owns much land' and *PKM* 25.1–2 (= *Pwyll* 582) *o ellwng Riannon o'r poen y mae yndaw* 'to release Riannon from the punishment which she suffers (*lit.* in which she is)'.

483 **ryfugus**: R *ryuygus*. Watkin (1958: xlviii) suggests that W's form shows a dialectal feature typical of Pembroke here, an assimilation of <y> to <u> before <u> as also in W 159 *a thunnu* (R *thynnv*), W 2512 *duffust* (R *dyffust*) and l. 642 *-lumun* (=*lymun*, but R *-lumyn*). ·

487 **yd oedwn ys llawer o amser yn damunaw y welet** 'for a long time I wished to see him': for the use of *ys*, present indicative 3 sg. of *bot*, in adverbial expressions denoting a period of time, see *GMW* § 147 (e) and also ll. 827–8 *yn y dinas yd wyf ys dydyeu* 'I have been in the town for days'. The periphrastic construction with the imperfect of *bot* plus *yn* plus verbal noun denotes continuous activity in the past; see *GMW* § 120 (a).

488 **ar yr Iessu Grist** 'by Jesus Christ' (?): Watkin (1958: 111) suggests emending to *Ac yr Iessu Grist* as part of the following sentence, i.e., 'And by Jesus Christ, dismount'. The scribe of W puts a full stop after *Grist*; R explicitly incorporates the phrase into the preceding sentence, *ar yr Iessu Grist y welet*. *Ar* is probably the preposition *ar* with the meaning 'for the sake of', also used in oaths and asseverations, see *GPC* s.v. *ar*[9]. However, this would be the only instance in W of the use of *Iessu Grist* with the definite article, compare, for example, l. 493 *my[n] Iessu Grist* 'by Jesus Christ'. Since *yr Iessu* is a common phrase (*GMW* § 29), the scribes may have conflated *Iessu Grist* with *yr Iessu*. Ingo Mittendorf

suggests emending to *ar yr Arglwyd Iessu Grist* 'by the Lord Jesus Christ'.

492 **gat e hunan**: probably best translated as 'leave [this idea] alone', compare *BdH* 1469 *tut ceo lessez ester* 'let all this be' and similarly W 2351–2 *gat vi yn llonyd ac yn hedwch* 'leave me at rest and in peace', which corresponds to *BdH* 2060 *lessez moi ester* 'let me be'.

493 **oed**: *oed* is used in a modal sense here, see *GMW* § 120 (f).

502 **o'm vncrys** 'with/wearing a single shirt', see on ll. 234–5 above.

514 **bei gall[ei]** 'if it were possible': not in R, the letters following *gall-* are illegible in W; Watkin (1958: 116) thinks that *-ei* was perhaps intended.

516 **A ffwy bynnac**: for the construction of the indefinite relative *pwy bynnac* 'whoever' with a pronoun referring back to the indefinite relative in the following clause, compare *GMW* § 90. This anaphoric pronoun is here contained in the verbal form *vydei*.

517 **yr kadarnet vei** 'however stout it [his heart] might be': see *GMW* § 45 for the use of equative adjectives with the prepositions *yr* and *rac*, to convey concessive and causal meanings respectively. The same phrase occurs in *BR* 16.1–2 *yr kadarnet vei y gallon* 'however stout his heart may be' and *YSG* 461 *callon, yr cadarnet uei nac yr kalettet* 'a heart, however stout or cold it may be'; for the construction compare also ll. 544–5 *rac calettet croen y ben* 'because of the hardness of the skin of its head' and l. 934 *yr daet darlleawdyr vei* 'however good a reader he might be'.

524–5 **Ef a vyd reit y'r llewot vynet drwy vy nwylaw i** 'It will be necessary for the lions to go through my hands': the expression *vynet drwy vy nwylaw i* is based on *BdH* 1699 *par me deus mains les covendra passer* 'through my two hands they will have to go'. The use of *ef a* as an expletive subject with *bot reit* 'be necessary' (see above on l. 63) fits the third sub-group established by Willis (1998: 151–2), i.e., of verbs which take clausal arguments. Compare ll. 693–4 *Ef a damchweinawd geni deu vab ym mywn fforest* 'It happened that I gave birth to two boys in a forest'.

529 **Na ellygaf**: *na* is used in answers before words beginning with a vowel after their initial /g/ has become Ø by lenition, see Morris-Jones (1913: 423).

531 *o dywettwn i* 'if I said': W has an imperfect subjunctive, which is rare after the conjunction *o* (compare *GMW* § 272 and Richards (1938: 17)), whereas R has imperfect indicative *dywedwn*.

536 *a thitheu a drigye yna* 'and you shall stay here': R has the expected form of the indicative present 2 sg. *drigyy*. Watkin (1958: ciii) considers *-e* to be an instance of *e* for *y*. See also above on l. 245.

536–7 **Iessu Grist a'thiffero** 'Jesus Christ may defend you': R *a'th differo*; further examples of the contraction *-th d-* (=/ ð/) > *-th-* are given in *GMW* § 20 N. 1 and Morris-Jones (1913: 183).

540 *o'r blaen*: the meaning of *o'r blaen* in this context is not clear; compare Watkin (1958: 117) who suggests that 'without delay' may be an appropriate meaning here, otherwise perhaps 'one of the lions, [the one] in front'?

545 **agori y safyn y'r llew** 'the lion opened its jaws': R *o'r llew*. Whereas W uses the rare construction with the preposition *y* to introduce the agent of a verbal noun (see above on l. 135 and l. 204), R has the common construction with the preposition *o*.

555–6 **gwedy hynny y cwplaawd Bown wassanaeth y llew yn dda digawn**: probably 'then Bown finished the laying out of the lion's corpse well enough' or, more sarcastically, 'finished the service for the lion well enough'. This phrase has no parallel in *BdH*.

559–60 **ar nys gwelsei eiroet y gyffelyb** 'the like of which he had never seen': compare above on ll. 85–6.

561 **degwyr**: this is the phenomenon called by Morgan (1952: 136) 'apparent lenition' of initial <gw-> with nasalizing numerals. It

originates in a wrong division of *de(n)gwyr* as *de(n)g* plus *wyr*. A
singular is more commonly used after a number (*GMW* § 51 (b)),
but compare l. 733 *trywyr* and *PKM* 69.3 *deguyr*.

568–9 *dan agori y safyn* 'opening his mouth': for the use of the
preposition *tan* or *dan* to form the equivalent of a present participle
with a verbal noun see *GMW* § 237.

571–2 *mur maen [. . .] nys diwreidei ef* 'a stone wall which he
would not destroy': the negative relative particle contains a
redundant infixed pronoun, compare above on l. 85–6.

580–1 *hwynt a dywedynt na bydei ohonaf inheu dim meint byth*
'they would say that I would never be of any size at all'.

**581–3 *Ac rac kewilid yd edeweis 'y gwlat ac y deuthum y'r wlat hon
ac y gwrheeis y Iuor o Mwmbrawnt ac y guesneitheis yn gywir***
'And from shame I left my country, and I came to this country and
paid homage to Ivor of Mwmbrawnt and served him loyally': for
'y as a variant of *vy*, see above on l. 246.

The adverbial phrase *rac kewilid* 'from shame' has scope only over
the immediately following clause *yd edeweis 'y gwlat*, and the
following clauses have the finite verb in sentence-initial position
(compare above on ll. 174–5). Parallel examples are discussed by
Willis (1998: 118–22), who suggests that such verb-initial clauses
are typically used 'in the second conjunct pair of conjoined clauses,
or in a longer sequence of conjoined clauses'; this suits the context
here. See also below on ll. 776–7.

584–5 *a'm ffon i y drom* 'with my heavy stick': for an adjective with
an article following a noun with a possessive pronoun, compare
GMW § 28 (f) N and Watkin (1958: cxlix). See also l. 586 *dy ben
di yr mawr* 'your big head' (on the form of the article here compare
above on l. 169) and l. 967 *Vy mab y tec* 'My dear son'. The
feminine form of the adjective *trwm* shows that *ffon* is feminine,
compare below on ll. 924–5.

587 *werth vn uanec* 'value of a single glove': this expression
corresponds to *BdH* 1797 *le vailant de un gant* 'the value of a single
glove'. Compare Watkin (1958: clxi–clxiii).

590–1 *ny chyffroes vn aylawt ar Gopart yr y vedru mwy noc yr na metrit*: since *kyffroi* can be transitive as well as intransitive, two translations appear possible: 'he did not move a single limb on Copart, despite striking him/it, any more than if he/it had not been struck' and 'not a single limb on Copart moved, despite striking it/ him, any more than if it/he had not been struck. Compare *BdH* 1801– 2: *l'Escopart se tint tot sus en estant, / ke il ne wakere tant ne kant* 'The Escopart stayed upright and on his feet, and never staggered'.

614 *nachaf Copart*: R *Gopart*: lenition of a noun is expected after *nachaf* (compare Morgan (1952: 434–5)), but personal names are treated differently: the name *Bown* remains consistently unlenited after *nachaf*. Compare also W 4196 *nachaf pedeir kennat*.

620–1 *'Nyt ef a wnel Duw y dyuot ef y'm llys a miui yn dragywyd'* '"May God make that he never enters / God forbid that he ever enter my court with me"': Compare *BdH* 1924–5 *'ne place a damedé / ke il entre ma meson jur de mon ayé'* '"God forbid he enter my house as long as I'm alive"'. R has *yn vyw* after *a miui* (i.e., 'with me alive'). For further examples of *nyt ef* with the present subjunctive of *gwneuthur* in negated wishes see Morgan (1952: 372). According to Willis (1998: 151–2) this use of *nyt ef* belongs to the sub-group of expletive *ef* with verbs which take clausal arguments. Compare also *KAA* 529–30 *'Nyt ef a wnel Duw llad o'r iarll y veibyon yr iechyt y'm corff i.'* '"May God forbid that the earl kill his sons for the health of my body"' and *YCM* 141.10–11 *'Nyt ef a wnel Duw'*, *heb y Rolond*, *'dielwi y Freinc trwydof i'* '"God forbid", said Roland, "that the French should be destroyed through me"'.

633 *wch lafur*: R *awch llauur*; Watkin (1958: cxx), gives five instances of a form *wch* of the possessive pronoun 2 pl. from W, all between columns 69 and 82. The form *ych* only occurs before column 69, whereas the form *awch* is only found after column 82. No lenition is expected after the possessive pronoun 2 pl. and Watkin (1958: cxi) therefore suggests that <l> is used for /λ/ here.

642 *yn hoeth-lumun* 'stark-naked': *hoeth* is a variant of *noeth*, the reading in R, arising from false division in the phrase *yn noeth* > *yn (h)oeth*. On *-lumun* for *-lymun* (but R *-lumyn*) as a dialectal feature typical of Pembroke, see above on l. 483.

646 *y'r neuad yd aethant oc eu bwyt* 'they went to the hall to their meal': R *y eu*; *oc* is a form of the preposition *y* 'to' used before possessive pronouns 3 pl., compare YSG 315 *oc eu porthi* 'to nourish them' and see glossary s.v. *o³*, GPC s.v. *o⁵*, YSG, p. 180, and Watkin (1958: cxxi).

647 *A gwedy daruot y Milys priodi Iosian o'e hanuod* 'and after Milys had married Iosian against her will': for *o anfodd* 'against one's will' see GPC s.v. *anfodd*.

670 *y kyuarchassant well*: lenition of *gwell* in the idiom *cyfarch gwell* 'to greet' is the rule after finite forms of *cyfarch*, whereas after the verbal noun the initial of *gwell* remains unlenited; compare l. 91.

670 In this reworking of the creed *yr hwnn* is the antecedent for a series of relative clauses (*a anet, ac a uu, ac a drywestawd, ac a diodefawd, ac a uu varw ac a gladwyt*), into which are inserted two sentences with the verb in initial position (*ac y gwerthawd, ac y daw*) and one sentence with an adverbial phrase preceding the verb (*a'r trydyt dyd y kyuodes*). Watkin (1958: clvii) thinks that the uses of *y* indicate a confusion of *y* and *a* (but see below on ll. 803–4 and compare Willis 1998: 118–9), but notes that the Anglo-Norman version also uses relative and main clauses side by side. The text of the Creed in Llyvyr Agkyr Llandewivrevi (1346) shows similar syntactic complexities, which here seem to reflect the wording of the Latin source: *Iessu Grist, yr hvnn a diodeuaud yr an guaret ni, a disgynnavd y vffernn, a'r trydydyd y kyuodes o veirv. Ac ef ymdyrchauavd y nef, ac y mae yn eisted ar deheu y Tat Duw Holl-gyuoethauc. [. . .] Ac odyna y dav ef y varnnv byv a marv* (Lewis 1929–31: 202–3) 'Jesus Christ, the one who suffered to redeem us, who descended to hell [*or possibly non-relative* descended], and on the third day he rose from the dead. And he ascended to heaven, and he is sitting to the right of the Father, almighty God. And from there he will come to judge the living and the dead'. Compare the Latin text, *[. . .] Christus. Qui passus est pro salutate nostra, descendit ad inferos, tertia die resurrrexit a mortuis. Ascendit ad caelos, sedet ad dexteram Patris. Inde venturus judicare vivos et mortuos* (Lewis 1929–1931: 202–3). Note the close similarities with regard to the fronting of *a'r trydydyd/tertia die* and *odyna/Inde*. See also above on 376–84.

674 *ar ugeint*: R *ar hugeint*; forms with and without initial <h> are attested in Middle Welsh, see Morgan (1952: 388).

692 *Mae*: *mae* is used here in a question with the meaning 'where is', see *GMW* § 148 (b)(2).

693 *Syr*: *Sire* also occurs in the corresponding line *BdH* 2755 as term of address.

697 *wely di* 'behold, here (is)': compare *GMW* § 280 for *wely dy* > *weldi* and *Ger*. 294 *wely dy y paladyr a oyd y'm law i* 'here (is) the spear which was in my hand'. As Thomson (*Ger.*, p. 81) notes, the phrase is interrogative in origin and demonstrative in function.

705 *gwledi*: R *gwladoed*. *gwledi* is a variant of the plural of *gwlat* and according to Watkin (1958: xlviii–xlix) a southern dialectal feature.

711 *ac ny welas hi erroyt llysewyn well* 'and she had never seen a better plant': for the lenition of a comparative in a negative clause see *GMW* § 46.

711–12 *kanys a hwnnw y gallei wneuthur y llyw y mynhei ar y hwyneb a'e chorff* 'because with this she was able to produce the colour that she wanted on her face and on her body': the preverbal particle *y* preceding *gallei* is supplied from R as the better reading; W has *a gallei*.

Watkin (1958: clvii) suggests that the relative particle *y* preceding *mynhei* is used for *a*, which is also the reading of R, *a uynnei*. W's *y* may be influenced by similar instances in which, however, the logical antecedent of the relative clause is part of a prepositional/adverbial phrase, as in *PKM* 33.35 (= *Bran*. 118–19) *ar y llun y mynho e hun* 'in the fashion that he himself wishes' and *PKM* 41.12–13 (= *Bran*. 304–5) *yn y lle y mynnych ditheu* 'in the place that/where you wish'.

Perhaps less likely is the translation 'because with this she was able to apply (*lit*. make) the colour *where* she wanted it on her face and on her body'.

724 *y maner* 'their banner': compare Anglo-Norman *baner(e)*; both *maner* and *baner* exist in Welsh, and the form *maner* is

extrapolated from forms with lenited initial, since both initial /m/
and /b/ become /v/ under lenition. The same applies to *beinc* and
meinc 'bench', Anglo-Norman *ba(u)nc*, which is, however, only
attested with lenited initial in *YBH* (l. 822, W 3741) and a decision
with regard to its radical initial is therefore impossible.

729–46 Stimming (1899: 159) notes that the passage beginning at line
2824 in the Anglo-Norman text (corresponding to l. 720) is
obviously corrupt ('liegt offenbar verstümmelt vor'); see also below
on ll. 732–3. Watkin (1958: 150) points out that the Welsh trans-
lation is based on a very defective Anglo-Norman manuscript but
that the Welsh translator attempted to derive some sense from his
source. Textual problems remain, and we have included this
passage as an example of a slightly confused translator at work.
Note that the differences between W and R are small and do not
contribute to a better understanding of the Welsh text.

729 **Pann deuth Bown ac eu hymlit** 'When Bown came and pursued
them': for the syntax, see above on ll. 324–5. Instead of *ac*, R has
oc, which is a form of the preposition *y* 'to' used before possessive
pronouns 3 pl.; see above on l. 646.

732 **oc yssyd yn y dref** 'that (*lit.* from what) is in the town': compare
above on l. 35 and *GMW* § 75 N.4 and *GPC* s.v. *o*^{1}(6.l) for the use
of the preposition *oc* here.

732–3 **ymwan a oruc Bown [ac Armiger]**: Watkin (1958: 150) notes
that the phrase *ac Armiger*, which is neither in W nor in R, was lost
after *Bown*, on the basis of *BdH* 2841 *Estevus Boun o Armiger justé*
'Then Boeve fought with Armiger'. Stimming (1899: 160) comments
that this passage in the Anglo-Norman text is confused and garbled
and that the Welsh translator made independent but clumsy
changes to improve the sense: 'Die ganze Stelle ist offenbar sehr in
Unordnung geraten und verstümmelt. W [i.e., the Welsh version] geht
auf die gleiche Vorlage zurück, die der Uebersetzer nicht verstand
und selbständig, aber ungeschickt, geändert hat'.

733 **ymhoylut a orugant oll at y trywyr**: the 'three men' have not
been mentioned before and it remains unclear who they are and
what their role is in the story. But compare *BdH* 2843 *trois presons*

ad Boves conquesté 'Boeve took (*lit.* conquered) three prisoners'. Watkin (1958: 150–1) suggests a rather complex and unlikely multilingual scenario, namely that they owe their existence first to the translator, who kept the French expression *a l'atravers* 'sideways' in *BdH* 2846 untranslated, and then to later scribes, who, influenced by the *trois presons*, interpreted something like *alatraver(s)* or *alatryvyr* as *trywyr*.

Since the adverbial meaning 'wholly' of *oll* is difficult to reconcile with the meaning of *ymhoylut* 'return', *oll* probably means 'everyone' here, with semantic agreement between the verb (plural) and *oll* (collective); see *GPC* s.v. *oll*[1].

733–4 *a'r trywyr hynny a orugant*: the meaning of this sentence remains doubtful; Watkin (1958: 151) suggests that *orugant* may be a form of *gorugo* 'to tear, pierce, conquer (?)' (which would then be a rather unlikely narrative present in a main clause) or that *a orugant* is a mistake for *a oruuant* 'they defeated (these three men)'.

735 *digyaw a oruc Bown wrth y bobyl hynny* 'Bown was angry with these people': the lenition following the feminine singular article and the plural form of the demonstrative show a mix of singular and plural syntax with *pobyl*, as in *PKM* 49.21 *y seith cantref hynny* 'these seven commots', with a noun in the singular and the demonstrative in the plural. Compare also the following examples noted by Morgan (1952: 11), *ar ysgymunyeit pobyl honno* 'these accursed people', with the plural form of the adjective and the singular form of the demonstrative, and *pobl feilchion* 'proud people', with lenition of the plural form of an adjective, as if following a feminine noun in the singular.

736 *y ergyt* 'at/by a blow': *y* here is the preposition originally meaning 'from', compare above on l. 105, and see Watkin (1958: 151) and Bromwich and Evans (1992: 202).

742–3 *a'e hanregawd*: presumably 'who [had] made her presents'. Compare *BdH* 2855–8: *Estevus les altres en la paleis entré, / e la pucele les ad mult mercié, / mes le meilur ad mult plus desiré, / ke les trois prisons li ad presenté* 'At that moment, the others entered the palace and the maiden thanked them profusely, but most of all she wanted the best man, who had presented her with the three prisoners'.

744–5 y erchi [idaw] vynet 'to ask him to go': W *y erchi vynet*, R *y erchi idaw mynet*; in the case of the verb *erchi*, the person asked is normally denoted by a prepositional phrase with *y* 'to'; W attests both lenition and non-lenition of the verbal noun describing a required action; compare W 3765 *erchi idaw vynet* versus l. 72 *erchi idaw mynet*. Although non-lenition of *mynet* is more frequent in W, the insertion of *idaw* appears preferable to the insertion of a possessive pronoun 3 sg., as is suggested by Watkin (1958: 151), *y erchi [y] vynet*.

746 ny ffynnyawd racdaw 'it did not succeed for him (= he did not succeed)': for a similar use of the preposition *rac* with *rhwyddhau* 'to prosper' see HGvK 28.13–14 *Oddyna eissyoes pob dryll y rhwyddhaws pob peth rhag Gruffudd* 'From then on, however, everything gradually prospered for Gruffudd'.

749–50 Duw yr hwnn a'n kreawd a'th iachao 'May God, who created us, save you': W *iacha*, R *iachao*; R's subjunctive appears to be better here; see Watkin (1958: 152) and l. 825 *Duw a'th iachao di* 'May God save you'. On the use of *yr hwnn* here to introduce a non-restrictive relative clause see Morris-Jones (1931: 98–9), who calls this type of relative clause 'coordinate'.

756 Vyg chwaer: R *vy chwaer*; Watkin (1958: xlvii) suggests that W's form represents an isolated southern (Pembroke) dialectal realization of the nasal mutation, as in *yngwâr* 'my sister'; see also above on l. 313.

769–70 ac eu bwyt yd aethant 'and they went to their meal': R *y eu*; for the forms of the combination of the preposition *y* 'to' with the possessive pronoun 3 pl. see GMW § 56 N.3.

776–7 A thrannoeth pan dwyrhaawd y dyd yd aeth duc Uascal a'y wyr ac a gyhyrdassant a duc Dostris 'And the next morning, when the day dawned (*lit.* rose), duke Vascal came with his men and they met with duke Dostris': this is an example of a particular type of clausal coordination in Middle Welsh, in which two conjoined clauses share the same subject. In the first clause an adverbial phrase precedes the verb and selects the particle *y*; the subject appears in postverbal position in the first clause but selects the particle *a* in the second clause. This type is discussed in detail by Willis (1998: 108–22), who suggests that it is 'part of a fully productive grammatical pattern' (Willis 1998: 273) which operates in contexts of special narrative continuity. For further examples compare ll. 803–4 *Ac odyna yd ymlidiawd ef duc Dostris ac a'e trewis ar y luruc dyrnawt mawr braf* 'and then he pursued count Dostris and gave him a heavy strong blow on his armour', ll. 924–5 *yna y kymerth Bown ffon bres ac a trewis Teruagawnt ac ef* 'then Bown took a staff of brass and struck Teruagawnt with it', l. 926 *yna y neidawd [. . .] ac a ffoawd* 'then he jumped [. . .] and fled' and l. 959 *yna y peris [. . .] ac a dywawt* 'then he caused [. . .] and said'; in the last three examples R has the preverbal particle *y* to introduce the second clause.

781 **trwy distryw y wlat** 'destroying the country': for *trwy* plus verbal noun denoting manner or attendant circumstances see *GMW* § 240.

787 **Terri [y] marchawc clotuorus** 'Terri, the celebrated knight': the insertion of *y* is suggested by Watkin (1958: 153), on the basis of sense and of *BdH* 2922 *Terri [. . .] le chevaler preysé* 'Terri, the famous knight'.

787–8 **ymlaen [y rei ereill] achub y Sore** 'in front of the others he attacked Sore': the insertion of *y rei ereill* is suggested by Watkin (1958: 153), on the basis of sense and of *BdH* 2925 *devant les altres va ferir Ysoré* 'in front of the others he goes to strike Ysoré'. The scribes of W and R seem to have interpreted the French name as containing the article, as there appears to be an extra space between <y> and <s>. In the Anglo-Norman version it is Boeve who fights against Ysoré (see *BdH* 2924), but in the Welsh version it may be Terri.

788–9 **yny ballwys idaw y luruc**: *lit.* 'until his mail-coat failed him'.

789–90 **Terri a achubawd [Lancelin]** 'Terri attacked Lancelin': the insertion of *Lancelin* is suggested by Watkin (1958: 154), on the basis of sense and of *BdH* 2928 *Terri fert Lancelin* 'Terri strikes Lancelin'.

796 A Therri, ny bu hwyra 'And Terri, he was not very slow': *hwyra* may be the superlative of *hwyr* 'late, slow', here with elative meaning and loss of final <f>; compare similarly l. 352 *eitha*. GPC s.v. *hwyraf* prefers to take it as a verbal noun, 'to delay, loiter', but the omission of the particle *yn* would be unusual. Compare Watkin (1958: 154) and *BdH* 2937 *e Terri n'est gueres targant* 'and Terri was not slow either'.

797 ef a ladawd agos y deugein 'he killed nearly forty': this appears to correspond to *BdH* 2938 *ke qu'el consuit, ne ad de mort garrant* 'those he reached had no protection from death'. Watkin (1958: 154–5) suggests that the translator may have confused *garrant* and *quaraunte* 'forty', possibly because the Anglo-Norman text was read out to him for translation.

798–9 ef a dorres Bown y wayw yndaw: *ef* is probably an expletive subject ('Bown broke his/the lance . . .'). The transitive verb *torri* 'to break' does not fit comfortably into the categories with which Willis (1998: 149–53) typically associates such subjects, but he notes some expletive subjects used with transitive verbs in his Middle Welsh corpus, which does not include *YBH*; see Willis (1998: 161–2). Alternatively, *ef* could be the subject and *Bown* a parenthetical modification ('he, Bown, broke the lance . . .').

Watkin (1958: cli–clii, 155) suggests emending *yndaw* to *ydaw*, parallel to l. 420 *y vreich ddeheu idaw* 'his right arm', with the article and a prepositional phrase with *y* 'to' denoting possession. Compare also *BdH* 2942 *La lance al duc brise meyntenant* 'The duke's lance broke at once'.

803–4 Ac odyna yd ymlidiawd ef duc Dostris ac a'e trewis ar y luruc dyrnawt mawr braf 'and then he pursued count Dostris and gave him a fine big blow on his armour': the verb *trewis* has two direct objects, the infixed object pronoun *'e* and *dyrnawt mawr braf*. Compare *BdH* 2948 *grant cope li done* 'he gave him a great blow', with a personal pronoun 3 sg. dat., and for the Welsh idiom *taraw dyrnawt* W 2579–80 *ac ef yn vab a'th trewis ar dy ben tri dyrnawt* 'and he as a boy gave you three blows on your head', ll. 877–8 *a tharaw Iuor ac ef ar y helym dyrnawt mawr* 'and [Bown] gave Ifor with it [i.e. his sword] on his helmet a big blow', and *Ow.* 131 *a tharaw karw a hi dyrnawt mawr* 'and he gave the stag with it [i.e., his staff] a big blow'.

811–12 *'A dybygy di caffel vy holl ewyllus i ual hynn?' 'Ef a'r allei ymi y gaffel.'* '"Do you think you will obtain my full passion like this?" "It is possible that I will obtain it"': compare *BdH* 2957–8 *"Ore tost de vus averai ma voluntez."* / *"Bien purra estre,"* dist *Boves li senez* '"Now I shall soon have my wish granted by you." "That may well be so," said Boeve the wise'. For the phrase *ef a'r allei* and its syntax compare *YSG* 861–2 *kanys ef a'r allei idaw ymgyfyrgolli yn ehegyr* 'since it is possible that he looses everything suddenly' and *YSG* 3353 *kanys ef a'r allei y dragwres beri y'r blodeu golli* 'since it is possible that the great heat causes the blossoms to fall'. The particle *ry* in *a'r* (< *a* + *ry*) appears to strengthen the sense of possibility already present in *(g)allei*; compare Modern Welsh *efallai* 'perhaps' < *ef a allai* and *YSG*, pp. 195–6.

820 **ynhy vrda**: note the spelling of the nasalization of <t> here. For further instances of lenition after *ty* see Morgan (1952: 109–10).

825 **Duw a'th iachao di ac a gerych** 'God may save you and the ones you love': the relative clause *a gerych* has no expressed antecedent and functions as object of *iachao*, see *GMW* § 77 (c).

828 **ys dydyeu** 'for (some) days': for the use of *ys*, indicative present 3 sg. of *bot*, in adverbial expressions with nouns denoting a period of time, see *GMW* § 147 (e).

835 **yd achubassant attaw** 'they hastened to him': *achub* means a non-hostile movement towards a person here; this is the only example of this meaning noted in *GPC* p. 1340.

854 **Iudas o Machabes**: in the extant Anglo-Norman text Yvori calls two warriors, *BdH* 3561, *Judas e Masebré* 'Judas and Masebré'; *Iudas o Machabes* appears to be a slightly garbled reference to Maccabeus, the second-century leader of the Jews in their war of liberation against the Syrians and a type of the brave and valorous warrior in the Middle Ages. There is a succinct description of his deeds in the thirteenth-century *Historia Gruffud vab Kenan*, in a comparison of his achievements and Gruffudd's: *megys yd amdiffynnvs Iudas Machabeus gulat er Israel y gan y brenhined paganyeit a'r kenedeloed kyttervyn, a ruthrei en eu plith en venych* 'as Judas Maccabeus defended the land of Israel from the pagan

kings and the neighbouring peoples who frequently made attacks
into their midst' (*HGvK* 9.15–17; see also *VGFC* § 12.8); and this
theme is again taken up in two further passages, *HGvK* 11.18–22
and 28.18–20. In *Cronicl Turpin* the fame of the dead Rolant is
compared to Judas's fame: *Kyffelyb o glot y Iudas Machabeus* 'of
the same fame as Judas Maccabeus' (*YCM* 162.27–8) and this
comparison is taken from the Latin original: *Iudae Machabeo
probitate comparatus* (*HKM* 205).

855 *os mi a gymer arnaf vrwydyr* 'if it is me who undertakes a
battle': the verb in the so-called mixed order is in the 3 sg. (see
Richards 1938: 100) but the suffixed pronoun refers to the logical
subject.

856 *y gyffelyb varchawc ny bu eiroet* 'a similar knight never
existed': Morgan (1952: 89) argues that *y* is the article in this
construction and gives other examples of the lenition of *cyffelyb*
after the article and before a masculine noun.

863–4 *mawr vyd hynny*: compare *BdH* 3572 *grant ert la perte*
'great will be the loss'. *GPC* notes uses of *mawr* with a meaning
'awful, terrible' and this would suit the context here. Watkin (1958:
174) believes that the original Welsh version had *y kyni* 'the battle/
the distress' instead of *hynny*.

864 *gwedy ymgymyscant* 'after they will fight with each other':
Watkin (1958: 174) prefers the reading of R, *gwedy yd ymgymyscant*,
but *GMW* § 266 notes examples of the conjunction with and
without subordinating *y*; *gwedy yd* occurs in W 1791.

864–5 *ymgyhyrdwn, myn duw, os mynhwn* 'let us meet [in single
combat], by God, if we wish (it)': R *mynnwn*; the scribe of W
appears to be fond of a spelling <-nh-> for <-nn->; compare, for
example, W 2855–6 *penhaf*, R *bennaf*, W 3132 *ny vynhaf* (present
indicative 1 sg.), R *mynnaf*, and l. 755 *os mynhy* (present indicative 2
sg.), R *mynny*. The form *mynhwn* can therefore be taken as present
indicative 1 pl.; see also above on l. 531. *os* may be either the
combination of the conjunction with the object pronoun 3 sg. or
the simple conjunction; see *GMW* § 272 (b), (c).

865–6 *ef a vyd tyghedic it pymthec brenhin* 'fifteen kings will owe allegiance to you': this is an example of *ef a* as an expletive subject with a form of *bot*. Similar examples are listed by Willis (1998: 150).

867 *minheu ym Mwmbrawnt*: Watkin (1958: 175) suggests that a phrase like 'my castle' may have been omitted before *minheu*, but then one would probably expect *inheu*.

871 *Ac yna y kerdassant ar lleilltu*: 'and then they went to one side': Watkin (1958: 175) suggests that the Welsh text is corrupt here. *BdH*'s 3583 *le gué passent, oltre se sont mis* ('they crossed the ford and reached the other side') implies that the single combat between Bown and the Saracen leader Ivori takes place on one side of a ford, perhaps in order to prevent others from interfering. The Middle English and the Old Norse versions refer to an island in the ford, a traditional place for single combat: *in an yle vnder þat cite, / þar þat scholde þe bataile be. / Ouer þat water þai gonne ride* 'they rode to an island below the city, where the combat was to take place; they rode across the water' (*Beues* 4141–43), *þeyr ridu nu vt j holmen* 'they rode out to the island' (*BS* p. 337). The reference to the ford in *BdH* 3583 at least explains the riverbank that is later mentioned without prior reference (l. 896): *Ac yna ar lann auon yd ymgynullassant y Sarascinyeit* 'and then the Saracens assembled on the bank of the river'.

875 *na thorassant* 'so that they did not break': for further examples of *na* introducing adverbial clauses of result see *GPC* s.v. *na*[1] (d).

878 *yny dygwydwys y blodeu a'r mein*: compare *BdH* 3600–2 *L'espé trait, grant coup li feri. / A mont sur le helme, ou l'or i fu, / peres e flors ad il abatu* 'He drew his sword and dealt him a great blow. On the top of the helmet, where the gold [i.e., the decoration] was, he knocked out precious stones and ornaments'. Helms, as well as armour, were often lavishly decorated in the Middle Ages; compare Blair (1958: 170–2).

884 *chwaen Ffragheid* 'a French feat': this corresponds to *BdH* 3604 *tor François* 'a French turn'. Stimming (1899: 168) notes that this phrase, which is well-attested in medieval French texts, appears

to describe a sudden attack after a feigned flight; compare also Weiss (2008: 91), who translates this phrase as 'turning suddenly at full gallop'.

889–90 *a da y traweint y Ffreinc a ffrwythlawn* 'and the French struck well and successfully': *BdH* 3614 *Bien firent François e par grant vertu* 'The French struck well and with great force'. Bown and his companions are characterized as French knights only in the final part of the text, starting with a passage in which the Saracen leader Yvori tells his counsellor that *"le roi Hermin ad François mandez / dru li est Josian, je sai de veritez"* '"King Hermin has sent for a Frenchman; I know for sure he is Josiane's lover"' (*BdH* 3160). Bown is clearly the Frenchman referred to here, but this information is not contained in W. References to the French or their fighting techniques then accumulate in the final encounter between Bown's and Yvori's hostile armies; compare *BdH* 3604 *a tor Francois li fert par vertu* 'turning suddenly at full gallop, he struck him with great force' (*A blyghau a oruc Bown a gwneuthur chwaen Ffragheid ffrywthlawn* (ll. 883–5)) 'and Bown grew angry and and did a successful French feat'), *BdH* 3622 *François i firent com pruz e hardiz* 'the French acted like bold and brave men' (W –), and *BdH* 3628 *Francois sunt armés, li chevaler vailant* 'The French are armed, the brave knights' (*canys clotuorus yw marchogyon Ffreinc mywn arueu* (ll. 900–1) 'for the French knights in arms are celebrated'). It appears that in the final part of the narrative Bown's/ Boeve's English origins have been forgotten; compare also Weiss (1986: 240): 'In the first half [of *Boeve de Haumtone*], Boeve is an English hero; in the second, apparently French', see also Weiss (2008: 83).

    R *trewynt*; the ending *-eint* of the imperfect indicative 3 pl. is a variant formed by analogy with the 3 sg. *-ei*; see *GMW* § 132 (c).

897–8 **yna y delit dec admiral ar hugeint a dec mrenhin ac a'e dugassant ganthunt y Vratmwnd** 'then thirty emirs and ten kings were caught, and they brought them with them to Bratmwnd': this is an example of clausal coordination similar to the one discussed above for ll. 803–4; there is, however, no identity of the subjects here. It is parallel in structure to the following pair of clauses quoted from *Ystoryaeu Seint Greal* by Willis (1998: 111), *Ac o'r diwed efo a delit o gernyt, ac a'e dugassant y'r fforest* 'And in the end he was caught by force, and they took him to the forest'. The insertion of *wy* before *a'e dugassant* suggested by Watkin (1958: 176) therefore seems unnecessary.

There is some confusion here as to the number of captives; compare *BdH* 3623 *treis amirals e quinze rois unt pris* 'they seized three emirs and fifteen kings' and l. 903 *pympthec mrenhin*. According to *BdH* 3624 the prisoners are taken to *Monbrant*; R has *y Vratfwrt*. *Bratmwnd* is the name of the king of Damascus but also occurs as a place-name in a number of instances in W; see Watkin (1958: xli) and Poppe and Reck (2008: 152–3).

900–1 *canys clotuorus yw marchogyon Ffreinc mywn arueu* 'for the French knights in arms are celebrated': possibly implying that the French knights will be victorious as soon as they have proper arms. This appears to correspond to a descriptive statement outside the direct speech in the Anglo-Norman text, *BdH* 3628 *François sunt armés, li chevaler vailant* 'the French are armed, the brave knights'.

911 *nyt arbedassant* 'they did not spare': the subject is Gi and his men; compare Watkin (1958: 177).

911–12 *Eithyr a alwei ar [vedit] onadunt ny welei na mam na mab* 'except those of them who demanded baptism, no one would see [again] mother or child': W has *vedic* 'a physician' (a perhaps more realistic approach); the emendation to *vedit* 'baptism' is suggested by Watkin (1958: 177) on the basis of *BdH* 3645–6 *si deu ne cleyment e baptisement, / jamés ne verrunt femmes ne enfant* 'if they did not invoke God and ask to be baptised, never again would they see wives or children'. R has *eithyr a welynt ar ureint medygon onadunt* and omits *ny welei na mam na mab*.

913 *hen Bown*: this corresponds to *BdH* 3647 *le duc Boves*; *hen* is perhaps used here to distinguish Bown, the hero of the narrative, from Terri's son of the same name. Compare l. 892 *Bown vab Terri* versus l. 893–4 *Bown o Hamtwn*.

914–15 *Ac yna yd aeth Gi vrenhin yn erbyn Bown a dywedut wrthaw. 'Syr,' heb y Bown, 'Duw a dalo it.'*: W has changed *heb ef*, referring to Gi, into *heb y Bown* by deleting *ef* and inserting *Bown*, and Gi's words appear to have been omitted, perhaps because they also began with the address *syr*; compare *BdH* 3649–51: *e le roi Gui li va encontrant.* / *"Sire," dist il, "jeo vus rent la terre de Monbrant."* / *"Bel sire," fet Boves, "merci vus rent."* 'and king Gui went to meet him. "Sir," he said, "I present you with the land of Monbrant." "Dear Sir," said Boeve, "I thank you."' R has *Syr heb y bown.*

915–18 ***Ac yna anuon a orugant yn ol Iosian [. . .] ac a vynhei gret ar gyhoed ac a vynhei heb ohir y vedydyaw*** 'they sent for Iosian [. . .] and for those who wanted the faith publicly and who wanted to be baptised without delay': The relative clauses function as complements to the prepositional phrase *yn ol* in the idiomatic expression *anuon yn ol* 'to send after'. R *uynnei*; the form *mynhei* could formally be imperfect indicative or subjunctive, see above on ll. 864–5; its use in two generalizing relative clauses makes it likely that it is subjunctive here.

924–5 ***yna y kymerth Bown ffon bres ac a trewis Teruagawnt ac ef*** 'then Bown took a staff of brass and struck Teruagawnt with it': for the syntax, see above on ll. 803–4. *Ffon* is otherwise a feminine noun, as is shown by the use of the feminine form of the adjective *trwm* in ll. 584–5, *a'm ffon i y drom*, as well as by the possessive pronoun 3 sg. in l. 561, *rac y thrymet*, with reference to *ffon* in l. 560, and the anaphoric reference with masculine *ef* is therefore incorrect. Watkin (1958: 178) suggests that the translator was thinking of masculine *mace* used in the Anglo-Norman text, *BdH* 3665 *Hil prist un mace si fiert Tervagant* 'He took a club and struck Tervagant'.

927 ***y pydiw yd oedewch yn credu*** 'in (*lit.* to) whom you were believing': *y pydiw* is a combination of the prepositional interrogative *pydiw* 'to whom' (used in direct and indirect questions) with the preposition *y* 'to'; compare *GMW* § 84 (a) and *GPC* s.v. *paddiw*.

929–30 ***Y neb [. . .], madeuit Duw vdunt*** 'Whoever [. . .], may God forgive him (*lit.* them)': like *pawb* (see above on ll. 158–9), *neb* can be used with singular or plural reference. Compare *ar neb a oedynt yn yr ynys a anryfedassant [. . .]* 'and whoever was (*lit.* were) on this island marvelled [. . .]', quoted *GPC* s.v. *neb*, from *Ystorya Daret*.

madeuit is a 3 sg. imperative with an ending *-it* instead of regular
-et, see *GMW* § 140 (b).

931 **yn [yn] bywyt** 'in our lifetime': the insertion of *yn* 'our' is
suggested by *BdH* 3673 *Ne li crerom mie en tut nostre vivant* 'We
will never believe in him in all our lives' and other instances with
preposition and possessive pronoun, such as W 3060–1 *eithyr na
bydaf lawen byth y'm bywyt* 'except that I shall never be happy in
my lifetime' (for *y'm* 'in my', see above on l. 232).

955 **or bydy varw di** 'if you die': for *or < o* plus *ry*, compare *GMW*
§§ 272 and 185(c); for the position of the affixed pronoun after the
predicate in copular clauses, compare *GMW* § 62 N.2.

957 **ny'm tawr ohonunt** 'I am not concerned about them': R *dawr*;
for the defective verb *dawr/tawr* and its syntax, see *GMW* § 162.

958 **tri meib** 'three children': Bown has two sons, Gi and Milys
(compare W 3555–61), and one daughter, Betris (compare W 3508–
10); *mab* therefore means 'child' here, rather than 'son'; compare
also *BdH* 3816 *trois enfans*.

966–7 **kymeint yw y duchan ac na bu eiroet y gymeint** 'his moaning
is so great that there never was its equal': for the various con-
structions of clauses expressing result after the equative, see *GMW*
§ 44.

967 **Vy mab y tec** 'My dear son': for the use of the article with an
adjective after a noun preceded by a possessive pronoun, see *GMW*
§ 28 N. and Watkin (1958: cxlix–cl), and also above on ll. 584–5.

969–77 Here we follow Watkin, who uses R to supplement W, which
is incomplete at the margins.

970 **A phan welas Bown hi** 'And when Bown saw her': an
independent pronoun is used as the object here, instead of an
infixed pronoun; compare *GMW* § 55 (a) and contrast l. 748 *A
phan y gwelas Bown hi yn dyuot* 'And when Bown saw her
coming', with a syllabic form of the infixed pronoun after *pan*; see
GMW § 59.

972 **wyll deu** 'both': R *wy ell deu*, *wyll* is a contracted from of *wy ell*; compare *GMW* § 107 (c).

977 **y'r eglwys a barassei ef ehun y wneuthur** 'to the church which he himself had caused to be built (*lit.* whose building he had caused)': R *gwneuthur*; *eglwys* is a fem. noun; the lenition of *gwneuthur* indicates that *y* is a possessive pronoun masc. 3 sg., but compare *GMW* § 69 N. for other examples of genitival relative clauses with an anaphoric pronoun masc. 3 sg. referring back to feminine or plural antecedents.

Glossary

The arrangement of the words in the glossary is guided by didactic principles. The order of the entries generally follows the sequence of the Roman alphabet suggested by the graphic shape of the letters. The following points should be noted:

<g> representing both /g/ and /ŋ/ is listed under <g>, but <ng> = /ŋ/ is inserted after <g>;

<c> and <k> are treated as one letter and inserted after <b>;

<ch> and <ff> are listed separately after <c>/<k> and after <f> respectively, notwithstanding whether the latter represents /f/ or /ff/;

<f> = /f/ is arranged with <f>;

words with initial <u> or <v> are listed under <f> or under <u>, depending on the phonetic value of the letter;

word-internal <u> and <v> are arranged according to their graphic shape, no matter whether they represent /v/ or /ü/;

<d> representing /d/ and /ð/ is treated as one letter, but <d> is rendered as <δ> in the glossary where it represents /ð/ (= ModW <dd>).*

In instances in which the relation between spelling and pronunciation may cause difficulties of interpretation for the student, a Modern Welsh form is given in brackets. The selection of a head word in cases of text-internal variation is always a difficulty and we have attempted to give ample cross-references in this case, as well as in other cases of orthographic and morphological variation which may present problems. Finite verbal forms are entered under the verbal noun. Where the forms of the imperfect indicative and the imperfect subjunctive are identical, we have refrained from committing ourselves to one definitive interpretation in the glossary. Mutated consonants are restored to their radical forms, except in a few instances in which the mutated form has become petrified, for example *dros*. We have indicated the initial mutations that are expected after prepositions etc., even if these are not always realized in our text.

Line numbers are given for the first three examples.

* This is a departure from Modern Welsh conventions according to which <dd> is listed separately after <d>.

Abbreviations

adj. adjective
adv. adverb
aff. affixed
art. article
asp. aspirates
comp. comparative
conj. conjunction
cons. consuetudinal
def. definite
dem. demonstrative
equat. equative
f. feminine
fut. future
h– Sandhi *h*
impf. imperfect
indep. independent
inf. infixed
interj. interjection
interrog. interrogative
intrans. intransitive
len. leniting
m. masculine
n. noun

nas. nasalizing
neg. negative
neutr. neuter
num. numeral
ord. ordinal
perf. perfect
pers. personal
pl. plural
plupf. pluperfect
poss. possessive
pref. prefixed
prep. preposition
pres. present
pret. preterite
pron. pronoun
redupl. reduplicated
refl. reflexive
rel. relative
sg. singular
subj. subjunctive
superl. superlative
vn. verbal noun

A

a¹ (len.) preverbal particle 1, 4, 7;
with perf. particle **a'r** 811;
with inf. obj. pron. 1 sg. **a'm**
241, 2 sg. **a'th** (len.) 71, 76, 155,
3 sg. m. **a'e, a'y** (h–) 128, 129,
350, 3 sg. f. a'e (h–) 728, 2 pl.
a'ch 730, 3 pl. **a'e** (h–) 724, 897.

a² (len.) relative particle *who,*
which, that 1, 5, 7; with inf.
obj. pron. 1 sg. **a'm** 312, 313,
392, 2 sg. **a'th** (len.) 228, 229, 3
sg. m. **a'e, a'y** (h–) 137, 632,
642, 3.sg. f. **a'e** (h–) 742, 1 pl.
a'n 749.

a³ (len.) interrog. particle 34, 36,
468.

a⁴ (len.) vocative particle 152,
277, 358.

a⁵, a(c)¹ (asp.) conj. *and* 1, 2, 4;
with def. art. **a'r** 7, 27, 138;
with inf. poss. pron. 1 sg. **a'm**
(h–) 147, 382, 393, 2 sg. **a'th**
(len.) 131, 488, 677, 3 sg. m.
a'e, a'y (len.) 11, 17, 42, 3 sg. f.
a'e (asp., h–) 380, 438, 457, 3
pl. **a'e** (h–) 185.

a⁶, a(c)² (asp.) prep. *with* 67, 184,
186; after equative *as* (with
negation **ac na(t)**) 24, 256, 322;
with def. art. **a'r** 63, 92, 201;
with inf. poss. pron. 1 sg. **a'm**
(h–) 151, 361, 410, 2 sg. **a'th**
(len.) 148, 585, 3 sg. m. **a'e, a'y**
(len.) 98, 122, 132; for **tu a(c)**
and **parth a(c)** see **tu** and **parth.**

a⁷ (len.) prep. *of* 87, 217, 279
(**truan a beth** *a wretched thing*)
(*GMW* § 39 (c)).

abreið see **breið.**

achos m./f. *cause, reason* 530; **o**
achos *because of* 71, 105, 116–
117.

achub vn. *to seize; to attack; to*
hasten 61, 204, 348; pret. 3 sg.
achubawð 550, 722, 790, pret.
3 pl. **achubassant** 835.

achydic see **ychydic.**

adar pl. (m.) *birds* 428.

adaw vn. *to leave* 165, 252; pret.
1 sg. **edeweis** 581, pret. 3 sg.
edewis 754, plupf. 3 sg.
adawssei 507.

aðfwyn, aðvwyn adj. *fine,*
pleasant; noble 709, 770,
842.

adlo m. *account;* **dala adlo am** *to*
take account of, grieve about
149, 227.

admiral m. *emir* 893, 897; pl.
admirales, -lys 848, 863, 931.

adnabot vn. *to know, be acquainted*
with; pres. 1 sg. **atwen** 453,
impf. 3 sg. **atwaynat** 452.

adolwyn, adolwc vn. *to beseech;*
to request 13, 92, 258.

adref, atref adv. *home* 68, 360.

ae interrog. particle *is it?* 191 578,
639; **ae** conj. *whether* 842; **ae . . .**
ae conj. *whether . . . or* 473
(*GMW* § 196).

aeth, aethant, af see **mynet.**

afluneiðet m. *ugliness, deformity*
576.

aflunyeið adj. *deformed, mis-*
shapen 573.

affreit [afraid] adj. *unnecessary,*
needless 708.

afwyneu pl. (f.) *reins* 726.

agharueið [angharuaidd] adj.
unpleasant, repulsive 569.

agheu [angau] m./f. *death* 286,
377, 522.

agori vn. *to open* 545, 568.

agos adj. *near;* comp. **nes** 361;

agos y deugein *nearly forty* 797.
allan adv. *out* 331, 720, 853; **o
hyn allan** *from now on* 210; **o
hynny allan** *from then on* 17,
52, 211.
am (len.) prep. *around; because
of, concerning; on; about* 33,
40, 97; **y am** *from about* 219; **y
am hynny** *besides* 208; with
suff. pers. pron. 2 sg. **ymdanat**
75, 707, 3 sg. m. **ymdanaw** 41,
45, 219, 3 sg. f. **ymdanei** 709, 3
pl. **ymdanunt** 159, 852, 870.
amdrymder m. *heaviness (of old
age)* 10.
amðiffyn vn. *to save, protect,
defend* 673.
amðiret [ymddiried] vn. *to trust;*
pres. subj. 3 sg. **amðireto** 151.
amgen adj. *other, different;* **nyt
amgen (no)** *namely* 141, 813–
814, 891.
amherawdyr m. *emperor, ruler* 5,
12, 19.
amhyl adj. *large, abundant* 563.
amkan y prep. *about,
approximately* 721.
amot m./f. *agreement* 761.
amouyn [amofyn] vn. *to ask,
inquire;* pret. 3 pl.
amouynassant 836.
amrysson m. *dispute* 764.
amryuaylon [amryfeilion] adj. pl.
various, diverse 946.
amser m. *time* 7, 155, 462.
am(m)ws m. *war-horse, destrier*
24, 246, 726.
amylder m. *multitude,
abundance* 292, 427.
amysgafyn adj. *agile, nimble* 368.
anawð adj. *difficult, hard* 153.
aneglur adj. *indistinct, mumbling*
569.

anfurueið [anffurfaidd] adj.
deformed, hideous 616.
angchwanec see **yghwanec.**
angerð m./f. *anger* 546.
anheilwg [annheilwng] adj.
unbecoming, improper 93.
aniueil [anifail] m. *animal, beast*
559.
annoc vn. *to urge, encourage* 58.
anoðyfyn adj. *deep, bottomless*
130.
anrec m./f. *present* 17, 736.
anregu vn. *to present, make
presents;* pret. 3 sg. **anregawð**
743.
anreithaw vn. *to plunder, destroy*
378; pres. impersonal **anreithir**
730.
anrydeð m./f. *honour* 277.
anrydeðus adj. *honoured,
respected* 244.
anryueðu [anrhyfeddu] vn. *to
wonder, marvel at* 86, 576.
ansawð m./f. *nature; condition;
state* 518.
anuon [anfon] vn. *to send* 12, 17,
46; **anuon yn ol** *to send for*
848, 915–6, 932; pres. 1 sg.
anuonaf 76, pret. 1 sg.
anuoneis 750, pret. 3 sg.
anuones 744.
anuoð [anfodd] m. *displeasure;*
o'e hanuoð *against her will* 647.
anurðedic adj. *dishonourable,
disgraced* 243.
anwylnei m. *dear nephew* 622.
ar¹ (len.) prep. *on, upon; for, for
the sake of; with* (before
ordinals)*; to* (**roði ar uaeth ar**
give into fosterage to) 8, 21,
37; **ar draws** prep. *all over,
throughout* 819; **ar hynny** adv.
thereupon 125, 332, 356; **ar**

hynt adv. *immediately, at once* 120, 202, 401; **ar hyt** prep. *along, throughout* 196, 318, 336–7; **ar uessur, ar vessur** [fesur] prep. *with the intenion of* 205, 545, 800; **ar warthaf** prep. *on top (of)* 98; **y ar** prep. *(mounted) on; from (upon)* 249, 367, 513; with suff. pers. pron. 1 sg. **arnaf** 154, 241, 635, 2 sg. **arnat** 229, 706, 3 sg. m. **arnaw** 115, 172, 220, 3 sg. f. **arnei, erni** 32, 55, 405, 1 pl. **arnam** 677, 3 pl. **arnunt, arnaδunt** 179, 516, 615.

ar² demonstrative particle, serves as antecedent to a relative clause 85, 559; for **o+ar** see **o¹**.

arall adj. *another, other* 76, 113, 231; pl. **ereill** 293, 742, 787.

arbennic adj. *principal; excellent* 230, 244.

arbet vn. *to spare*; pret. 3 pl. **arbedassant** 911.

archaf, archassei, archyssit see **erchi**.

archescob m. *arch bishop* 595, 767, 947.

arδerchawc adj. *fine, excellent* 5.

arfawc, aruawc adj. *armed, bearing arms* 14, 49, 722.

arglwyδ m. *lord* 35, 37, 80; pl. **arglwyδi** 177.

arglwyδes f. *lady* 65, 398, 489.

argysswr m. *fear, terror* 179.

argyweδ m. *harm, injury* 544.

arllost f. *shaft of a weapon* 372.

aros vn. *to wait* 861.

aruawc see **arfawc**.

aruer [arfer] m./f. *rule; attire* 1, 707.

arueu [arfau] pl. (m./f.) *arms, armour* 42, 51, 78.

arwein vn. *to carry, bear; to guide, lead* 167, 841; pres. 2 sg. **arweδy** 705.

aryant m. *(piece of) silver* 24, 615, 674.

asgwrn m. *bone* 660, pl. **esgyrn** 511.

asseu [aswy] adj. *left* 421, 539.

at, att (len.) prep. *to, towards* 12, 25, 28; **hyt at** *to* 747, 841; with suff. pers. pron. 1 sg. **attaf** 78, 751, 2 sg. **attat** 750, 828, 3 sg. m. **attaw** 357, 824, 835, 3 sg. f. **attei, etti** 46, 135, 405, 3 pl. **attunt** 747, 888.

athoeδ see **mynet**.

athiffero (= a'th differo) see **diffryt**.

atref see **adref**.

attal [atal] vn. *to hold, detain* 528.

atwaynat, atwen see **adnabot**.

auon [afon] f. *river* 896.

auory [afory] adv. *tomorrow* 39, 317.

awch, wch poss. pron. 2 pl. *your* 633, 635, 663.

awchus adj. *sharp* 793.

awn see **mynet**.

awr f. *hour* 818, 894; **yn (n)awr, yr awr hon(n)** adv. *at this hour, now* 63–4, 355, 486.

aylawt m./f. *limb* 186, 591.

aythant see **mynet**.

B

baeδ coet m. *wild boar* 36, 37, 38.

bara m. *bread* 425.

barn f. *judgement* 260.

barnu vn. *to judge* 381, 669, 677.

barwn m. *baron, lord* 898, 905; pl. **barwneit** 677, 862.

bedyδ, bedyt, bedit [bedydd] m. *baptism* 632, 911, 936.

bedyδlestyr, betyδlestyr m. *font* 624, 630.

bedyðyaw vn. *to baptise* 622, 698,
  918; impf. (subj.) impersonal
  bedyðjit 623, pret. impersonal
  bedyðywyt 629, 936.
begythyaw vn. *to threaten,*
  menace; pret. 3 sg.
  begythyawð 759.
bei see **pei** for the conj. or **bot.**
beichogi m. *conception;*
  pregnancy 6.
beiðaw vn. *to dare*; pres. subj. 3
  sg. **beiðo** 470.
beinc f. *bench* 822.
bellach adv. *henceforth, further,*
  now 847.
beth interrog. pron. *what; why*
  87, 127, 191.
betyðlestyr see **bedyðlestyr.**
bilein (1) adj. *villainous* 269;
  (2) m. *villain; villein, feudal*
  tenant 242, 245, 246; pl.
  bileineit 246.
blaen m. *point* 339; **deudroet**
  ulaen/vlayn *forefeet* 541, 552;
  o flaen/vlaen *in front of, before*
  558, 615, 796; **o'r blaen** *in front,*
  ahead; without delay (?) 161,
  167, 540; **ymlaen** *before* 787.
blew pl. *hair* 168.
blewawc adj. *shaggy*; comp.
  blewogach 168.
blingaw, bligaw vn. *to flay, skin*
  131, 198, 315; pres. subj.
  impersonal **blinger** 65, pret.
  impersonal **blingwyt** 198.
blodeu pl. *flowers* 878, 883.
blwg [blwng] m. *indignation* 251.
blwyðyn f. *year* 454; pl. (after
  numerals) **blyneð** 310, 498,
  671.
blyghau [blynghau] vn. *to grow*
  angry 884.
blyneð see **blwyðyn.**

bocsach m./f. *brag, boast* 586.
bocsachu vn. *to vaunt, boast*;
  impf. (subj.) 1 sg. **bocsachun**
  532.
boð m. *will* 285.
boði vn. *to drown* 383, 639.
bon m. *base, bottom* 323.
bonheðic adj. *noble, gentle* 234,
  457, 808.
bore m. *morning* 720, 753;
  tran(n)oeth y bore, y bore
  drannoeth adv. *the following*
  morning 82, 661, 766; **yn vore**
  adv. *in the morning, early* 39,
  752, 782.
bot vn. *to be* 13, 18, 33; **bot yn**
  well gan (genhyf &c.) *to*
  prefer 234, 383, 743; pres. 1 sg.
  wyf 231, 278, 300, pres. 2 sg.
  wyt, vyt 96, 119, 355, pres. 2
  sg. + aff. pers. pron. 2 sg. (ti)
  wyti 95, pres. 3 sg. **yw, ydiw,**
  (y) mae, may, oes, (y) taw, ys,
  ysy 20, 34, 35, pres. rel. 3 sg.
  yssyð 77, 149, 732, in interrog.
  clauses **mae** *where is?* 692,
  pres. 3 pl. **ynt** 697, cons.
  pres./fut. 1 sg. **byðaf** 226, 403,
  443, cons. pres./fut. 2 sg. **byðy**
  358, 955, cons. pres./fut. 3 sg.
  byð 35, 63, 73, cons. pres./fut.
  2 pl. **byðwch** 730, impf. 1 sg.
  oeðwn, yttoyðwn 487, 694,
  impf. 3 sg. **oeð, yttoeð, ydoeð**
  1, 4, 5, impf. 1 pl. **oeðem** 928,
  impf. 2 pl. **oeðewch** 927, impf.
  3 pl. **oeðynt, oyðynt, yttoyðyn**
  48, 163, 213, pret. 1 sg. **bum**
  533, 579, pret. 2 sg. **buost** 923,
  pret. 3 sg. **bu** 23, 30, 93, pret. 3
  pl. **buant** 809, 908, plupf. 2 sg.
  buassut 119, plupf. 3 sg.
  buassei 84, 175, 430, pres.

subj. 1 sg. **bof** 531, pres. subj.
3 sg. **bo, boet** 314, 361, 677,
impf. subj. 2 sg. **beut, byðut**
146, 498, impf. subj. 3 sg. **bei,
pei, byðei** 55, 229, 240,
imperative 2 sg. **byð** 72,
imperative 3 sg. **bit** 706,
imperative 1 pl. **byðwn** 177.

bradwr m. *traitor* 574.

braf adj. *big, huge; fine* 199, 804.

brathu vn. *to pierce, stab, to
bite; to spur (a horse)* 171,
172, 200; pret. 3 sg. **brathawð**
889, pret. 3 pl. **brathassant**
904.

brawt m. *brother* 408.

brawtuaeth, -waeth, -wayth
[brawdfaeth] m. *fosterbrother*
257, 438, 472.

breich m./f. *arm, fore limb* 420,
421, 509; pl. **breicheu** 185, 554,
570.

breið na, abreið na adv. *nearly,
almost* 250, 965.

brenhin m. *king* 144, 152, 228; pl.
brenhineð 863, 930, 941.

brenhin(y)aeth f. *kingdom* 147,
235, 249.

brenhinawl adj. *royal, kingly* 775.

brenhines f. *queen* 492, 759, 951.

brethyn m. *cloth* 264.

breuðwyt m./f. *dream* 679, 680.

briwaw vn. *to break, shatter;*
pres. 1 sg. **briwaf** 584.

briwedic adj. *wounded, bruised*
278.

bron(n) see **rac**.

brwydyr f. *battle* 807, 855, 895.

brynn m. *hill* 795.

bryssyaw vn. *to hurry, hasten;*
imperative 2 sg. **bryssya** 970.

bugeil m. *shepherd* 88, 625, 639.

bugeilffon f. *sheperd's crook* 90.

bwgeileið adj. *belonging to a
shepherd, shepherdly* 75.

bwn m. *bittern, owl* 569.

bwrw vn. *to throw; to hit* 70,
416, 592; **bwrw neit** *to jump*
386, 637, 641; pret. 1 sg.
byryeis 129, pret. 3 sg.
byryawð, -wys 386, 637, 641,
pret. impersonal **byrywyt** 290,
325.

bwyt m. *meat, food* 341, 357, 400.

bwyt(t)a [bwyta] vn. *to eat* 220,
222, 431; pret. 3 sg. **bwytaawð**
428.

bychan adj. *little, small* 95, 327,
911.

byðin f. *army, host*; pl. **byðinoeð**
806, 888.

bynhac, bynnac see **pwy**.

byt m. *world*; **o'r (y) byt, yn y byt
(+neg.)** *(not)* . . . *at all* 389,
463, 619–20.

byth adv. *(for) ever, always* 189,
302, 411.

byw (1) adj. *living, alive* 55, 65,
198; **(2)** m. *the living* 381.

bywyt m. *life; lifetime* 226, 931.

C, K

cadarn adj. *strong, firm, stout*
90, 158, 295; pl. **kedeirn** 875;
equat. **kadarnet** 374, 428, 517.

cadarn-gryf adj. *firm and strong*
599.

cadarn-wychyr adj. *strong and
brave* 79.

kadeu pl. (f.) *armies, hosts* 794.

cadw vn. *to keep, guard* 74.

kadwyneu pl. (f.) *chains* 343.

caffel, kael, cael, vn. *to get,
obtain, have; to win; to find;
to come upon* 191, 300, 308;
pres. 1 sg. **caf, caffaf** 403, 761,

pres. 2 sg. **keffy, key** 192, 445,
489, pres. 2 pl. **keffwch, kewch**
189, 731, impf. (subj.) 1 sg.
kawn 35, 36, 235, impf. (subj.)
3 sg. **kaei, cai** 298, 362, 424,
impf. 3 pl. **keynt** 136, 137,
impf. (subj.) impersonal **keit**
37, pret. 2 sg. **kefeist** 354, 355,
pret. 3 sg. **kauas, cauas, cafas**
6, 294, 296, pret. 1 pl. **kawssam**
177, pret. 3 pl. **kawsant** 717,
plupf. 3 sg. **kawssei, kawssoeðei**
340, 743.
Kalanmei see **Duw**.
calet adj. *hard* 665; equat.
calettet 544, 570.
calet-lym adj. *hard and sharp* 570.
callon [calon] f. *heart* 106, 153,
250.
cam¹ (1) adj. *wrong, unjust* 284;
(2) m. *wrong* 118, 214.
cam² m. *step* 561.
kan conj. *since, because* 669; with
neg. **canny, kany** *because not*
227, 269, 823; with neg. and inf.
obj. pron. 3 sg. **kanys, cannys**
104, 604; with pres. 3 sg. of *bot*
canys, kanys 104, 304, 494; see
also **canys**.
can(t), kant num. *hundred* 166,
325, 326.
canlyn vn. *to follow* 906.
canmwyaf *majority* 193.
canu vn. *to sing, say; to blow*
411; pres. 2 sg. **keny** 130, 245,
pret. 3 sg. **cant** 158, 767.
canys, kanys conj. *since, because,
as* 104, 177, 198; see also **kan**.
car m. *kinsman, relative* 453.
carchar m. *prison; restraint* 214,
310, 495.
carcharor m. *prisoner, captive*;
pl. **carcharoryon** 197.

carcharu vn. *to imprison* 494.
caredic adj. *beloved, dear* 750, 829.
karu vn. *to love* 4, 218, 494; pres.
1 sg. **caraf** 71, 442, 487, pres.
subj. 2 sg. **kerych** 825, impf. 3
sg. **karei** 26, 808, 823, pret. 1
sg. **kereis** 442, 486, pret. 3 sg.
carawð 167.
caryat m. *love* 11,13, 224.
cassau vn. *to hate* 494.
castell, kastell m. *castle, fortress*
48, 231, 396; pl. **kestyll** 207.
cau vn. *to shut, close* 649.
cawr m. *giant; mighty man* 401,
404, 411.
cayat adj. *closed* 322.
kedernyt m. *strength, power* 387.
kedymdeith, kedymðeith m.
companion, friend 77, 332; pl.
cedymdeithon, kydymdeithon
93, 101, 176.
kefyn see **drachefyn**.
keinawc f. *penny* 326, 732.
keissaw vn. *to seek, search for; to
attempt* 230, 412, 418.
kelerdy [selerdy] m. *cellar* 124.
kelu vn. *to conceal* 223; pres. 1
sg. **kelaf** 223, 618, imperative 2
sg. **kel** 35.
kelwyð m. *lie, falsehood* 97, 130,
245; pl. **kelwyðeu** 929.
kenedyl f. *tribe, clan* 857.
kennadwri f. *message; mission*
23, 262, 264.
ken(n)at¹ f. *messenger* 12, 19, 23;
pl. **kenhadeu** 848.
kennat², kenhat f. *leave,
permission* 102, 944, 945.
kerðeu pl. (f.) *songs* 84.
kerðet vn. *to walk, go, travel* 90,
100, 243; **kerðet rac (ragof
&c.)** *to go ahead* 100, 137–8,
271 (*GMW* § 235); pres. 1 sg.

kerðaf 490, pres. 2 sg. kerðy
707, pret. 3 sg. kerðawð 271,
347, 369, pret. 3 pl. kerðassant,
-yssant 137, 628, 713, imperative
2 sg. kerða 161.
kereis, kerych see karu.
kerwyn f. *tub, vat* 631, 637, 641.
keryðus adj. *blameable* 118.
kewilið m. *shame, disgrace* 581.
kic m. *meat, flesh* 36, 56, 427.
kicleu, cicleu, kigleu see clybot.
kilið: y gilið pron. *each other* 794,
845–6.
kilyaw vn. *to retreat*; pret. 3 pl.
kilyassant 795.
kiniaw m./f. *food, meal* 402, 445.
citeð [sitedd] f. *city* 207.
claðu vn. *to dig, bury* 242, 378, 516;
pret. impersonal claðwyt 676.
claf adj. *ill, sick* 33, 55, 953.
claf-gorweiðawc adj. *ill and
recumbent* 951–2.
Clanmei see nos.
claret m. *claret (red wine)* 428.
clawð m. *moat, ditch*; pl. cloðyeu
242.
clawðwr m. *digger; common
labourer* 242.
cleðyf, cleðeu m. *sword* 42, 184,
304; pl. cleðyfeu 793.
cledyr y ðwyuron/ðwyfron/eu
dwyuron f. *his/their breast-
bone* 589, 597, 938.
cleuyt [clefyd] m. *sickness, disease*
32, 34, 814.
cloðyeu see clawð.
clotuorus [clodforus] adj. *famous,
celebrated* 723, 787, 792.
clust m./f. *ear* 323; pl. clusteu 99.
clybot vn. *to hear; to feel, sense*
439, 480, 782; pres. 1 sg.
clywaf 480, pres. 2 sg. clywy
479, pres. 3 sg. clyw 526, impf.

3 sg. clywei, klywei 84, 436,
441, pret. 1 sg. kicleu [ciglef]
468, pret. 3 sg. kigleu, cicleu
54, 476, 512 plupf. 3 sg.
clywssei 85.
knewillin m. *centre, middle* 307.
koch adj. *red* 926.
coesseu pl. (m./f.) *legs* 564.
coet, koet f. *forest, trees* 36, 37,
38; pl. coydyð 607.
coeth adj. *pure* 141.
cof m. *memory*; dyuot cof iði *she
recollects* 655.
colli vn. *to lose* 684; pret. 1 sg.
colleis 224, 443, 463, pret. 3 sg.
colles 470, 965.
colubyr m. *viper* 292, 307.
corff, korff m. *body* 382, 555,
669; pl. kyrff 977.
corn m. *horn, trumpet* 158.
coron f. *crown* 301.
coronawc adj. *crowned* 940.
coronhau vn. *to crown*; pret.
impersonal coronawyt 978.
kostawcki m. *mastiff* 926.
costi vn. *to cost*; pres. subj. 3 sg.
costo 35.
craf [craff] adj. *close, intent* 465.
creawdyr m. *creator* 902.
credu (y) vn. *to believe (in)* 609,
927, 928; pres. 1 sg. credaf 286,
605, 901, pres. 2 sg. credy 398,
578, pres. 1 pl. credwn 931, pres.
subj. 3 sg. cretto 152, impf. 1 sg.
credwn 467, impf. subj. 2 sg. +
aff. pers. pron. 2 sg. (ti) crettuti
146, pret. 3 sg. credawð 929.
kreu vn. *to create*; pret. 3 sg.
kreawð 750.
creu m./f. *blood* 313.
kreulawn adj. *cruel, fierce* 140.
cret f. *belief, faith* 918.
kri m./f. *cry* 792.

Cristawn m. *Christian* 400, 640, 919.
Cristonogaeth, -ayth f. *Christianity* 148, 151, 287.
croc, crog, crok f. *cross, crucifix; gallows* 287, 313, 377; **yg groc** *hanging on the cross; hanging on the gallows* 358.
croen m. *skin, hide* 545.
crogi vn. *to hang* 121, 192, 315; pres. impersonal **crogir** 317, pres. subj. impersonal **crocker** 65.
croyssaw m. *welcome* 446.
cryf adj. *strong* 561.
cryf-fenedic adj. *strong and stout* 659.
cryfder m. *strength* 431.
kuδyaw vn. *to hide* 123.
kussan m./f. *kiss* 41, 289.
kussanu vn. *to kiss* 104.
kwbyl adj. *whole, entire, total* 310, 498, 572.
kwplau vn. *to fulfil, carry out* 44, 654; pret. 3 sg. **cuplaawδ** 556.
kwrt m. *courtyard* 484.
kychwynnu vn. *to set off*; pres. 1 sg. **kychwynnaf** 752.
kydymdeithon see **kedymdeith**.
kyfagos, kyuagos adj. *near, adjoining* 48, 715.
kyfamser m. *meantime, time*; **yn y kyfamser hwnnw** *at that time* 5–6.
kyf(f)arch, kyuarch, kywarch (g)well/(g)uell [cyfarch] vn. *to greet* 22, 91, 824; pret. 3 sg. **kyuarchawδ** 749, pret. 3 pl. **kyuarchassant** 670.
kyfelybrwyδ [cyffelybrwydd] m. *likeness, the like of* 86.
kyflenwi vn. *to fulfil, accomplish* 52.

kyflym adj. *quick, swift* 420, 835, 852.
kyfnesseuieit [cyfneseifiaid] pl. (m./f.) *near relations; friends* 933.
kyfodi, kyuodi, cyuodi vn. *to rise, arise* 40, 132, 288; **kyfodi y vyny(δ)** *to rise up* 61, 113, 123; pret. 3 sg. **kyfodes, kyuodes** 255, 414, 641.
kyfoeth, kyuoeth m. *country, kingdom* 156, 208, 209; pl. **kyfoetheu** 956, 958.
kyfoethawc, kyuoethawc adj. *powerful, mighty; wealthy* 8, 61, 77.
kyfranc f. *battle* 163; pl. **kyfrageu** 739.
kyfrwy m. *saddle* 170.
kyfryw (len.) adj./pron. *of the same kind, such* 186.
kyfyl m. *vicinity*; **yn y gyfyl** *near to him, close to him* 470.
kyffarch see **kyfarch**.
kyffelyb adj. *like, similar* 560, 856.
kyffes m./f. *confession*; **ym kyffes** interj. *by (my) confession!* 360, 535.
kyffessu vn. *to confess*; pret. 1 sg. **kyffesseis** 496, pret. 3 sg. **kyffessawδ** 961.
kyffroi vn. *to move, be moved*; pret. 3 sg. **kyffroes** 590.
kyghor [cyngor] m. *advice, counsel* 636, 855; **bot wrth kyghor, gwneuthur kyghor** *to follow advice, yield to counsel* 72, 119, 359.
kyhoeδ adj. *public*; **ar gyhoeδ** *publicly* 918.
kyhwrδ vn. *to meet, fall in with* 881; pret. 3 sg. **kyhyrδawδ** 691, pret. 3 pl. **kyhyrδassant** 777.

kylch see **yghylch.**

kymedrolder m. *moderate quantity* 431.

kymeint see **mawr.**

kymhell (ar) vn. *to compel (s.o.)* 385; pret. 3 sg. **kymhellawð** 651.

kymorth m. *assistance, help* 335.

kymryt vn. *to take; to feel; to put on (clothing)* 69, 74, 90; **kymryt** *to feign, pretend* 32, 54–55; **kymryt y** *to feign, pretend* 272; **kymryt kennat** *to take leave* 945; pres. 1 sg. **kymer(h)af** 287, 611, 761, pres. 3 sg. **kymer** 855, impf. (subj.) 1 sg. **kymerwn** 497, impf. (subj.) 3 sg. **kymerei** 608, 684, pret. 2 sg. + aff. pers. pron. 2 sg. (ti) **kymereisti** 105, pret. 3 sg. **kymerth** 32, 42, 67, pret. 3 pl. **kymerassant, -yssant** 665, 769, 807, imperative 2 sg. **kymer** 161, 247, 264.

kyn¹ (len.) before equat. *as, so* 85, 340, 374.

kyn², kynt prep. *before, previous to* 194, 291; **val kynt** adv. *all the same* 964.

kyny (len.) conj. with neg. *although . . . not* 153.

kynðeirawc adj. *furious, raving mad* 780, 850.

kynhal, kynnal vn. *to hold; to rule* 209, 958; pres. 3 sg. **kynheil** 956.

kynhen f. *discord, strife* 758.

kynneu vn. *to light, kindle;* pret. impersonal **kyneuwyt** 667.

kynnic vn. *to offer* 206.

kynt adj. & adv. *earlier, swifter* 192, 201, 809; see also **kyn²**, superl. **kyntaf** *first, earliest; swiftest* 182, 202, 325.

kynteð m. *part of the hall in which the king sat in medieval times (entry, court)* 100.

kynulleitua [cynulleidfa] f. *assembly, host* 862, 935.

kyr llaw prep. *by, beside* 822.

kyrchu vn. *to approach, go to; to fetch; to attack* 171, 253, 739; pret. 3 sg. **kyrchawð** 689, 890, pret. 3 pl. **kyrchassant** 769, pret. impersonal **kyrchwyt** 631.

kyseuyll [cysefyll] vn. *to stand, stop* 440.

kysgu, kyscu (1) vn. *to sleep, slumber* 273, 306, 679; **(2)** f. *sleep* 224.

kyssyr m. *state of mind* 464.

kystal see **da.**

cyt see **y gyd.**

kytknawt m. *sexual intercourse* 500, 809.

kytunaw vn. *to agree, consent;* pres. 1 sg. **kytunaf** 901.

kythreul m. *devil, demon* 618, 644; pl. **kythreuleit** 422.

kyuagos see **kyfagos.**

kyuarch see **kyfarch.**

kyuaruot [cyfarfod] vn. *to meet* 122, 132, 538; cons. past 3 sg. **kyuaruyðei** 119, impf. subj. 3 sg. **kyuarfei** 186.

kyueillt [cyfaillt] m. *friend* 77.

kyueir [cyfair] see **yghyueir.**

kyuodi, cyuodi see **kyfodi.**

kyuoeth see **kyfoeth.**

kyuoethawc see **kyfoethawc.**

kyuot [cyfod] m. *rising;* **kael kyuot ar** *to start or rouse (game); to catch sight of* 37, 761–2.

kywarch see **kyfarch.**

kyweir adj. *well attired;* superl. **kyweiraf** 126.

kywir adj. *faithful, loyal* 583.

kywirdeb m. *loyalty, fealty* 211.
kywreinyaw vn. *to adjust* 539.

CH

chue [chwe] num. *six* 310.
chwaen f. *feat, exploit* 884.
chwaer f. *sister* 756.
chwant m. *appetite, craving;*
    caffel chwant *to eat one's fill* 56.
chwedleu pl. (m./f.) *news, tidings*
    837.
chwerthin vn. *to laugh* 577.
chwi[1] aff. pers. pron. 2 pl. 899.
chwi[2] indep. pers. pron. 2 pl. 901.
chwitheu[1] indep. conj. pers.
    pron. 2 pl. 161.
chwitheu[2] aff. conj. pers. pron. 2
    pl. 634.
chwrnu vn. *to snore* 273.

D

da (1) adj. *good; valiant* 146, 177,
    229; equat. **daet** 592, 934,
    kystal 355; comp. **gwell, guell**
    22, 91, 175; superl. **goreu** 528,
    856; **(2)** m. *wealth, goods* 149,
    189.
dabre see **dyuot.**
dachymygu vn. *to devise* 334.
dagreu see **deigyr.**
dala, daly vn. *to seize, catch; to*
    hold 112; **dala adlo am** *to take*
    account of, grieve about 149,
    227; impf. 3 sg. **dallei** 211, impf.
    3 pl. **delynt** 623, 632, pret. 3 sg.
    delis 659, pret. impersonal **delit**
    897, pluperf. 3 sg. **dalyssei** 533,
    imperative 2 sg. **dala, daly** 149,
    227.
damunaw vn. *to wish, long for*
    487.
damunedic adj. *desired* 45, 52.
damwein m. *event; state* 694.

damweinaw vn. *to happen;* impf.
    (subj.) 3 sg. **damweinei,**
    damchweinei 56, 727 pret. 3 sg.
    damchweinawδ 693.
dan, y dan (len.) prep. *under,*
    below, beneath 174, 211–12,
    294; with suff. pers. pron. 3 sg.
    m. **y danaw** 201, 207, 209.
danneδ pl. (m.) *teeth* 567.
danys *(one) deer* 508.
darlleawdyr m. *reader* 934.
darpar m. *intention* 197.
daruot [darfod] vn. *to finish; to*
    happen 193, 248, 532; as
    auxiliary denoting anterior
    action or event see *GMW* §
    154; pres. subj. 3 sg. **darffo**
    502, 529, impf. 3 sg. **daroeδ**
    194, 669, pret. 3 sg. **darfu,**
    daruu 384, 717, 768.
datseinaw vn. *to resound;* pret.
    3 sg. **datseinawδ** 607.
daw see **dyfot.**
day(a)r f. *earth, ground* 149, 312,
    516.
dec, deg [deg] (nas.) num. *ten* 235,
    386, 561.
dechreu (1) vn. *to begin;* pret. 3 sg.
    dechreuis 310, 375, 449; **(2)** m.
    beginning 177.
degweith [dengwaith] adv. *ten*
    times 617.
degwyr [dengwyr] m. *ten men* 561.
deheu (1) adj. *right* 83,420; **(2)** f.
    right (hand/side) 380.
deigyr m. *tear(-drop)* 224; pl.
    dagreu 122, 239, 280.
delw f. *form, shape* 312, 643; **ar**
    δelw *in the shape (of)* 312.
derwen f. *oak-tree* 593.
deu (len.) num. m. *two* 135, 196,
    213.
deudroet pl. *two feet* 422, 554,

637; **deudroet ulaen/vlayn**
forefeet 541, 552; **deudroed ol**
hindfeet 596.
deugein (nas.) num. *forty* 164, 673,
797.
deuwr m. *two men* 316.
dewr adj. *brave, bold* 61, 401,
455; superl. **dewraf** 619.
dewrder m. *bravery, valour,*
prowess 731.
diagon m. *deacon* 361.
diangk, diagk vn. *to escape* 113,
394; impf. (subj.) 1 sg. **diagwn**
301.
dial vn. *to avenge* 456, 522; pres.
1 sg. **dialaf** 328, 524.
diannot adj. *without delay,*
immediate 373, 606, 629.
diawl m. *devil* 939.
diawt f. *drink* 358.
dicyouein [dig(i)ofaint] m.
sorrow; anger 94, 226.
diðadleu adj. *without dispute* 422.
dideruysc [diderfysg] adj.
undisturbed 18.
didi see **tidi**.
didlawt adj. *abundant, plentiful*
220, 448.
diffryt vn. *to guard, protect;*
pres. subj. 3 sg. **differo** 537,
impf. (subj.) 3 sg. **differei** 290.
digawn (1) adj. *enough, sufficient*
428, 556; **(2)** m. *plenty,*
abundance 424, 431, 829; see
also **digoni**.
digelwyð m. *truth* 705.
digoni vn. *to be able;* pres. 3 sg.
digawn 335, 410, 505.
digyaw vn. *to take offence, to be*
offended/angry 735; pret. 3 sg.
digiawð 758.
dihafarch adj. *fierce, brave,*
vigorous 401.

diliwaw vn. *to lose/change colour*
237.
dillat sg./pl. (m.) *clothes* 69, 645.
dim pron. *anything, any* 34, 134,
259; **o ðim** adv. *in any way, at*
all 781.
dinas m. *city, large town* 159,
347, 623.
dioðef vn. *to suffer, endure* 672;
pret. 3 sg. **dioðefawð** 286, 377,
675.
diogel adj. *certain, assured* 869.
diogi vn. *to loiter;* pret. 2 sg.
diogeist 751.
diolwch (1) vn. *to thank;* pres. 1 sg.
diolchaf 754, 957, pres. subj.
3 sg. **diolcho** 832, impf. 3 sg.
diolchei 425, pret. 2 sg. + aff.
pers. pron. 2 sg. (ti) **diolcheisti**
279, pret. 3 sg. **diolches** 833;
(2) m. *thanks* 742, 814, 941.
diruawr [dirfawr] adj. *very great,*
huge 139, 438, 451.
dirgeledic adj. *secret* 22.
diryueð [diryfedd] adj. *not*
surprising, not strange 429.
discleiraw vn. *to shine* 784.
disgynnu, discyn vn. *to dismount;*
to descend 204, 317, 320; pret.
3 sg. **disgynnawð, discynnawð**
367, 881, imperative 2 sg.
disgyn 488.
distryw m. *destruction* 781.
disynwyr adj. *mad, senseless*
429.
ditheu see **titheu**.
diuachellu [difachellu] vn. *to*
evade (a blow); pret. 3 sg.
diuachellawð 593.
diuetha [difetha] vn. *to slay* 333.
diwarnawt m. *day* 75, 340, 673.
diwreiðaw vn. *to destroy; to be*
uprooted; impf. (subj.) 3 sg.

diwreiðei 572, pret. 3 sg.
diwreiðawð 594.
diwygyat, diwycyat m. *form; dress,
attire* 444, 466, 559; **ar diwycyat**
in the form of 559.
dodi vn. *to put, place* 40, 103,
111; **dodi llef/kri** *to raise a
shout/cry* 111, 792; pret. 3 sg.
dodes 657, 792, imperative 2
pl. **dodwch** 635.
doe, ðoe adv. *yesterday* 88, 128,
409.
dogyn m./f. *sufficiency, fill* 717,
718, 741.
doluryaw vn. *to grieve*; pret. 3 sg.
doluryawð 33.
dos see **mynet**.
drachefyn, dracheuyn, adv. *back*
25, 27, 215; with poss. pron.
2.sg. **dra'th gefyn** 359.
draenawc m. *hedgehog* 169.
draw adv. *yonder, there*; **o'r parth
draw** prep. *from beyond* 265;
tu draw *from beyond* 4.
dromwnt f. *dromond (a large
medieval ship)* 139.
dros (len.) prep. *over, across* 657,
794, 946; see also **tros**.
drut adj. *dear, expensive* 141,
248, 313.
drwc (1) adj. *bad; sad* 75, 279,
462; comp. **gwaeth** 233, 514;
(2) m. *evil; harm* 537, 538,
881.
drws m. *door* 649, 662, 664; pl.
drysseu 379.
drwy see **trwy**.
drwoð adv. *through* 388, 389,
394.
drycyruerth [drygyrferth] m.
sorrow, grief 282, 464, 514.
dryll m. *fragment, part*; pl.
drylleu 173, 542, 584.

drywestu vn. *to fast*; pret. 3 sg.
drywestawð 672.
du adj. *black* 589, 597; comp.
duach 563.
duaw vn. *to turn dark* 237.
duc[1] m. *duke* 776, 777, 797.
duc[2], ducsei see **dwyn**.
duces f. *duchess* 8421.
dugassant, dugost see **dwyn**.
duhunaw vn. *to awake* 308, 682;
imperative 2 sg. **duhun** 275.
duludaw vn. *to press upon, tread
on*; pret. 3 sg. **duludawð** 599.
duw, dyw, Duw m. *god* 80, 146,
167; **y rof a Duw** interj.
between me and God! 236,
263, 353.
Duw Kalanmei adv. *on the first
of May* 14.
dwfyn adj. *deep* 373.
dwfyr, dwuyr m. *water* 70, 130,
297; **dwfyr sswyn** *holy water*
925.
dwrn m. *fist; hilt* 322, 595.
dwy (len.) num. f. *two* 108, 566.
dwyl(y)aw see **llaw**.
dwyn vn. *to carry, bring; to carry
away, steal* 78, 318, 335; pres.
2 sg. **dygy** 359, impf. (subj.) 1 sg.
dygwn 301, pret. 3 sg. **duc** 373,
425, pret. 3 pl. **dugassant** 897,
pret. 2 sg. **dugost** 575, 583,
plupf. 3 sg. **ducsei** 407,
imperative 2 pl. **dygwch** 921.
dwyrhau vn. *to rise into view*;
pret. 3 sg. **dwyrhaawð** 776.
dwyuron see **cledyr y ðwyuron**.
dy[1] (len.) poss. pron. 2 sg. *your*
72, 95, 120.
dy[2], di, ti aff. pers. pron. 2 sg. 36,
72, 95.
dybryt adj. *ugly, horrid, atrocious*;
equat. **dybrytet** 643.

dyð m. *day* 27, 31, 47; pl. **dyðyeu** 828.

Dyðbrawt m. *the Day of Judgement, Doomsday* 381, 676.

dyðgweith adv. *one day* 299, 810.

dyfot, dyuot vn. *to come* 46, 125, 133; pres. 2 sg. **doy** 361, pres. 3 sg. **daw** 72, 120, 269, impf. 3 sg. **do(e)i** 30, 266, impf. 3 pl. **doent** 746, pres. subj. 2 sg. **delych** 155, impf. subj. 3 pl. **delynt** 623, pret. 1 sg. **deuthum** 581, pret. 3 sg. **dyfu, dyuu, doeth, deuth** 7, 21, 27, pret. 3 pl. **doethant, deuthant, deuthont** 143, 661, 703, imperative 2 sg. **dabre** 78, 335, imperative 2 pl. **dowch** 634.

dyfryn [dyffryn] m. *valley* 196.

dyffust vn. *to batter, smite* 308.

dygwch, dygwn, dygy see **dwyn**.

dygwyðaw vn. *to fall* 21, 205, 238; pres. 3 sg. **dygwyð** 174, 366, 413, pret. 1 sg. **dygwyðeis** 327, pret. 3 sg. **dygwyðawð, -wys** 110, 204, 261.

dylyu vn. *to be obliged to; to have a right to*; pres. 1 sg. **dylyaf** 500, pres. subj. 2 sg. **dylyych** 134, impf. (subj.) 1 sg. **dylywn** 217.

dyn f. *person, man* 429, 462, 464; pl. **dyn(n)yon** 632, 636, 975.

dyrchaf(el), dyrchauel vn. *to raise, lift* 62, 98, 109; pret. 3 pl. **dyrchafyssant** 142.

dyrnawt m. *blow, stroke* 117, 203, 302; pl. **dyrnodeu** 737, 793, 874.

dyro see **roði**.

dyuot see **dyfot**.

dyuynnu [dyfynnu] vn. *to summon, order to appear* 45.

dyw see **duw**.

dywededic adj. *said, mentioned* 689.

dywedut vn. *to say, speak* 26, 50, 55; pres. 1 sg. **dywedaf** 500, pres. 2 sg. **dywedy** 96, 97, 409, impf. 1 sg. **dywedwn** 467, impf. (subj.) 2 sg. **dywedut** 532, impf. 3 sg. **dywedei** 569, impf. 3 pl. **dywedynt** 580, impf. subj. 1 sg. **dywettwn** 531, impf. subj. 3 sg. **dywettei** 302, 568, impf. impersonal **dywedit** 833, pret. 1 sg. **dywedeis** 284, pret. 2 sg. + aff. pers. pron. 2 sg. (ti) **dywedeisti** 240, pret. 3 sg. **dywawt, dywot** 32, 34, 71, pret. 3 pl. **dywetyssant** 317, pret. impersonal **dywetpwyt** 454, plupf. 3 sg. **dywedyssei** 259, imperative 2 sg. **dywet** 578, 705, imperative 1 pl. **dywedwn** 847.

E

e hun, e hunan (1) refl. pron. 3 sg. m. *himself* 195, 977, 3 sg. f. *herself* 446; **(2)** adv. *alone* 335, 746–7; **(3)** *own* 67, 260, 518.

ebrwyð adj. *quick, swift* 189, 745.

echdoe adv. *the day before yesterday* 753.

edeweis, edewis see **adaw**.

ediuar [edifar] adj. *sorry* 106.

ediuarwch [edifeirwch] m./f. *repentance* 256, 937.

edrych vn. *to watch, look (for)* 83, 163, 373; pres. 3 sg. **edrych** 83, 508, 520, imperative 2 pl. **edrychwch** 927.

eðiw see **mynet**.

ef (1) indep. pers. pron. 3 sg. m. *he* 14, 49, 51; **(2)** expletive pron. (*GMW* § 191) 72, 120, 182.

ef aff. pers. pron. 3 sg. m. 13, 26, 27.

effeirat m. *priest* 354, 355, 360.

efferen f. *mass* 411, 767, 768.

eglur adj. *bright, clear* 720.

eglwys f. *church* 628, 689, 691.

egylyon [engylion] pl. (m.) *angels* 973.

ehag [eang] adj. *broad* 346.

ehalaeth adj. *large, broad* 563, 650.

ehedec vn. *to fly*; pres. 3 sg. **eheta** 99, impf. subj. 3 sg. **ehettei** 201, impf. subj. 3 pl. **ehettynt** 202.

ehofyn-wychyr adj. *bold and brave* 101–2.

ehut-hwimwth adj. *quick and swift* 656–7.

ehwybyr adj. *nimble, swift* 414.

eiδaw *owning* 235.

eil ord. num. *second* 804.

eilweith adv. *a second time, again* 391.

eillaw vn. *to shave* 626.

eiroet, erroyt adv. *ever* 126, 344, 560.

eissoes, eisswys adv. *however, yet, nevertheless* 5, 89, 109.

eiste(δ) vn. *to sit, be seated* 274, 288, 380; pret. 3 sg. **eisteδawδ** 653.

eisteδfa f. *seat* 652.

eitha [eithaf] m. *end* 352.

eithyr prep. *but, except* 911.

el, elewch, elwn, elych see **mynet**, for **elych** see also **dyuot**.

elchwyl adv. *once more, again* 417.

elw m. *possession* 232.

ellwg vn. *to drop, shed; to let go* 92, 280, 529; see also **gellwg**.

emennyδ m. *brain* 99, 330, 351.

emyl m./f. *side, edge* 396, 440.

eneit m./f. *soul* 382, 422, 668; pl. **eneideu** 644, 973.

enill vn. *to win*; **enill y maes** *to win the field, be victorious*; pret. 1 sg. **enilleis** 248, 304, pret. 3 sg. **enillawδ** 795.

enkyt m. *space, period*; **enkyt un awr** adv. *within the space of an hour* 894.

enw m. *name* 60, 145, 307.

enwi vn. *to name* 476, 480, 934.

erbyn see **yn erbyn**.

erchi vn. *to ask, request, demand* 25, 46, 112; pres. 1 sg. **archaf** 314, pret. 2 sg. + aff. pers. pron. 2 sg. (ti) **ercheisti** 128, pret. 3 sg. **erchis** 423, 649, 683, plupf. 3 sg. **archassei** 26, plupf. impersonal **archyssit** 29.

erchwyn m./f. *bedside* 274, 652.

erδynt see **yr**.

ergyt m./f. *throw, cast*; **y ergyt** *at one blow* 736.

ereill see **arall**.

erni see **ar¹**.

erroyt see **eiroet**.

escob, esgob m. *bishop* 355, 616, 620; pl. **escyb** 916, 977.

esgyrn see **asgwrn**.

esmwyth adj. *comfortable* 717.

etiueδ [etifedd] m. *offspring, heir(s)* 147.

et(t)o, etwa adv. *again, yet, still* 106, 454, 501.

etti see **at**.

eu (h–) poss. pron. 3 pl. *their* 52, 136, 163; with prep. **y** *to* **eu** 769; see also **y⁵**.

eur m. *gold* 24, 141, 615.

ewineδ pl. (m./f.) *nail, claw* 570, 571.

ewch see **mynet**.

ewyllus, ywyllus m./f. *will, wish, desire; last will* 29, 45, 260.

ewythyr m. *uncle* 360, 619.

F (V, U)

val, ual, vel [fel, fal] prep. *like* 304, 749, 811; **val kynt** adv. *all the same* 964.

vegys see **megys**.

vi, ui aff. pers. pron. 1 sg. 78, 760; see also **i**.

velly, y velly [felly] adv. *so, thus* 659, 810, 903.

uot [fowt] f. *vault, arched roof* 345.

vychyr see **gwychyr**.

vy hun, vy hunan, fu hunan refl. pron. 1 sg. *myself* 162, 587, 634.

vy(n), 'y(n) [fy] (nas.) poss. pron. 1 sg. *my* 72, 74, 88.

vyny(δ), y vyny(δ) [fyny(δ)] adv. *up* 61, 62, 113.

vyt (=wyt) see **bot**.

Ff

ffalst m. *a false person, deceiver* 847.

ffenedic adj. *bold, brave, stout* 456, 730.

ffenestyr f. *crenel, battlements; window* 397.

ffiol m./f. *cup, bowl* 154; **ffiol y penn** *scull-cap, scalp* 351.

ffo (1) vn. *to flee, retreat* 113, 200, 910; pret. 3 sg. **ffoawδ** 926, pret. 3 pl. **ffoyssant** 196, imperative 2 sg. **ffo** 94; **(2)** m. *flight* 115.

ffol adj. *foolish, silly* 107.

ffon(n) f. *stick, staff* 98, 109, 560; pl. **ffynn** 702.

fforch f. *forked stick; supports of a bed* 651.

fforδ f. *road, way* 291, 346, 817.

fforest f. *forest* 14, 16, 38.

fforestwyr pl. (m.) *foresters* 38.

Ffragheiδ [Ffrangaidd] adj. *French* 884.

Ffreinc (1) *France* 901; **(2)** pl. (m.) *Frenchmen* 890.

ffroen f. *nostril* 108.

ffrowyllaw vn. *to scourge, whip* 674–5.

ffrwst m. *haste* 653, 654.

ffrwyth m./f. *strength; feat, act* 178; pl. **ffrwytheu** 923.

ffrwythlawn adj. *fruitful, successful* 884–5, 890.

ffrystaw vn. *to hurry, hasten* 333.

ffuruaw [ffurfo] vn. *to form, create*; pret. 3 sg. **ffuruawδ** 312.

ffustaw vn. *to beat* 938.

ffyδlawn adj. *faithful, loyal* 611.

ffynio (rac) vn. *to succeed*; pret. 3 sg. **ffynnyawδ** 746.

G

gadael vn. *to leave; to let*; pres. subj. 2 sg. **gettych** 314, pres. subj. 3 sg. **gatto** 481, imperative 2 sg. **gat** 278, 492, imperative 2 pl. **gedwch** 634.

gaflach m. *arrow, lance, spear* 406, 416, 417.

galon pl. (m.) *enemies* 185.

gallel vn. *to be able*; pres. 1 sg. **gallaf** 223, 609, 752, pres. 2 sg. **gelly** 610, pres. 3 pl. **gallant** 958, pres. subj. 2 sg. **gellych** 78, pres. subj. 3 sg. **gallo** 34, impf. (subj.) 2 sg. **gallut** 523, impf. (subj.) 3 sg. **gallei** 16, 44, 51, impf. (subj.) 3 pl. **gellynt** 17, 623, impf. impersonal **gellit** 630.

gallu m. *power; fighting force, army* 193, 195.

galw vn. *to call; to demand* 257, 332, 511; **galw ar** *to call upon* 257, 332, 511; pres. impersonal **gelwir** 20, impf. 3 sg. **galwei**

911, impf. impersonal **gelwit**
1, 8, 452, pret. 3 sg. **gelwis**
854, pret. impersonal **gelwit** 7,
630, imperative 2 sg. **galw** 968.
gan(n) (len.) prep. *with, by; in*
the opinion of 93, 149, 197;
with suff. pers. pron. 1 sg.
genhyf 234, 383, 2 sg. **genhyt**
469, + aff. pers. pron. 2 sg. (ti)
genhyti 621, 3 sg. m. **gant(h)aw**
229, 241, 259, 3 sg. f. **genthi** 30,
738, 743, 3 pl. **ganthun(t)**,
gantu(nt) 138, 197, 696.
ganet, ganydoeð see **geni**.
garanot pl. (m./f.) *cranes, herons*
427.
gartref adv. *at home* 175, 181.
garw adj. *rough, coarse*; comp.
garwach 168; superl. **garwaf**
169.
gefyn see **drachefyn**.
geir m. *word* 303, 904; pl. **geireu**
284.
gellgi bwn m. *game-dog (used in*
hunting the bittern) 569.
[g]ellwg [gellwng] vn. *to let go;*
to drop, shed 92, 122, 239;
pres. 1 sg. **gellygaf** 529, 536,
pres. 2 sg. **gellygy** 535, pret. 3
sg. **gellygawð** 212, imperative 2
sg. **gellwg, ellwg** 535, 640.
geneu m. *mouth* 108, 568.
geni vn. *to bear, to be born* 685,
693; pret. impersonal **ganet** 7,
376, 451, plupf. impersonal
ganydoeð 450, **genyssit** 735.
geol f. *gaol, prison* 290, 292, 296.
glan(n) f. *bank, shore* 370, 896.
glas adj. *green* 264.
glaschwerthin vn. *to laugh*
(sardonically) 190.
glew adj. *brave, valiant, courageous*
187; superl. **glewaf** 180.

glewder m. *courage, prowess* 432,
519.
glin m. *knee* 21, 206, 261.
glo m. *charcoal* 237.
gloðest m./f. *revelry* 85.
gobraf(f) [gobraff] adj. *large, huge*
559, 568.
godric m. *delay, tarrying*; **heb**
odric adv. *without delay, at*
once 799.
gofalu vn. *to harass* 293.
gofit, gofut m. *grief, sorrow,*
trouble 120, 132, 300.
gofyn, gouyn vn. *to ask (for),*
request; to enquire about 102,
115, 127; **gouyn y** *to ask*
someone, demand from s.o.
102, 115, 127; pres. 2 sg.
govynny 127, pret. 3 sg.
gofynnawð, gouynnawð 19,
472, 826.
gogonyant m. *glory* 938.
gogwyðaw vn. *to lean* 398.
gogyfu(w)ch adj. (equat.) *as*
high; **ar ogyfu(w)ch a(c)** *as*
high as, level with 322, 652.
gohir m. *delay*; **heb ohir**
immediately 704, 913, 918.
goledrat adj. *stealthy, clandestine*
196.
goluð m. *hindrance*; **heb oluð** *at*
once 548, 588, 612.
gorawenus adj. *joyful* 30, 477.
gorchymyn (1) vn. *to command; to*
commend, entrust to the care of
971; pres. 1 sg. **gorchymynnaf**
382, pret. 3 sg.
gorchymynnawð, -mynwys
496, 783; **(2)** m. *command,*
order 960.
gorchyuygu [gorchfygu] vn. *to*
overcome, defeat; pret. 3 sg.
gorchyuygawð 806.

goreu see da.
gorf(f)owys vn. *to rest* 279, 713;
pret. 3 sg. gorffwysawð 688,
pret. 3 pl. gorffwyssassant
715, 780, 949.
gormoð m. *excess, superfluity* 585.
gorthrwm adj. *very heavy,*
grievous 55.
gorthodaf see gwrthot.
goruc, gorugant[1] see gwneuthur.
gorugant[2] see notes.
goruot [gorfod] vn. *to survive,*
prevail; to overcome, defeat;
cons. pres./fut. 3 sg. goruyð
118, pres. impersonal goruyðir
865, pres. subj. 3 sg. gorffo
151.
gorweð vn. *to lie, recline* 254.
gosper m./f. *evening; vespers* 818.
gossot vn. *to appoint; to place*
171, 364, 541; gossot ar *to*
attack; to strike s.o. 171–2, 364,
541; pret. 3 sg. gossodes 415,
419, pret. 3 pl. gossodassant
922, impf. impersonal gossodet
298.
gouyn see gofyn.
grawth adj. *greedy, voracious* 429.
grymus adj. *strong, powerful;*
superl. grymussaf 853.
gu- see also gw-.
guastat [gwastad] adj. *steadfast*
152.
guesneitheis see gwassanaethu.
gwaelot m. *bottom* 290.
gwaet m. *blood* 69, 108.
gwaeth see drwc.
gwaethiroeð (Duw), guaethiroeð
interj. *alas (God)!* 198, 212.
gwahanredawl adj. *special* 77.
gwala f. *sufficiency* 297.
gwalch f. *hawk, falcon* 202.
gwalyeit f. *bellyful, fill* 399.

gwalop m. *gallop* 484.
gwallt m. *hair* 565, 626.
gwanhau vn. *to weaken;* pret. 1 sg.
gwanheeis 324.
gwarandaw vn. *to listen* 277, 316;
imperative 2 sg. gwarandaw 760.
gwarant m./f. *guarantor* 610.
gwarchadw vn. *to guard* 298,
316.
gwaret (1) vn. *to save, help* 34;
(2) m. *recovery* 814.
gwarthaf see ar[1].
gwarthafleu pl. (f.) *stirrups* 170.
gwarthec sg./pl. *cattle, cows* 426.
gwas m. *servant* 619, 620 .
gwassanaeth m./f. *service; laying*
out for burial of a corpse 556.
gwas(s)anaethu, -aythu vn. *to*
serve 154, 220, 770; pret. 1 sg.
guesneitheis 582, pret. 3 sg.
gwassnaethawð 447.
gwaeret, gwayret m. *bottom* 318,
337.
gwaew, gwayw m. *spear, lance*
42, 172, 173.
gweð m./f. *manner;* yn vnweð
adv. *any way, any manner* 600;
pa weð interrog. pron. *how*
442–3, 622, 705.
gweði f. *prayer* 385, 387.
gweðiaw, gweðyaw, gueðiaw vn.
to pray; worship 342, 375, 500;
pres. subj. 2 sg. gweðiych 153.
gweðu vn. *to suit, befit; to be*
suited; to be proper; pres. 3 sg.
gweða 227, impf. (subj.) 2 sg.
+ aff. pers. pron. 2 sg. (ti)
gueðuti 242, impf. (subj.) 3 sg.
gweðei 233.
gwedy, guedy prep. *after* 2, 69,
76; gwedy na conj. *after* with
subordinating neg. 512.
gwðost see gwybot.

gweirglawð f. *meadow* 74, 82, 185.
gweithret m./f. *act, deed* 382.
gwelet vn. *to see* 10, 179, 487;
  pres. 2 sg. **gwely** 192, 697, 830,
  pres. 3 sg. **gwyl, guyl** 272, 281,
  320, pres. 2 pl. **gwelwch** 178,
  impf. (subj.) 1 sg. **gwelwn** 466,
  impf. (subj.) 3 sg. **gwelei** 228,
  397, 510, pret. 1 sg. **gueleis** 455,
  pret. 3 sg. **gwelas** 642, 691, 711,
  plupf. 3 sg. **gwelsei** 126, 560, 566.
gwely, guely m. *bed* 274, 650, 658;
  pl. **gwelyeu, guelyeu** 253, 718.
gwell, guell see **da**.
gwenith *wheat*; **gwenith peilleit**
  wheat flour 394.
gwenwynic adj. *venomous;
  angry, fierce* 293, 306, 550.
gwerth m. *value* 189, 587, 731.
gwerthu vn. *to sell; to betray* 137;
  pret. 3 sg. **gwerthawð** 673.
gweryru vn. *to neigh* 477, 515.
gwin m. *wine* 428.
gwir (1) adj. *true, right* 458, 486,
  500; **(2)** m. *truth* 96, 240, 409.
gwisc f. *dress, garment* 75, 264, 265.
**gwiscaw, gwisgaw, guiscaw
  (ymdan)** vn. *to dress, put on,
  arm (oneself)* 159, 160, 645;
  pres. 2 sg. **gwisky** 706, pret. 3
  sg. **gwiscawð** 51, 785.
gwisgawc adj. *well dressed;*
  superl. **gwisgocaf** 126.
gwlad, gwlat f. *country* 76, 191,
  212; pl. **gwledi** 705, 946.
gwlychu vn. *to wet; to dip* 69;
  pret. 3 sg. **gwlychawð** 280.
gwn see **gwybot**.
gwneuthur vn. *to do, make; to
  cause* 656, 712, 884; pres. 1 sg.
  gwnaf 65, 73, 80, pres. 2 sg.
  gwney 359, pres. 3 sg. **gwna**
  604, pres. 1 pl. **gwnawn** 635,

678, 813, pres. subj. 3 sg.
  gwnel 620, impf. 1 sg. **gwnawn**
  757, impf. 3 sg. **gwnaei** 26, 28,
  260, pret. 2 sg. **gwnaethost** 118,
  pret. 3 sg. **gwnaeth** 1,12, 39,
  goruc 53, 482, 682, pret. 3 pl.
  gwnaethant, ay- 142, 160, 163,
  gorugant 695, 714, 716, pret.
  impersonal **gwnaethpwyt** 649,
  imperative 2 sg. **gwna** 923, 960.
gwr m. *man* 4, 7, 146; pl. **gwyr**
  183, 188, 196.
gwra see **gwrhau**.
gwrawl adj. *manly* 709.
gwrda m. *nobleman* 837; pl.
  gwyrda 531.
gwregis m. *girdle, belt* 656, 658,
  659.
gwreic f. *woman* 2, 3, 25; pl.
  gwrageð 125, 845, 932.
gwreic(c)a [gwreica] **(1)** vn. *to
  marry, take to wife* 229, 241,
  pret. 3 sg. **gwreickaawð** 3; **(2)**
  f. *wife* 497.
gwreicða f. *lady* 403.
gwreicyangk f. *young lady,
  noblewoman* 397.
gwrhau, gwra (y) vn. *to pay
  homage (to); to submit (to)*
  209, 603; pret. 1 sg. **gwrheeis**
  582.
gwrogaeth m./f. *homage* 206,
  211, 612.
gwrtheb vn. *to answer* 867.
gwrthot vn. *to refuse, forsake;*
  pres. 1 sg. **gwrthodaf** 236, 902,
  919 pres. 2 sg. **gwrthody** 225,
  pret. 2 sg. + aff. pers. pron. 2 sg.
  (ti) **gwrthodeisti** 241, imperative
  2 sg. **gwrthot** 225, 234.
gwrthwyneb adj. *disagreeable,
  vexatious* 259.
gwrych pl. (m.) *bristles* 169.

gwybot vn. *to know, perceive* 200,
506, 523; pres. 1 sg. **gwn** 37, 486,
pres. 2 sg. **gwðost** 36, cons. pres./
fut. 1 sg. **gwybyðaf** 481, impf.
3 sg. **gwyðat** 57, 823, 837, impf.
3 pl. **gwyðynt** 734, impf. subj.
3 sg. **gwypei** 229, pret. 3 sg.
gwybu 783.

gwybyðus adj. *learned, knowing*
916.

gwychyr-lew adj. *brave and
courageous* 187.

gwyl, guyl see **gwelet**.

gwylaw vn. *to watch over* 973.

gwyry f. *virgin* 377, 671.

gyrru vn. *to drive; to spur; to send*
614, 779; imperative 2 sg. **gyr**
502.

gyt see **y gyt**.

H

hagyr adj. *ugly, hideous* 573;
equat. **hacret** 643.

han(n)er m. *half* 194, 291, 370.

hanuot [hanfod] vn. *to be (from),
descend (from)*; pres. 1 sg.
hanwyf, henwyf 246, 450, impf.
3 sg. **hanoeð** 450, impf. 3 pl.
hanoyðynt 734.

hayach adv. *almost* 296, 652, 954.

hayarn adj. *of iron* 560; pl. **heyrn**
343.

hayðu (ar) vn. *to deserve (from)*;
plupf. 1 sg. **hayðysswn** 303.

hawl see **holi**.

heb[1] (len.) prep. *without* 42, 231,
430.

heb[2], heb y(r) def. verb *said*
(*GMW* § 170) 35, 63, 73.

heðiw adv. *today* 64, 88, 249.

heibyaw adv. *past, by* 76.

heint m./f. *disease* 55.

hela vn. *to hunt* 59, 437.

helym f. *helmet* 351, 804, 878; pl.
helmeu 784.

hen adj. *old* 569, 913.

henbeis f. *old threadbare
garment* 551.

heneint m. *old age, senility* 3, 11.

henwyf see **hanuot**.

herlot m. *young boy; rascal*
95,106, 116.

herwyð prep. *according to; by*
381, 515, 726; **herwyð y(ð)**
conj. *according as, as* 528.

heuyt, heuet [hefyd] adv. *also*
495, 903, 917.

heyrn see **hayarn**.

heyern(n)yn adj. *(made of) iron*
402, 406.

hi[1] indep. pers. pron. 3 sg. f. 120,
258, 259.

hi[2] aff. pers. pron. 3 sg. f. 6, 13,
26.

hidleit adj. *abundant* 280.

hihi indep. redupl. pers. pron. 3 sg.
f. 272.

hir adj. *long, tall* 429; pl. **hirion**
570; comp. **hwy** 314, 567;
superl. **hwyaf** 567.

hir-lymyon adj. *long and bare* 564.

hithe(u) indep. conj. pers. pron.
3 sg. f. 15, 424, 447.

hithe(u) aff. conj. pers. pron. 3 sg.
f. 17, 30, 39.

hoeth-lumun adj. *stark-naked* 642.

hof [hoff] adj. *beloved; pleasant*
680, 738.

holi vn. *to claim, demand* 89,
134; subj. pres. 2 sg. **holych**
134, imperative 2 sg. **hawl** 134.

holl pron. (adjectival before nouns)
(len.) *all the, complete* 156, 173,
193 (*GMW* § 107 (b)).

hollti vn. *to break, split*; pres. 3 sg.
hyllt 349, pret. 3 sg. **holltes** 788.

hon(n) dem. pron. sg. f. *this* 64,
191, 300.
honno dem. pron. sg. f. *that* 4, 58,
139.
hoydyl f. *lifetime, life* 226.
hugein(t) see **ugein(t)**.
hun(an) see **e, fu, vy hun(an)**.
hur m./f. *recompense, fee* 727.
hwch f. *sow; pig* 68, 69, 168.
hwnn dem. pron. sg. m. *this* 64,
639, 670.
hwnnw dem. pron. sg. m. *that* 6, 8,
50.
hwy¹, hwyaf see **hir**.
hwy² see **wynt²**.
hwyeit pl. (f.) *ducks, wild geese*
427.
hwyl f. *sail* 142.
hwylaw vn. *to sail* 142.
hwynt see **wynt¹**.
hwynteu see **wynteu**.
hwyr adj. *slow, difficult*; comp.
hwyrach 232; superl. **hwyra**
[hwyraf] 796.
hyfrydu vn. *to console* 964.
hyllt see **hollti**.
hyn(n)¹ dem. pron. neut. sg. *this*
76, 88, 210.
hyn(n)² dem. pron. pl. *these* 314,
706, 762.
hynny¹ dem. pron. neut. sg. *that*
2, 17, 52; **ar hynny** adv.
thereupon 125, 332, 356; **yn
hynny** adv. *during that time, in
the meantime* 695–6.
hynny² dem. pron. pl. *those* 293,
305, 734.
hynny³, hyny see **yny**.
hynt f. *course; military campaign,
march* 888; **ar hynt** adv.
immediatly, at once 120, 202,
401.
hyspys adj. *well-known, sure* 453.

hyt¹ f. *length, while*; **yr hyt
honno** adv. *for that period,
that long* 498–9; **ar hyt** prep.
along, throughout 196, 318,
336–7.
hyt² (len.) prep. *as far as, until, to*
216, 274, 352; **hyt at** prep. *to*
747, 841; **hyt hyn** adv. *so far*
501; **hyt na(t)** conj. *so that
not, in order that not* 302, 551,
599; **hyt pan(n)** conj. *until, so
that* 758, 869; **hyt tra** conj.
while, as long as 296, 533, 724;
hyt yn prep. *as far as, to, until*
27, 143, 352.

I, J

i aff. pers. pron. 1 sg. 74, 88, 96.
iachau vn. *to save, redeem*; pres.
subj. 3 sg. **iachao** 677, 750,
825.
iach-lawen adj. *safe and sound*
456.
iarll m. *earl* 1, 10, 14; pl. **ieirll** 771.
iarllaeth m. *earldom* 47.
iarlles f. *countess* 10, 28, 32.
iawn, jawn (1) adj. *right, proper*;
comp. **iawnach** 493; (2) adv.
very 152, 637, 653; (3) m. *truth;
atonement* 260, 285, 815.
iðaw, iði see **y⁵**.
ie *yes* 458, 697, 843.
iechyt m./f. *health* 36.
ieirll see **iarll**.
ieuanc, ieuank adj. *young* 4, 12.
ieueigtit m. *youth* 2.
im(i), ini see **y⁵**.
in(h)eu aff. conj. pers. pron. 1 sg.
315, 327, 328.
ir adj. *fresh* 36.
it, itti see **y⁵**.
iubet (<i> = /dʒ/) m. *gibbet,
gallows* 192.

LL

llað vn. *to kill, slay; to cut off; to behead* 16, 51, 64; pres. 1 sg. **lladaf** 586, 605, pres. 2 pl. **lleðwch** 189, pres. impersonal **lleðir** 865, impf. 3 sg. **lladei** 608, pret. 1 sg. **lleðeis** 128, pret. 3 sg. **lladawð** 213, 725, 797, pret. impersonal **llas** 183, 703, imperative 2 pl. **lleðwch** 188.

llafur m. *labour, toil* 279, 633.

llall: y llall pron. *the other* 530, 533.

llamsachus adj. *prancing* 483.

llamysten f. *sparrow-hawk* 202.

llathrut m. *abduction*; **dwyn yn llathrut** *to abduct (a woman)* 575, 583.

llaw f. *hand, side* 83, 90, 98; pl. **dwyl(y)aw** 40, 62, 103.

llawen adj. *joyful, glad* 23, 30, 66; **bot yn llawen wrth** *to be delighted with* 23; comp. **llawenach** 344, 389.

llawenhau vn. *to rejoice*; pret. 3 sg. **llawenhaawð** 845.

llawer adj. *many, much; many a* 223, 224, 299.

llawn adj. *full* 140.

llawr m. *floor, ground*; **y'r llawr** adv. *down* 204, 238, 250.

lle m. *place* 36, 407, 449.

llechua [llechfa] f. *hiding-place* 133.

lledrat m. *theft*; **dwyn yn lledrat** *to steal* 407–8.

llef m./f. *cry; voice* 111, 700, 729; **dodi llef** *to raise a shout/cry* 111.

llefein, lleuein vn. *to cry, weep* 461, 521, 669.

lleilltu: ar lleilltu *one by one; (on) one side; seperately* 771–2, 871.

llenwi vn. *to fill* 631.

lles m. *benefit* 73.

llet m. *width* 371.

lletty m. *lodging* 716, 727, 820; pl. **llettyeu** 739.

llettywr m. *host* 726, 740.

lleuein see **llefein.**

llew m. *lion* 532, 543, 544; pl. **llewot** 520, 524, 526.

llewenyð m. *joy, gladness* 344, 439, 451.

llewycua, llewygua [llewygfa] f. *swoon, faint* 255, 461.

llewygu vn. *to swoon, faint* 111, 238, 250; pret. 3 sg. **llewygawð** 513.

llinin m. *string, small rope* 129.

llit m. *anger, wrath* 108, 127, 239.

llithraw vn. *to slip* 10.

llityaw, llidyaw vn. *to become angry; to spur (a horse)* 107, 385.

llitiawc adj. *angry, furious* 254, 414, 550.

llitiawc-wenwynic adj. *angry and furious* 550.

lliw, llyw m. *colour, hue* 712, 839.

llong, llog f. *ship* 139, 371, 687; pl. **llogheu** 943.

llom adj. f. *bare; threadbare, worn* 551; pl. **llymyon** 564.

llosgi vn. *to burn* 131, 666; plupf. impersonal **lloscyssit** 728.

lluðedic adj. *tired, weary* 277.

lluruc, llurug f. *coat of mail* 551, 789, 804; pl. **llurugeu** 784, 875.

llwrw(f) m. *path, direction*; **yn llwrw y benn** *headlong* 290; **yn llwrwf y deudroet** *feet first* 637.

llygat m./f. *eye* 562; pl. **llygeit** 565.

llyma interj. *look here* 133, 488.

llymyon see **llom.**

llyn m. *drink* 448.

llys m./f. *court, palace* 20, 62, 67.

llysewyn m. *herb, plant* 710, 711.
llystat m. *step-father* 116.
llyw see **lliw**.

M

mab m. *boy, son, child* 7, 8, 60;
pl. **meibon, meib** (after num.)
children, sons 932, 958.
mackwy m. *a youth, page* 358;
pl. **maccwyeit** 661.
macrayth *reproach, insult* 247.
maðeu vn. *to forgive*; pret. 3 sg.
maðeuawð 379, imperative 3 sg.
maðeuit 930.
mae, may see **bot**.
maen, mayn m. *stone* 129, 571;
pl. **mein** 397, 878, 883.
maes m. *(open) field* 352, 795; (y)
maes o prep. *out of* 641, 666.
maeth m. *fosterage, rearing*; **roði
ar uaeth** *to give in fosterage* 8.
mal y(ð) conj. *when, while* 678–9,
810; **mal na(t)** *that . . . not* 679.
mam f. *mother* 85, 104, 105.
man adj. *small, little* 427.
manec f. *glove* 587.
maner f. *banner, flag* 724.
march m. *horse* 174, 348, 356; pl.
meir(y)ch 164, 166, 565;
meirych gre *stud-horses* 565.
marchawc m. *horseman, knight* 8,
43, 60; pl. **marchogyon** 14, 49,
112.
marchnat f. *market* 710.
marchogaeth vn. *to ride (a horse)*
78, 481.
marchocau vn. *to ride (a horse)*;
pret. 3 sg. **marchocaawð** 796,
pret. 3 pl. **marchoccaassant**
850.
marmor m. *marble* 397, 976.
marthyrolyaeth m./f. *slaughter*
907.

marw (1) adj. *dead* 174, 227, 330;
(2) m. *the dead* 381; pl. **meirw**
676.
mawr adj. *great, big; heavy;
terrible; deep* 33, 49, 70;
equat. **kymeint** 24, 566, 578;
comp. **mwy** 464, 591, 809;
superl. **mwyaf** 25, 486, 566.
mawreð m. *greatness,
magnificence* 790.
mawrhydic adj. *magnificent* 923.
með defective verb *says*; impf. 3 sg.
meðei 38.
medru (ar) vn. *to strike, hit* 364,
416, 419; pret. 3 sg. **metrawð,
medrawð** 412, 418, 593, impf.
(subj.) impersonal **metrit** 591,
plupf. 3 sg. **metrassei** 415.
meðylyaw vn. *to think,
contemplate, intend* 362; pret.
1 sg. **meðylyeis** 752.
megys, vegys prep. *like, as* 184,
237, 241; **megys y(ð), vegys
y(ð)** conj. *as, so that* 51, 128,
162.
meint m./f. *size, number* 139; 559,
580.
menegi vn. *to relate, tell* 22, 28,
261.
merch f. *daughter* 147, 150, 218.
merthyru vn. *to martyr* 384.
messur see **ar¹**.
metrassei, metrawð, metrit see
medru.
mi indep. pers. pron. 1 sg. 36, 71,
73.
mil num. f. *thousand* 164, 166, 207.
milltir m./f. *mile* 370.
minneu, min(h)eu indep. conj.
pers. pron. 1 sg. 39, 65, 80.
mis m. *month* 763, 936.
miui [myfi] indep. redupl. pers.
pron. 1 sg. 133, 270, 535.

moð m. *manner, mode* 45, 670,
824; **pa voð** interrog. pron.
how 44.

moes def. verb imperative 2 sg.
give 433.

moli vn. *to esteem, praise*; pres.
1 sg. **molaf** 587.

mor[1] m. *sea, ocean* 4, 38, 265.

mor[2], **ymor** (len.) conj. (before the
equat.) *how, so* 256, 616, 842.

morðwyt m./f. *thigh* 416, 417, 510.

morwyn f. *virgin* 377, 497, 498.

muchyð m. *jet* 563.

mur m. *wall* 571.

mwy, mwyaf see **mawr**.

myn interj. *by* 268, 300, 392; **myn
Duw** interj. *by God!* 402–3, 530.

mynwgyl, mwnwgyl m. *neck* 40,
103, 129; **mynet ðwylaw
mynwgyl** *to embrace* 504.

mynych, myneich adj. *frequent,
often* 294, 468, 874.

mynet vn. *to go* 16, 25, 50; **mynet
dros** *to cross, retrace; intercede*
793–4; pres. 1 sg. **af** 39, 89,
263, pres.1 pl. **awn** 815, pres.
subj. 2 sg. **elych** 491, pres.
subj. 3 sg. **el** 75, impf. subj. 1
sg. **elwn** 162, impf. subj. 2 pl.
elewch 162, pret. 3 sg. **aeth** 67,
82, 173, pret. 3 pl. **aethant,
aythant** 43, 388, 629, perf. 3
sg. **eðiw** 774, plupf. 3 sg.
athoed 741, 962 imperative 2
sg. **dos** 244, imperative 1 pl. **awn**
501, imperative 2 pl. **ewch** 162.

mynnu (y) vn. *to want (from),
wish, desire, seek* 62; pres. 1 sg.
myn(n)af 154, 208, 247, pres.
2 sg. **mynny, mynhy** 639, 755,
pres. 1 pl. **mynnwn, mynhwn**
622, 865, pres. 2 pl. **mynwch**
899, 902, impf. (subj.) 1 sg.

mynnwn 223, 276, 534, impf.
(subj.) 3 sg. **mynnei, mynhei**
2, 24, 180, pret. 2 sg. + aff.
pers. pron. 2 sg. (ti) **mynneisti**
191, pret. 3 sg. **mynnawð** 3.

mywn see **y mywn**.

N

na[1], **nat** subordinating negation
that not 1, 55, 198; with inf.
obj. pron. 1 sg. **na'm** 314, 2. sg.
na'th 466, 3 sg. **nas** 213, 290,
512.

na[2], **nac** (asp./len.) negation with
imperative and answer 35, 148,
208 (*GMW* § 197); **na vi** *not so*
467.

na[3] conj. *(n)or, (n)either* 150, 464,
643; **na(c) . . . na(c) . . .** conj.
neither . . . nor . . . 119–20,
178, 226.

nachaf interj. *lo!, behold!* 125,
356, 507.

nadreð pl. (f.) *snakes, serpents* 292.

namyn[1], **namwyn**[1] conj. *except,
but* 226, 491, 752.

namyn[2], **namwyn**[2] prep. *except,
besides* 147, 168, 412.

nawð m./f. *protection; sanction*
206.

nawr see **awr**.

neb pron. *anyone* 126, 137, 363; **y
neb** (before relative clauses)
the one, whoever 929.

nef m./f. *heaven* 87, 312, 324.

nei m. *nephew* 356, 627.

neidaw vn. *to jump, leap*; pret. 3
sg. **neidawð** 344, 345, 926.

neill: y neill (len.) pron. *the one*
528, 533, 540.

neillaw: ar neillaw prep. *on one
side (of)* 103.

neit m./f. *jump, leap* 386, 637, 641.

neithawr m./f. *wedding feast* 85.

neithwyr m./f. *last night* 664.

nepell: ny . . . nepell *not for long* 953.

nerth m./f. *strength; help, support* 178, 342, 387.

nes see **agos**.

neu (len.) conj. *or* 64, 65, 98.

neu ry prev. particle with perf. part 194 (*GMW* § 188).

neuað f. *hall* 100, 646.

newyð adj. *new; fresh* 360, 626.

ni¹ indep. pers. pron. 1 pl. 177, 622, 635.

ni² aff. pers. pron. 1 pl. 38, 378, 671.

nifer, niuer m./f. *number; host, company* 13, 15, 49.

ninheu indep. conj. pers. pron. 1 pl. 930.

no(c) (asp.) conj. *than* (after comp.) 85, 175, 201; with def.art. **no'r** 168, 563; with inf. poss. pron. 1 sg. **no'm** (h–) 383, 2 sg. **no'th** (len.) 494.

nos f. *night* 224, 495, 647; **Nos Clanmei** adv. *on May-day's eve* 32.

nosweith adv. *one night* 306.

notwyð f. *needle* 190.

ny¹, nyt, nyd (asp./len.) negation in main clause 119, 134, 146; **nyt ef** neg. *not* 474, 620 (*GMW* § 191, see also note on ll. 620–1); with inf. obj. pron. 1 sg. **ny'm** 957, 3 sg. **nys** 118, 412, 418.

ny² negation in relative clause 229, 240, 872; with redundant inf. obj. pron. 3 sg. **nys** 85, 559.

O

o¹, oc¹ (len.) prep. *of, from; because of; about; with*

(wearing, carrying) 11, 13, 15; **o achos** prep. *because of* 71, 105, 116–17 (**o'e hachos hi** *because of her*); **o ðim** adv. *at all, in any way* 781; with def. art. **o'r** 6, 10, 112; with dem. pron. as antecedent to a relative clause **o'r a** 26, 29, 186 (*GMW* § 75); with inf. poss. pron. 1 sg. **o'm** (h–) 117, 154, 189, 2 sg. **o'th** (len.) 224, 234, 3 sg. m. **o'e** (len.) 133, 814, 947–8, 3 sg. f. **o'e** (asp., h–) 103, 105, 255; with suff. pers. pron. 1 sg. **ohonaf** 580, 2 sg. **ohonot** 209, 3 sg. m. **ohonaw** 342, 391, 431, 3 sg. f. **ohonei** 256, 446, 3 pl. **ohonunt, onaðunt** 180, 318, 505.

o² (asp.) conj. *if* 35, 136, 258; with inf. obj. pron. 3 sg. **os** 225, 752, 755; with neg. **ony(t)** 55, 131, 328 (len.) *if not, unless; except*; with forms of **bot os** *if it is* 513, 855, 865, **osit** *if there is* 133 (*GMW* § 272 (b) i); with inf. obj. pron. 1 sg. **ony'm** 502, 3 sg. **onys** 137, 189, 535.

o³, oc² form of prep. **y** *to* (*GMW* § 56, N. 3); with inf. poss. pron. 3 sg. m. **o'y, o'e, oe y** (len.) 123, 212, 298, 3 sg. f. **o'e** (asp., h–) 103, 3 pl. **oc eu** (h-) 646.

obry adv. *down below* 74.

och interj. *alas! woe!* 469.

odidawc adj. *fine, splendid* 265, 267.

oð uch prep. *above* 338.

oðy vaes adv. *from without* 649, 906.

oðy vywn adv. & prep. *(from) within* 762, 775, 909.

oðyma adv. *from here* 301, 315, 752.
oðyna adv. *then, afterwards* 681, 803.
oðyno adv. *from there, then* 342, 378.
oeð, oeðem, oeðewch, oeðwn, oeðynt see bot.
oer adj. *cold* 637.
oet, oed m./f. *appointed time, date*; oet (y) dyð *appointed day* 27, 30–1, 47.
oetran m. *age, period (of life)*; oetran gwr *adulthood* 155.
ofer, ouer adj. *vain, futile, useless* 400, 633, 663.
ofnocau vn. *to fear* 121; pret. 3 sg. ofnocaawð, ouynoccaawð 375, 888.
of(f)yn [ofn] m. *fear* 346, 363, 368.
offrwm m. *offering, sacrifice* 689.
oi a interj. *oh* 87, 299, 311.
ol adj. *rear, hind-* 596; yn ol prep. *after* 848, 905, 915–6; yn ol hynny *after that, then* 421, 426–7.
oll pron. *all* 53, 281, 296 (*GMW* § 107 (a)).
ony(t), onys see o².
or conj. *if* with perf.part. ry 621, 955.
os conj. *if* 225, 513, 752.
ouer see ofer.
ouereð [oferedd] m. *vanity; folly* 380.
oyð, oyðynt see bot.

P

pa (len.) interrog. pron. *what* 115; pa voð, pa weð *how* 44, 442–3, 622; pa le, py le *where* 36, 450, 734–5; o ba le, o py le *from where* 407, 449, 734; pa ryw *what kind of* 618.

Padriarch m. *patriarch* 435, 496.
pagan m. *pagan, heathen* 326, 327, 329; pl. pagann(i)eit 150, 383, 395.
paladurwr m. *reaper* 184.
paladyr m. *spear(-shaft)* 590.
paleis m. *palace* 775.
palmer m. *palmer (itinerant monk)* 444, 452, 465.
pallu vn. *to be destroyed; to fail*; pret. 3 sg. pallwys 788.
pan¹, pann (len.) conj. *when, as* 2, 7, 54; yr pan *since* 454, 470; hyt pan(n) *until, so that* 758, 869.
pan² interrog./rel. *whence* 450, 734 (*GMW* § 87).
paradwys m./f. *paradise* 376.
paraf, parassei, parei, paryssant see peri.
parawt adj. *ready, prepared* 718, 740.
parhau vn. *to last, survive*; pres. 1 sg. parhaaf 953, pret. 3 sg. parhaawð 724, 936.
parth m./f. *side* 326, 509, 607; parth a(c) prep. *towards* 3, 10; o'r parth draw y prep. *from beyond* 265.
pauwneit pl. *paynims* 900, 908, 910.
pawb pron. (sg./pl.) *everyone, all* 159, 162, 187.
pechaduryeit pl. (m.) *sinners* 671.
pechodeu pl. (m.) *sins* 380.
pedeir num. f. *four* 391, 650.
peðestyr m. *footman, pedestrian* 243.
pei, bei conj. *if* 35, 119, 145; pei na conj. *if not* 727; with inf. obj. pron. 2 sg. bei na'th (len.) 466, 3 sg. pei nas 290.

peidaw (a(c)) vn. *to stop; leave off,
refrain (from)*; imperative 2 sg.
peit 756.
peilleit *flour* 394, 426.
pen(n) (1) adj. *chief, head, supreme*
156; superl. **penhaf** 898, 905;
(2) m. *head; top, end* 16, 21, 38;
pl. **penneu** 185.
penyadur m. *leader, lord* 721.
penyt m. *penance* 672.
perchein meirych pl. (m.) *horse-
owners, knights* 164, 166.
pererin m. *pilgrim* 686, 708, 827;
pl. **pererinyon** 701.
peri vn. *to cause; to bid* 68, 197,
303; pres. 1 sg. **paraf** 131, pres.
2 sg. **pery** 64, pres. 3 sg. **peir**
120, impf. (subj.) 3 sg. **parei**
15, 50, pret. 3 sg. **peris** 494,
648, 698, pret. 3 pl. **paryssant**
199, plupf. 3 sg. **parassei** 977.
perueð [perfedd] m. *middle, centre*
347; **ymherueð** prep. *in the
middle (of)* 172.
peth m. *thing; part* 26, 29, 36.
petrogyl [pedrongl] adj. *four-
cornered, square* 295.
petwar num. m. *four* 762, 931, 936.
petwarcant m. *four hundred* 183,
207.
petwyryð ord. num. m. *fourth*
43.
pieu def. verb *to belong to; to
own* (also in relative clauses)
(*GMW* § 88, 89); impf. 3 sg.
pioeð 737.
piliaw vn. *to peel, strip* 510.
piliedic adj. *peeled* 328.
pob pron. *each, every* 154, 186,
607; **pob peth** *everything* 26, 29.
pobyl f. (sg./pl.) *people, folk* 673,
735.
poeneu pl. (m.) *pains, agony* 314.

poeni vn. *to torment, punish* 645,
674.
pont f. *bridge* 371, 766.
pony interrog. pron. *do you not
. . .?* 192, 479 (*GMW* § 196).
porth m. *gate* 91, 853.
porthawr m. *porter, door-keeper*
91, 93.
porthcwlis m. *portcullis* 908.
porthmon, porthman m.
merchant, townsman 253, 716;
pl. **porthmyn** 702.
porthua [porthfa] f. *harbour* 136,
138, 943.
prafder [praffter] m. *(large) size*
576.
praf(f) [praff] adj. *great, big,
strong* 324, 505, 560.
praff-froenuoll [froenfoll] adj.
big and wide-nostrilled 564.
pregethu vn. *to preach* 937.
pren m. *timber, wood* 313, 377,
392.
pres adj. *(made of) brass* 924.
presswylyaw vn. *to inhabit* 48.
priawt adj. *married* 7, 843.
priodas f. *marriage, wedding* 768.
priodi vn. *to marry* 457, 647.
profadwy, prouadwy adj. *proven*
242, 847.
proui [profi] vn. *to test, examine*
710.
pryf m. *worm, snake* 306, 308; pl.
pryfet, pryuet *vermin* 292, 295.
prynu vn. *to buy; to redeem* 142,
248, 378; impf. (subj.) 3 sg.
prynei 137, pret. 3 sg. **prynawð**
313, 392, pret. 3 pl. **prynyssant**
140.
putein f. *whore* 96, 97.
pwy interrog. pron. *who; what* 102,
145, 267; **pwy byn(h)ac/ bynnac**
whosoever 516, 642.

pwys m. *weight*; yr y petwarpwys
o eur coeth *for his weight in
pure gold four times* 141 (see
Watkin 1958:85).

py see pa.

pyðiw: y pyðiw *to whom* 927.

pymptheg, pym(p)thec (nas.)
num. *fifteen* 75, 345, 778.

pynneu pl. (m.) *packs* 615.

R

rac prep. *before; because of; from*;
with vn. *lest, for fear that* 108,
121, 132; with equat. used
substantivally *on account of*
544, 561, 592; rac bron(n) prep.
before 21, 101, 133; with suff.
pers. pron. 1 sg. ragof 490, 2 sg.
ragot 223, 619, 3 sg. m. racðaw
100, 369, 396, 3 sg. f. rocði 274,
3 pl. racðun(t), rocðun 138, 628,
712.

rac(c)o adv. *over there* 178, 264,
384.

racðywededic adj. *afore-mentioned*
6, 11, 57.

raf [rhaff] f. *rope* 318, 337.

rawn m. *(coarse) hair, horsehair*
565.

redec vn. *to run* 834; pret. 3 sg.
redawð 201, 969.

redecuagyl [rhedegfagl] f. *slip-
knot, noose* 656.

rei pron. *some* 112; y rei *the ones*
741–2, 787, 795.

reit m. *obligation, necessity* 63,
73, 426.

riuedi [rhifedi] m. (sg./pl.)
numbers, total 935.

rodyaw vn. *to walk (around)* 710.

roði vn. *to give, bestow* 24, 40,
135; pres.1 sg. roðaf 147, 831
pres. 2 sg. roðy 131, impf.

(subj.) 1 sg. roðwn 302, 326,
328, pret. 1 sg. roðeis 117, pret.
2 sg. + aff. pers. pron. 2 sg. (ti)
royssosti 247, pret. 3 sg. roðes
433, 447, 726, pret. impersonal
roðet 8, plupf. 3 sg. royssei 102,
104, 267 imperative 2 sg. dyro
399, 489, 831.

rubalt m. *ribald person* 95, 98.

rwng, rwg, y rw(n)g prep.
between 62, 562, 971; y rwg
a(c) *both . . . and . . .* 207; with
suff. pers. pron. 1 sg. y rof 236,
263, 353, 3 sg. m. y ryðaw 599,
3 pl. (y) rygthunt, y ryðunt 521,
758, 764.

rwygaw vn. *to tear, rend*; pret.
3 sg. rwygawð 550.

rwymaw vn. *to tie, bind* 70; pret.
1 sg. rwymeis 129, pret. 3 pl.
rwymyssant 665.

ry-[1] (len.) prefix *very, too.*

ry[2] (len.) prev. particle 84, 126,
194 (denoting perf. meaning);
with expletive pron. ef a'r
811.

rydrwm adj. *very heavy, too heavy*
334.

ryð adj. *free* 216, 866.

ryðhau vn. *to free, release* 315,
342; pret. 3 sg. ryðhaawð 213.

ryðideu pl. (m./f.) *fief (?)* 772.

ryfic m. *boldness* 477, 479.

ryfugus adj. *bold* 483.

ryhir adj. *very long, too long*
640.

ryueð [rhyfedd] adj. *wonderful,
strange* 459, 755.

ryueðawt [rhyfeddod] m. *wonder,
surprise* 499, 935.

ryuelu (a(c)/ar) [rhyfelu] vn. *to
wage war (with/on)* 778; pres.
1 pl. ryuelwn 79.

ryw (len.) pron. *some, such, kind*
479, 559, 680; **pa ryw** *what kind
of* 618 (*GMW* § 99).
rywyr adj. *very slow, too slow* 30.

S

safyn m./f. *mouth, jaws* 545, 547,
569.
sarllach m. *mirth, merriment* 85.
sawl, y sawl (len.) pron. *so much,
so many* 84.
sawsser f. *saucer* 566.
sef 3, 39, 45 (*GMW* § 55 f).
seith (nas./len.) num. *seven* 497,
762, 808.
serch m./f. *affection, love, lust* 52.
serchawl adj. *wanton, amourous*
44.
serth adj. *uncivil, insulting* 256.
seuyll [sefyll] vn. *to stand (erect)*;
kyuodi yn seuyll, *to stand up*
40, 321, 600; impf. 3 sg. **safei**
371.
s(s)on m./f. *noise, clamour* 278,
585, 663.
sorri vn. *to be(come) angry* 108.
sswyn see **dwfyr.**
s(s)ynwyr m./f. *sense; feeling* 515,
965.
synsgal, synyscal m. *seneschal* 156,
744.
syr m. *sir* 693, 862, 915.

T

tagu vn. *to choke (to death),
strangle* 545; pret. 1 sg. **tegeis**
664, pret. 3 sg. **tagawð** 660.
tal m. *forehead* 307, 563.
talu vn. *to pay; to repay, reward*
773; pres. subj. 3 sg. **talo** 80,
915.
talym m. *part; while* 351, 554, 663.
tan m. *fire* 666.

taraw vn. *to strike, give a blow* 98,
110, 322; impf. 3 pl. **traweint**
890, pret. 3 sg. **trewis, -wys** 350,
421, 723, pret. 3 pl. **trawssant**
702, plupf. 3 sg. **trawssei** 415.
tarðu vn. *to gush* 108.
taryan f. *shield* 42, 172, 349; pl.
taryaneu 874.
tat m. *father* 72, 80, 84; pl. **tadeu**
929, 933.
tatmaeth, -mayth m. *fosterfather*
60, 114, 122.
taw see **bot** or **tewi.**
tawr: ny'm tawr *I am not
concerned* 957.
tebic (y) (1) adj. *similar (to)* 355,
408, 644; equat. **tebyccet,
tybycket** 830, 832; **(2)** m.
opinion; **o'm tebic** *in my view*
117, 410.
tebygasswn see **tybygu.**
tec adj. *beautiful, fair; dear* 222,
227, 233; superl. **teckaf** 126.
tegeis see **tagu.**
teir num. f. *three* 207, 562, 671.
teirgweith adv. *three times* 110.
teruynedic [terfynedig] adj.
appointed 47.
teruynu [terfynu] vn. *to end,
finish; to die* (intrans.); pres. 3
sg. **teruyna** 979, pret. 3 sg.
teruynawð, -wys 739, 764, 806,
pret. 3 pl. **teruynassant** 972,
pret. impersonal **teruynwyt**
894.
tewi vn. *to be silent, hold one's
tongue* 678, 813; **tewi a son** *to be
quiet, hush* 278, 585; imperative
2 sg. **taw** 106, 278, 585.
teyrnget f. *tribute, sign of respect*
774.
ti[1] indep. pers. pron. 2 sg. 79,
119, 354.

ti², di, dy aff. pers. pron. 2 sg. 36, 72, 96.

tidi, tydi, didi indep. redupl. pers. pron. 2 sg. 233, 234, 443.

tir m. *land* 149, 866, 899; pl. tyroeδ 208.

titheu¹, ditheu indep. conj. pers. pron. 2 sg. 64, 241, 497.

titheu², ditheu aff. conj. pron. 2 sg. 97, 150, 225.

tlawt adj. *poor, needy* 493.

toll adj. f. *perforated, full of holes* 551.

torri vn. *to break, shatter; to cut* 337, 343, 626; pres. 3 sg. tyr(r) 172, 590, pret. 3 sg. torres 365, 379, 542, pret. 3 pl. torassant, torryssant 664, 875, plupf. 3 sg. torrassei 291.

torth f. *loaf* 393.

tra (len.) conj. *while* 694, 961; hyt tra *while, as long as* 296, 533, 724.

traet see troet.

traethu vn. *to relate, tell, say;* pres. impersonal treithir 194.

tragywyδ adj. *eternal* 621.

trallawt m./f. *affliction, distress, sorrow* 120, 122, 199.

tran(n)oeth adv. *on the morrow* 41, 776; tran(n)oeth y bore, y bore drannoeth adv. *(on) the following morning* 82, 661, 766.

traweint, trawssant, trawssei see taraw.

traws: ar draws prep. *all over, throughout* 819.

trayan m./f. *a third, the third part* 297.

traytwr, traytur m. *traitor* 112, 317, 699.

trebelit adj. *quick, fast, nimble* 553, 948.

tref(f) [tref] f. *town* 89, 165, 232; tref tat f. *patrimony* 89.

treis m./f. *force, violence;* y dreis *by force* 105, 405.

tremygu vn. *to despise* 11.

treuledic adj. *worn, threadbare* 551.

trewis, trewys see taraw.

tri (asp./nas.) num. m. *three* 117, 340, 958.

trigyaw vn. *to stay, remain* 175; pres. 2 sg. trigye 536, impf. (subj.) 3 sg. trigyei 917, plupf. 3 sg. triciassei 437.

Trindawt f. *Trinity* 629.

trist adj. *sad* 395, 908.

trist-aflawen adj. *sad and unhappy* 395.

tristwch m. *sadness* 938.

troet m./f. *foot* 509, 510; pl. traet *feet* 170, 174, 243.

troetueδ, troedueδ, troytueδ [troedfedd] m./f. *(measure of a) foot* 345, 386, 391.

troi vn. *to turn; to walk (around)* 695; troi y agheu *to turn to death, kill;* pret. 3 sg. troes 725.

trom see trwm.

tros, dros (len.) prep. *over, across* 657, 766, 794.

trossawl [trosol] m./f. *staff, bar* 294, 308, 329.

trossi [trosi] vn. *to convert* 153.

truan(t), truawnt adj. *miserable, wretched* 87, 95, 97; comp. truanach 464.

truanhau (wrth) vn. *to take pity (upon), feel compassion (for)* 144, 282, 444.

truansayth f. *wretchedness, disreputableness (?)* 96.

trugarawc adj. *merciful* 668.

trugareδ m./f. *mercy, pity, compassion* 206, 682, 801.

trugarhau vn. *to have mercy (on)*
781; imperative 2 sg. **trugarhaa**
284.

trwm adj. *heavy*; f. **trom** 562, 585;
pl. **trymyon** 794; equat. **trymet**
561.

trwy, drwy (len.) prep. *through; by
means of, in* 94, 108, 113; with
def. art. **trwy'r** 687; with suff.
pers. pron. 3 sg. m. **trwyδaw**
173, 365, 415.

trwyn m. *nose* 564.

trydyt [trydydd] ord. num. m.
third 676.

trywyr m. *three men* 733, 743.

tu m./f. *side* 4, 20, 43; **tu a(c)**
prep. *towards* 20, 43, 67; **tu
draw** *from beyond, from the
other side (of)* 4.

tuchan m./f. *moaning* 967.

twyllwr m. *deceiver, traitor* 130,
574, 697.

ty m. *house* 232, 271, 716.

tybygu vn. *to think, suppose,
imagine*; pres. 2 sg. **tybygy** 811,
impf. (subj.) 3 sg. **tybygei** 473,
pluperf. 1 sg. **tebygasswn** 248,
pluperf. 3 sg. **tybygassei** 625.

tybyeit vn. *to think, suppose* 191.

tydi see **tidi**.

tyfu vn. *to arise* 758.

tyghedic [tynghedig] adj. *sworn,
bound by oath* 866.

tyghetuen [tynghedfen] f. *fate,
destiny* 463.

tygyaw [tycio] vn. *to avail*; impf.
(subj.) 3 sg. **tycyei** 232, pret. 3
sg. **tygawδ** 231.

tyngu, tygu vn. *to swear, take an
oath* 63, 392.

tynnu vn. *to draw, pull; to take
off* 219, 331, 349; pret. 3 sg.
tynnawδ 184, 350, 414.

tyrnas f. *kingdom, realm* 853.

tyroeδ see **tir**.

U, V

uch, vch [uwch] (len.) prep. *above,
overhead* 38, 338, 344; **uch/vch
penn** *above* 38, 338, 344–5.

uchel, vchel adj. *high; loud* 111,
188, 273; superl. **uchaf, vchaf**
319, 338.

vchel-orawenus adj. *loud and
joyful* 477.

ucheneidaw vn. *to sigh* 655.

uδunt, vδunt see **y⁵**.

vfyδ adj. *obedient, humble* 960.

uuuδhau [ufuddhau] vn. *to obey* 52.

ugein(t), vgein, hugein(t) (nas.)
num. *twenty* 387, 672, 674.

uffern f. *hell, inferno* 379.

un, vn (len.) num. *one*; as adj.
only, single 113, 125, 147.

vnbeis f. *single shirt* 235.

unben, vnben m. *lord, prince*
233, 234, 499.

unben(n)es, vnbennes f. *lady,
noblewoman* 227, 245, 277.

vncrys m. *single shirt* 502.

vnuiniawc [unfiniog] adj. *single-
edged (sword)* 562.

vnweδ: yn vnweδ adv. *at all (?)* 600.

vnweith adv. *once* 480.

urδaw, vrδaw vn. *to ordain* 354,
360; pres. 1 sg. **vrδaf** 155, pret.
1 sg. **urδeis** 409.

vrδawl adj. *dignified; knightly,
dubbed* 156, 244; pl. **vrδolyon**
770.

urδedic, vrδedic adj. *noble,
splendid* 818, 956, 976.

W

wch see **awch**.

wedy, wedi see **gwedy**.

weithon adv. *now, from now on, hereafter* 678, 813, 940.
wely di interj. *behold!, look (here), here is* 697.
wligaw see **bligaw**.
wrth (len.) prep. *at, by, beside, to, because of, according to* 23, 33, 71; **wrth hynny** *therefore* 72, 232, 534–5; **y wrth** prep. *from* 391, 555, 823; with suff. pers. pron. 1 sg. **wrthyf** 278, 284, 2 sg. **wrthyt** 276, 284, 446, 3 sg. m. **wrtha(w)** 175, 275, 283, 3 sg. f. **wrthi** 34, 282, 444, 3 pl. **wrthunt** 176, 781.
wugeil see **bugeil**.
wy m. *egg* 328.
wyf, wyt(i) see **bot**.
wylaw vn. *to weep, cry* 122, 239, 283; pret. 1 sg. **wyleis** 224.
wyll see **yll**.
wyn pl. (m.) *lambs* 74.
wyneb m. *face* 281, 465, 712.
wynt¹, hwynt indep. pers. pron. 3 pl. 137, 580, 628.
wynt², hwy aff. pers. pron. 3 pl. 975.
wynteu¹, hwynteu¹ indep. conj. pers. pron. 3 pl. 178, 187, 395.
wynteu², hwynteu² aff. conj. pers. pron. 3 pl. 18, 527, 772.

Y

y¹, yr def. art. *the* 5, 10, 13; also with vocative (*GMW* § 28 (c)).
y², yð preverbal particle 3, 16, 17; with inf. obj. pron. 1 sg. **y'm** 451, 462, 2 sg. **y'th** (len.) 442, 826, 3 sg. **y** (h–) 290, 297, 657.
y³, yð rel. pron. 37, 45, 48.
y⁴ (1) poss. pron. 3 sg. m. *his* (len.) 2, 11, 13; **(2)** poss. pron. 3 sg. f. *her* (asp./h–) 7, 13, 28; **(3)**

poss. pron 3 pl. *their* (h–) 165, 384, 932.
y⁵ (len.) prep. *to; for* 4, 11, 59; with def. art. **y'r** 15, 16, 19; with inf. poss. pron. 2 sg. **y'th** (len.) 244, 248, 3 sg. m. **y** (len.) 674, 726, 783; 3 pl. **eu** (h–) 769; with suff. pers. pron. 1 sg. **im, imi, ym, ymi** 39, 78, 128, 2 sg. **it, itt, itti, yt, ytti** 34, 63, 73, 3 sg. m. **iðaw, yðaw** 13, 20, 22, 3 sg. f. **iði** 17, 26, 56, 1 pl. **ini** 188, 2 pl. **ywch** 633, 900, 3 pl. **uðunt, vðunt** 136, 526, 690.
'y⁶ see **vy(n)**.
y⁷ see **yn²**.
y⁸ syllabic obj. pron. 3 sg. m. 454, 3 sg. f. 691, 748, 841.
ychydic, achydic adj. and adv. *(a) little, few; a small amount, some* 15, 83, 195.
ydiw see **bot**.
y gyt adv. *together* 18, 70, 160; **(y) gyt a(c)** (asp.) prep. *together with* 14, 82, 195–6; **(y) gyt a(c) y(ð)** conj. *as soon as* 255, 272, 320.
yghwanec, yg(ch)wanec, angchwanec adj. *further, more, additional* 25, 42, 150; **yn yghwanec y** *more than* 972.
yghylch [ynghylch] prep. *around, about* 99, 330, 662.
yghyueir [yng nghyfair] prep. *towards* 597.
yll: hwy yll cant *all hundred* 326; **wyll deu** *both, the two of them* 972.
y mywn, mywn prep. *in* 70, 92, 130; **y mywn y** *into* 423.
y vyny(ð) adv. *up* 61, 62, 113.
ym¹ prep. *by*; **ym kyffes** interj. *by (my) confession!* 360, 535.

ym² syllabic obj. pron. 1 sg. 325.
ym³ see yn¹.
yma adv. *here* 176, 325, 409.
ymadaw vn. *to renounce,*
    forsake, give up 148; pres. 1 sg.
    ymadawaf 285, impf. (subj.)
    1 sg. ymadawn 150.
ymadrawð m./f. *speech*; pl.
    ymadroðyon 94, 254, 305.
ymbil vn. *to entreat, implore* 400.
ymchoelut see ymhoylut.
ymdanat, ymdanei, ymdanaw,
    ymdanunt see am.
ymðeith adv. *away* 95, 421, 503.
ymðiðan (1) vn. *to talk, converse*
    258, 627; (2) m. *talk, conver-*
    sation 276, 627.
ymðiarchenu vn. *to take off one's*
    shoes 653.
ymðiffyn, ymðiffin see amðiffyn.
ymðifregu vn. *to beseech,*
    implore 311, 341, 667.
ymðirgelu vn. *to conceal oneself;*
    to lie in ambush 49, 58.
ymdreiglaw vn. *to turn oneself;*
    to approach; pret. 3 sg.
    ymdreiglawð 2.
ymgadarnhau vn. *to confirm (a*
    pact with each other) 869.
ymgaru vn. *to love one another*;
    impf. 3 pl. ymgerynt 504.
ymgeinaw vn. *to abuse, insult*;
    pret. 3 sg. ymgeinawð 638.
ymguðyaw vn. *to hide oneself, lie*
    in ambush 15.
ymgyffelybu vn. *to marry into a*
    family, take in marriage 233.
ymgyhwrð vn. *to meet (in single*
    combat); pres. 1 pl.
    ymgyhyrðwn 857, imperative
    1 pl. ymgyhyrðwn 864.
ymgymhwyssaw vn. *to stand*
    erect 748.

ymgymyscu vn. *to fight (with*
    each other); pres. 3 pl.
    ymgymyscant 864.
ymgynnull vn. *to gather, assemble*;
    pret. 3 pl. ymgynullassant 896.
ymgyrchu vn. *to assault, attack*
    182.
ymgyuaruot (a(c)) [ymgyfarfod]
    (1) vn. *to come across, meet*
    (with), befall; pret. impersonal
    ymgyfarfuwyt 354; (2) m.
    meeting, encounter, battle 182.
ymgywreinyaw vn. *to steady*
    oneself 170.
ymherueð [ym mherfedd] prep.
    in the middle (of) 172.
ymhoylut, ymchoelut vn. *to turn,*
    return, go back 176, 215, 574;
    pres. 2 sg. ymhoyly 359, pret.
    3 sg. ymhoelawð 798, 963,
    ymhoyles 887, pret. 3 pl.
    ymhoylyssant 395.
ymhwyth interj. *please* 225, 278.
ymi see y⁵.
ymiachau vn. *to take leave, depart*
    714.
ymlað (1) vn. *to fight*; pres. subj.
    1 pl. ymlaðom 586; (2) m.
    combat, battle; fighting 794.
ymlaen prep. *before* 787.
ymlit vn. *to pursue, follow* 369,
    729; pret. 3 sg. ymlidiawð,
    ymlidyawð 797, 803.
ymoglyt vn. *to beware* 708.
ymolchi vn. *to wash oneself*;
    pret. 3 sg. ymolches.
ymor see mor².
ymorðiwes vn. *to overtake; to*
    come up with 203.
ymplith prep. *among, amidst*
    531, 975.
ymswynaw vn. *to cross oneself*;
    pret. 3 sg. ymswynawð 616.

ymwan vn. *to joust, fight* 732, 859.

ymwarandaw vn. *to listen;*
imperative 2 sg. ymwarandaw
693.

ymwelet vn. *to visit, meet* 92, 262,
266.

ymysgytweit vn. *to shake oneself*
390.

yn¹, y, ym (before m-) (nas.) prep.
in 1, 2, 5; yn hynny adv. *during
that time, in the meantime*
695–6; with inf. poss. pron. 1 sg.
y'm (h–) 232, 325, 358, 2 sg. y'th
(len.) 106, 578; with suff. pers.
pron. 3 sg. m. ynδaw 48, 254,
272, 3 sg. f. ynδi 15, 352,
452.

yn², y (len.) with adjectives
forming adverbs 18, 22, 24.

yn³ particle preceding verbal
noun 4, 10, 15; with inf. poss.
pron. 2 sg. y'th (len.) 230.

yn⁴ (len.) predicative particle 17,
88, 97.

yn⁵ (h–) poss. pron. 1 pl. *our* 37,
378, 931.

yna adv. *then; there* 16, 33, 40.

yn erbyn prep. *against* 165, 321,
855.

ynni m. *vigour* 479.

yno adv. *there* 20, 39, 49.

ynt see bot.

ynteu¹ indep. conj. pers. pron. 3 sg.
m. 195, 330, 339.

ynte(u)² aff. conj. pers. pron. 3 sg.
m. 16, 111, 145.

ynuydu [ynfydu] vn. *to become
mad, rage* 954.

yny, hyn(n)y (len.) conj. *until, so
that* 75, 99, 100.

ynyal adj. *secluded* 47.

yr prep. *during; from; for (the sake
of); for, because of; despite,*

notwithstanding 13, 35, 141;
yr na conj. *as though . . . not*
591; yr pan conj. *since* 454,
470; with suff. pers. pron. 1 sg.
yrof 328, 3 sg. m. yrδaw 247,
1 pl. yrom 671, 3 pl. erδunt 326.

yr hwnn dem. pron. m. *who* 670,
723, 749 (*GMW* §70 N.2, §74).

yr hyn(n) dem. pron. neutr. *which,
that* 426, 683 (*GMW* §70 N.2,
§74).

ys syllabic obj. pron. 3 sg. neutr.
223.

ys, ysy, yssyδ see bot.

yskaelussaw vn. *to neglect, slight*
11.

yscolheig m. *cleric, learned
person;* pl. yscolheigon 916.

yscynnu, ysk-, ysg- vn. *to mount*
391, 433, 482; pret. 3 sg.
yscynnawδ, ysgynnawδ 368,
860.

yscyrnic adj. *bony* 565.

yscyuala, yskyuala [ysgafala]
adj. *unarmed; small (of
number)* 16, 51.

ysgathru vn. *to cut* 184.

ysgithreδ pl. (m.) *tusks, fangs*
567.

ysgraf f. *boat* 372.

ysgrin f. *coffin* 976.

ysgwier m. *squire* 522.

ysgwyδ f. *shoulder* 420, 539; pl.
ysgwyδeu 99.

ysparduneu pl. (m./f.) *spurs* 171,
201, 385.

yspeilaw vn. *to sack (a town),
spoil, plunder;* plupf.
impersonal yspeilyssit 728.

yspodol, yspodyl f. *sword* 562,
595.

yssigaw [ysigo] vn. *to break,
shatter, crush* 885.

ystabyl f. *stable* 963.
ystafell, ystauell f. *chamber,*
room 220, 252, 648.
ystlys m./f. *side, flank* 561, 795;
gan y ystlys *along his side*
418–19.
ystondardwr m. *standard-bearer*
157, 180.
ystonder(d) m./f. *standard, banner*
161, 167.
ystorya f. *story* 979.
ystwg [ystwng] vn. *to lower;*
pret. 3 pl. **ystygassant** 908.

ystrywyaw vn. *to devise, scheme,*
plot 44.
ystyryaw vn. *to consider,*
contemplate; pret. 3 sg.
ystyryawð 45.
ystynnu vn. *to extend, stretch*
170, 801.
ystyr m./f. *meaning, sense* 783.
yttoyðyn, yw see **bot**.
yuet [yfed] vn. *to drink* 431, 717,
741.
ywyllus see **ewyllus**.

Personal Names and Places

Abraham a heathen warrior 889, 892.
Almaen, Almayn Germany 5, 13, 19.
Amulis a city in the east 819.
Apolin a heathen god 873.
Arwndel Bown's stallion 171, 200, 519.
Belsabub Beelzebub 886.
Bethlem Bethlehem 377.
Bon(y)fei Josian's fosterbrother 507, 509.
Bown de/o Hamtwn, hen Bown Bown of Hamtwn 7, 127, 132.
Bown vab Terri Terri's son 892.
Bradmwnd king of Mwmbrwnt and Bown's antagonist 165, 179, 183.
Calys the German emperor's place of residence 20, 21.
Carusalem Jerusalem 434.
Ciuil a foreign city 893.
Copart a giant, Ifor's and Josian's servant 589, 591, 600.
Cwlwyn Cologne 945.
Damascyl Damascus 410.
Dostris a hostile duke, enemy of the lady of Amulis 777, 803.
Egipt Egypt 143.
Ermin king of Egipt, Josian's father 160.
Ffreinc (1) France 901; **(2)** pl. (m.) Frenchmen 890.
Garsi a merchant of Amulis 716.
Gi Bown's son 887, 889, 905.
Giwn Bown's father, earl of Hamtwn 1, 6, 47.
Grandon Bradmwnd's nephew 356, 364.
Gris archbishop of Amulis 767.
Hamtwn an English city; Bown's birthplace 1, 28, 442.

Iessu Grist Jesus Christ 151, 286, 311.

Iuor [Ifor] king of Mwmbrawnt, Bown's rival 437, 498, 501.

Idewon Jews 674.

Iosian princes of Egypt 192, 222, 254.

Iudas (o Machabes) one of Iuor's counsellers 674, 854.

Lancelin a pagan warrior 790.

Lloegyr England 490.

Mahom, Mahwn Mohammed 146, 168, 268.

Meir Madlen Mary Magdalen 379.

Milys[1] Bown's son 887, 890

Milys[2] Josian's suitor in Cologne 647, 662.

Morglei Bown's sword 184, 800, 877.

Mwmbrawnt, Mwnbrawnt, Mamwrawnt a city/kingdom in the east 582, 867, 899.

Pedyr Saint Peter 300.

Rodefon Bradmwnd's standard bearer 166, 171, 174.

Ruuein Rome 947.

Sabaot(h), Saboth, Sebaot Bown's fosterfather 9, 60, 678.

Saras(s)inieit, Sarascinyeit, Sarasinyeit Saracens 140, 149, 696.

Seint Gilys Saint Giles 682, 688.

Seint Lawrens Saint Laurence 978.

Sore a pagan warrior 788.

Terri Sabaoth's son; Bown's fosterbrother and friend 787, 789, 830.

Teruygawnt a heathen god 579, 920, 921.

Uascal a hostile duke, enemy of the lady of Amulis 776.

Bibliography

Ball, Martin J. (1989–90), 'The Mutation of Prepositions in Welsh', *SC* 24/25, 135–138.

Blair, Claude (1958), *European Armour circa 1066 to circa 1700* (London).

Borsley, Robert D., Maggie Tallerman and David Willis (2007), *The Syntax of Welsh* (Cambridge).

Bromwich, Rachel and D. Simon Evans, eds (1992), *Culhwch and Olwen* (Cardiff).

Davies, Sioned (1995), *Crefft y Cyfarwydd* (Caerdydd).

Evans, D. Simon (1966–8), 'The Sentence in Early Modern Welsh', *BBCS* 22, 311–337.

Evans, D. Simon (1971), 'Concord in Middle Welsh', *SC* 6, 42–57.

Evans, D. Simon (1986), *Medieval Religious Literature* (Cardiff).

Evans, Emrys (1958–60), 'Cystrawennau '*sef*' mewn Cymraeg Canol', *BBCS* 18, 38–54.

Jenkins, Dafydd (1986), *The Law of Hywel Dda* (Llandysul).

Jones, Glyn E. (1984), 'The Distinctive Vowels and Consonants of Welsh', in *Welsh Phonology*, ed. M. J. Ball and G. E. Jones (Cardiff), 40–64.

Lewis, Henry (1927–9), 'Y Berfenw', *BBCS* 4, 179–189.

Lewis, Henry (1929–31), 'Credo Athanasius Sant', *BBCS* 5, 193– 203.

Lewis, Henry (1943), *Yr Elfen Ladin yn yr Iaith Gymraeg* (Caerdydd).

Mac Cana, Proinsias (1966), 'An Old Nominal Relative Sentence in Welsh', *Celtica* 7, 91–115.

Manning, Paul (2002), 'Orderly Affect: The Syntactic Coding of Pragmatics in Welsh Expressive Constructions', *Pragmatics* 12:4, 415–446.

Morgan, T. J. (1937–9), 'Braslun o gystrawen y berfenw', *BBCS* 9, 195–215.

Morgan, T. J. (1952), Y *Treigladau a'u Cystrawen* (Caerdydd).

Morris-Jones, John (1913), *A Welsh Grammar. Historical and Comparative* (Oxford).

Morris-Jones, John (1931), *Welsh Syntax. An Unfinished Draft* (Cardiff).

Ó Gealbháin, Séamas (1991), 'The Double Article and Related Features of Genitive Syntax in Old Irish and Middle Welsh', *Celtica* 22, 119–44.

Poppe, Erich (1995), 'Notes on the Narrative Present in Middle Welsh', in *Hispano-Gallo-Brittonica. Essays in Honour of Professor D. Ellis Evans on the Occasion of his Sixty-Fifth Birthday*, ed. J. E. Eska et al. (Cardiff), 138–50.

Poppe, Erich (1999), 'Adaption und Akkulturation. Narrative Techniken in der mittelkymrischen Y*storya Bown de Hamtwn*', in *Übersetzung, Adaptation und Akkulturation im insularen Mittelalter*, ed. E. Poppe and L. C. H. Tristram (Münster), 305–17.

Poppe, Erich (2000), 'Constituent Order in Middle Welsh: The Stability of the Pragmatic Principle', in *Stability, Variation and Change of Word Order Over Time*, ed. Rosanna Sornicola et al. (Amsterdam), 41–51.

Poppe, Erich and Regine Reck (2006), 'A French Romance in Wales: Y*storya Bown o Hamtwn*. Processes of Medieval Translations', part 1, *ZCP* 55, 122–80.

Poppe, Erich and Regine Reck (2008), 'A French Romance in Wales: Y*storya Bown o Hamtwn*. Processes of Medieval Translations', part 2, *ZCP* 56, 129–64.

Reck, Regine (1999), 'Heiligere Streiter und keuschere Jungfrauen. Religiöse Elemente in der kymrischen Adaption des anglo-normannischen *Boeve de Haumtone*', in *Übersetzung, Adaptation und Akkulturation im insularen Mittelalter*, ed. E. Poppe and L. C. H. Tristram (Münster), 289–304.

Rejhon, Annalee C., ed. (1984), *Cân Rolant: The Medieval Welsh Version of the Song of Roland* (Berkeley, Los Angeles, London).

Richards, Melville (1938), *Cystrawen y Frawddeg Gymraeg* (Caerdydd).

Rodway, Simon (2004), 'The Red Book Text of «Culhwch ac Olwen»: A Modernising Scribe at Work', *Studi Celtici* 3, 93–161.

Sayers, Dorothy L. (1957), *The Song of Roland* (Harmondsworth).

Schumacher, Stefan (2000), *The Historical Morphology of the Welsh Verbal Noun* (Maynooth).

Stimming, Albert (1899), 'Einleitung', in *Der anglonormannische Boeve de Haumtone*, ed. Albert Stimming (Halle), i–cxciii.

Surridge, Marie E. (1985), 'The Number and Status of Romance Words Attested in *Ystorya Bown de Hamtwn*', *BBCS* 32, 68–78.

Thomas, Peter Wynn (1993), 'Middle Welsh Dialects: Problems and Perspectives', *BBCS* 40, 17–50.

Thomas, Peter Wynn (2000), 'Cydberthynas y Pedair Fersiwn Ganoloesol', in *Canhwyll Marchogyon. Cyd-destunoli Peredur*, ed. Sioned Davies and Peter Wynn Thomas (Caerdydd), 10–49.

Watkin, Morgan (1939), 'Albert Stimming's *Welsche Fassung* in the *Anglonormannische Boeve de Haumtone*. An Examination of a Critique', in *Studies in French Language and Mediæval Literature Presented to Professor Mildred K. Pope* (Manchester), 371–379.

Watkin, Morgan (1958), 'Rhagymadrodd', 'Nodiadau', 'Geirfa', in *Ystorya Bown de Hamtwn*, ed. Morgan Watkin (Caerdydd), xxi–clxxiii, 69–182, 185–247.

Watkins, T. Arwyn (1997), 'The *sef* [. . .] Realization of the Welsh Identificatory Copula Sentence', in *Dán do Oide: Essays in Memory of Conn R. Ó Cléirigh*, ed. A. Ahlqvist and V. Capková (Dublin), 579–93.

Weiss, Judith (1986), 'The date of the Anglo-Norman *Boeve de Haumtone*', *Medium Ævum* 55, 237–41.

Weiss, Judith (2008), *Boeve de Haumtone and Gui de Warewic: Two Anglo-Norman Romances*. The French of England Translation Series 3 (Tempe).

Williams, J. E. Caerwyn (1995), 'Notulae', *Hispano-Gallo-Brittonica*, ed. J. F. Eska et al. (Cardiff), 304–18.

Williams, Stephen J. ed. (1968), *Ystorya de Carolo Magno* (Caerdydd).

Willis, David W. E. (1998), *Syntactic Change in Welsh. A Study of the Loss of Verb-Second* (Oxford).

Wmffre, Iwan (2003), *Language and Place-Names in Wales. The Evidence of Toponymy in Cardiganshire* (Cardiff).